No. 1518
$18.95

GROWING FRUITS AND BERRIES

BY DAVID A. WEBB

TAB **TAB BOOKS Inc.**
BLUE RIDGE SUMMIT, PA. 17214

To Charles, Robert, Merry, and my mother, Marion

FIRST EDITION

FIRST PRINTING

Copyright © 1983 by TAB BOOKS Inc.

Printed in the United States of America

Library of Congress Cataloging in Publication Data

Webb, David A.
   Growing fruits and berries.

   Includes index.
   1. Fruit-culture.   2. Berries.   I. Title.
SB355.W38   1983   634   82-19451
ISBN 0-8306-0118-X
ISBN 0-8306-0518-5 (pbk.)

Photo Credits
Most of the photographs used in this book were provided courtesy of Stark Bro's Nurseries & Orchards Co., Louisiana, Missouri, and the United States Department of Agriculture.

Cover illustration by Al Cozzi.

Contents

Introduction   vii

Acknowledgments   viii

PART 1   BEFORE PLANTING   1

1 **Plan Your Fruit Garden**   2
   Climate—Soil—Topography—Size of Your Growing Area—
   Existing Trees and Shrubs—Your Time Schedule—Best Varieties

2 **Nibblers, Gnawers, and Urchins**   13
   Rodents—Deer—Pets—Children—Adults—Mechanical Injuries
   to Fruit Plants—Weather—Safety in the Garden

3 **Soil Fertility**   22
   Organic Matter—Soil—Caution!—Compost—Mulch

4 **Getting Started**   29
   Tools—Pollination—Shade Tolerance—Upon Plant Arrival—
   Planting Fruit Trees—It Takes Time—Pruning—Forced
   Bearing—Photoperiodism—The Q 10 Factor—Botanical Names

PART 2   SMALL FRUITS   41

5 **Strawberries**   42
   Junebearers and Everbearers—Climate—Site—Planting—
   Culture—Winter Care—The Strawberry Plant—Renewal—Pest
   Control—Diseases—Reducing Losses—Buying Plants—Cash
   Crop—Pick-Your-Own Operations

6 Raspberries   **62**
Climate—Site—Types of Raspberries—Planting—The Raspberry
Plant—Training—Culture—Pruning—Insect Pests—Diseases

7 Blackberries and Dewberries   **75**
Blackberries—Dewberries—Insect Pests—Diseases

8 Grapes   **86**
Site—Planting—Culture—Training Systems—Harvest—Diseases—Insect Pests—Grape Classifications—Cultivars

9 Gooseberries and Currants   **98**
Varietal Selection—Site—Culture—Pruning—Diseases—Insect
Pests

10 Elderberries   **105**
Site—Planting—Culture—Pruning—Harvest

11 Rhubarb   **109**
Fruit or Vegetable?—Site—Planting—Culture—Mulch—Re-
producing Plants—Harvest—Varietal Selection—Diseases—
Insect Peasts—Forcing for Indoor Growth

PART 3   TREE FRUITS   **117**

12 Apples   **118**
Site—Planting—Pruning—Pollination—Dwarf Trees—Culture—Apple Insect Pests—Diseases

13 Pears   **136**
Climate—Site—Planting—Culture—Pruning—Fireblight—Insect
Pests—Harvest

14 Quinces   **145**
Japanese Flowering Quince—Climate—Site—Planting—
Culture—Pruning—Harvest—Pests

15 Cherries   **151**
Climate—Site—Planting—Culture—Pruning—Insect Pests—
Diseases

16 Apricots   **160**
Site—Planting—Culture—Pruning—Insect Pests—Diseases

17 Plums   **168**
European Plums—Japanese Plums—Pruning—Culture—
Diseases—Insect Pests

18 Peaches   **177**
Climate—Site—Planting—Culture—Pruning—Diseases—Insect
Pests

19 Nectarines   **186**
Climate—Site—Soil—Planting—Culture—Pruning—Harvest

20 Mulberries   **194**
Climate—Site—Planting—Culture—Pruning Hedges—Pruning
Trees—Insect Pests—Diseases—Harvest

PART 4 NATIVE FRUITS AND MELONS   **201**

21 Juneberries: The Birds' Favorite Fruit   **202**
Climate—Site—Planting—Culture—Pruning—Pests

22 Cranberries   **207**
Climate—Site—Planting—Culture—Pests—Harvest—Highbush
Cranberries

23 Blueberries   **214**
Types—Site—Planting—Culture—Pruning—Pest Control—
Varietal Selection

24 Huckleberries   **220**
Site—Planting—Culture—Diseases—Insect Pests—True Huck-
leberries

25 Bush Cherries   **224**
Climate—Site—Planting—Pruning—Varietal Selection

26 Unusual Fruits   **228**
Chokecherries—Persimmons—Pawpaw

27 Jelly Fruits   **238**
European Mountain Ash—Rosehips—Russian Olives—Crab Ap-
ples

28 Marvellous Melons   **244**
Fruit or Vegetable?—Dessert Melons—Watermelons

PART 5 AFTER PLANTING   **253**

29 Preserving Produce   **254**
Causes of Food Spoilage—Fresh Storage—Canning—Freezing
Fruit—Drying Fruits—Jellies, Jams, and Preserves

30 Why Fruit Plants Fail   **269**
Failure to Bear Fruit—Plant Death

31 Natural Methods for Control of Insects and Diseases   **276**
Resistant Varieties—Cultural Control—Biological Control—
Diseases

32 Sources for the Beginner   **285**
Mail-Order Houses—Retail Outlets—Guarantees—Insurance—
Addresses

Index   **293**

Introduction

There is serenity in watching nature work her annual miracles. Yet there is also excitement as a barren twig is transformed into a creation of beauty with showy blossoms and, finally, laden heavily with mouth-watering, luscious fruit.

In addition to enjoying the taste delights of freshly picked cherries, plums, and apples—grown with your own hands in your very own yard—fruit trees and bushes can also be a landscaper's dream. They provide the ideal combination of the aesthetic and the practical.

Growing fruit is an increasingly popular activity. There are many reasons to grow your own fruit. There is an economic advantage of beating the high prices at the market or as a way to earn a little extra money. Many people grow fruit for a hobby as part of their recreation. For homeowners, it is a wholesome activity the whole family can enjoy. For people who rent, there are container plantings and miniature varieties that grow indoors. Inner-city residents can improve their nutrition and beautify their surroundings by growing fruits near southern-exposure windows, in their own yards, or in cooperative urban gardening lots.

Growing Fruits and Berries will help anyone interested in growing fruit to do so successfully. This book deals only with temperate-zone fruits that can be easily grown in almost any yard. The book is divided into five parts for reference: before planting, small fruits, tree fruits, native fruits and melons, and after planting.

Along with the joys of "growing your own" will come an onslaught of problems the beginner must try to overcome. What's the best location? When should you plant? Is your climate right? Are your winters too cold or long enough for the fruit you have in mind? And what should you do about pests?

This book deals with the problems gardeners face. There is advice on natural pest controls and the selection of plant varieties best suited to climate and disease and insect resistance for a particular region. *Growing Fruits and Berries* is one book the home fruit grower will not want to be without. It will help turn your garden into a showplace and it will show beginners how to grow fruit the professional way.

Acknowledgments

I would like to thank the following people and organizations for the help they provided:

Ada V. Murr, assistant to marketing services manager, Stark Bro's Nurseries & Orchards Co., Louisiana, Missouri.

Marion Michaels of Black River Falls, Wisconsin.

Merry Michaels of Black River Falls, Wisconsin.

Charles Webb of Black River Falls, Wisconsin.

Dr. Robert I. Webb of Santa Monica, California.

Leonard Doud of Black River Falls, Wisconsin.

Star Przybilla of Whitehall, Wisconsin.

Evelyn Tester, Public Library, Black River Falls, Wisconsin.

Paul & Alvalina Nandory of Black River Falls, Wisconsin.

Mary Borofka of Chippewa Falls, Wisconsin.

Helen Blicher of Elk Mound, Wisconsin.

Part 1
Before Planting

Chapter 1

Plan Your Fruit Garden

Before you start to plant anything—even if it's only one apple tree—it's always a good idea to have a plan. For one thing—if you plant only one apple tree—it might never bear fruit. Almost all apples require another apple tree of a different variety nearby to cross-pollinate them. See Figs. 1-1 and 1-2. A mulberry tree not only requires cross-pollination, but the male of the species does *not* bear fruit and is sold only for ornamental purposes. It is not necessary that you know how to tell the sex of trees. Just be sure to order from a reputable nursery—specifying what you want. As you can see, some of your planning requires careful consideration.

The climate in your area, your soil, the topography (hilliness or flatness) of your land, the size of your lot or acreage, your existing trees and shrubs, your time schedule, and the fruits you want are other factors that must be considered before you begin planting.

CLIMATE

The most important factor in your decision about what to grow is your climate. Unless you are growing plants in a greenhouse, you will not be able to change the growing conditions. If you live in an area that has subzero winters, you are going to have to select fruits that are able to survive extreme cold. Face up to that reality. Do *not* try to grow plants that are too tender for your area. You will be wasting your time and causing yourself to bear unnecessary grief when they fail. Always select plants that will thrive in your climate.

Fig. 1-1. Apple Blossoms. Almost all apples require another apple tree of a different variety nearby to cross-pollinate them (courtesy United States Department of Agriculture).

Temperature

Temperature is probably the first thing that comes to mind when discussing climate. Winter injuries are caused by severely cold or fluctuating temperatures. The average (mean) of cold temperatures is the guide used by horticulturists to determine the plant hardiness of a particular region.

Fruit growers will often try to create a "microclimate" for plants that are only somewhat hardy. Such devices as windbreaks,

Fig. 1-2. Apple tree in fruit. Dwarf fruit trees or semidwarfs are practical for most homeowners (courtesy Paul & Alvalina Nandory).

planting in a sheltered location, southern exposure, or using a northern exposure to delay flowering are all tricks that can help a marginally hardy plant to survive.

When fruit plants are grown in areas for which they are not suited, the result is usually disastrous. It will save you much work and grief to select for planting only those fruits that will grow in your area. Plant hardiness is a key issue.

If peaches are your favorite fruit and you live in North Dakota, forget it. If they manage to survive one winter, they probably will *winterkill* (die) the next. Instead of fighting nature, make a checklist of other fruits you like that are more compatible to your area. Strawberries, bush cherries, and hardy selections of apples and plums can do quite well in the far north. A rugged fruit such as the Juneberry will grow even in parts of Alaska.

If you live in the South, you could have a different problem; your fruit plants might not receive sufficient winter chilling. There are new varieties of fruits that have low chill requirements. These are the fruits to plant in areas where insufficient chill is a problem. Those living in the deep South might consider growing semitropical fruits such as oranges, grapefruit, or lemons.

Some temperate-zone fruits such as strawberries can grow practically anywhere. Plant only those cultivars (varieties) suited to your *photoperiod* (amount of daylight received during the growing season). For an in-depth discussion on photoperiodism and its effects upon fruits—especially the strawberry—see Chapter 4.

Rainfall

Another aspect to your climate, one that also influences your choice of fruit, is the amount of rainfall your area receives each year. Regions that commonly get considerable rain are more humid than those areas that seldom receive rain. Humidity has its own effects upon plants. In areas that are very humid, good air circulation around plants will have to be maintained. This is necessary to discourage fungus diseases that seem to thrive in moist, warm conditions. Air circulation and exposure to sunlight reduces the incidence of these diseases.

Ordinarily, the amount of rainfall varies with the region of the country where you live. The Eastern half of the United States generally receives more rainfall than the Western half. If you live in the West or other dry areas, you will probably have to rely upon irrigation.

Some fruits will survive in dry climates. Buffaloberries are quite tolerant of drought and sandcherries will survive even under prolonged periods of water-stress conditions. With sufficient water, however, they do much better and are more productive. No matter what fruit you plant, it is necessary to have a reliable source of water. All fruits require an adequate water supply to produce. When needs for water are not met, the plant will react with yellowing leaves and stunted growth. Your newly set and young plants are highly vulnerable. Death will follow long periods of drought.

Be sure to water your plants thoroughly during dry periods. Even in those areas with ample yearly rainfall, it is essential to keep a close watch on your plants and their water and other needs. Plant energy required to maintain life can then be used for growing and fruiting.

SOIL

Before you begin planting, you will want to become well acquainted with your soil. Is your soil acidic or alkaline? Do you know? The nature of the soil in which you grow your fruit plants will have a bearing on many things. Knowing your soil lets you know which fruits will grow best on your land. It also tells you what changes are needed for you to grow what you want.

5

pH

Most fruits prefer a slightly acidic soil. Acidity in soils is measured in terms of degrees called *pH*. Soil pH can determine the success or failure of your fruit plants. You can test your soil pH by using one of the soil pH testing kits that are commercially available. Or you can have your county agricultural extension service test your soil for its pH—usually for a small fee. They can also test your soil for nutrient deficiencies or toxins that might be present. Many old orchard lands have unsafe levels of lead and arsenic in their soils as the result of yearly accumulations of pesticides.

The soil pH is the most important thing you will need to know when planting blueberries. Blueberries require a very acidic soil to perform well. The prime soil modifier for pH is *barnyard lime* or *garden lime*. When added to soils, it will "sweeten" them and make the soil less acidic. Never add lime to blueberry soil.

Soil Type

Another feature you will want to be aware of is your soil type. Soils are classified into three general categories: *sandy, loam* (rich, black dirt), and *clay*. Most soils will be a combination of these types. It is not necessary to have your soil tested to determine its type. A good "look and feel" on your part will tell you.

Soil type is partly determined by soil texture. The texture of the soil tells how rough or smooth the grains of minerals are in it. The soil texture is responsible for many of the important qualities of the soil. For example, the aeration and water-holding capacities of a soil are the result of its texture. The smoother the texture the better the compaction and water-holding capacity, but the poorer the aeration.

Sandy soil looks sandy. It has a gritty feel to it because it is rough textured. Such soil is usually low in organic matter and not very fertile. It also has a poor water-holding capacity. Fruit plants grown in sandy soil will require more frequent waterings than those grown in other soil types. When you place sandy soil in the palm of your hand and squeeze, it does not compact very well.

Clay soil is the opposite of sandy soil. The particles that compose clay soils are very fine and will compact tightly when squeezed. Clay soils are smooth to the touch. This gives them very good water-holding capabilities. Nevertheless, soil compaction can present a problem. During periods of drought and heat, the clay will bake into almost the consistency of brick. During rainy seasons, too much water will be held by the soil. This can cause injuries to the roots and crowns (area of plant at the soil line). Most clay soils will need to be altered to allow for better drainage and aeration.

Loam soils are best described as rich, black dirt. They are high in humus (organic matter in decay). Loam soils have more capacity to hold water than sandy soils, and better aeration and drainage than clay soils. As a rule, loam soils are higher in fertility than either sandy soils or clay soils. This is because the amount of fertility of the soil is affected by the levels of humus in it. The more humus in a soil the more fertile that soil is likely to be.

If you have sandy soil or clay soil, do not despair. Generally, all soils can be improved with the addition of organic matter (leaves or composts) to it. In the case of sandy soils, you might have to build up the humus levels over several years. Check each chapter for the soil preferences of individual fruits. See Chapter 3 for more information on soils.

TOPOGRAPHY

Is your yard flat or does it slope or have small hills on it? This is what is meant by the topography of the land. Most land is not flat. Sometimes bulldozers are used to flatten land. In addition to paying for the cost of that operation, it will be necessary to replace topsoil where it has been scraped off.

You will save yourself trouble and expense by planting according to your property's existing contours. You do not need a flat piece of land to grow fruit. For example, you can plant strawberries on a hill or slope provided you plant them in horizontal rows along the side. If you plant them in vertical rows, every time it rains your soil will be washed downhill. This will leave your yard a muddy mess and ruin your strawberry patch.

Low Areas

There are likely to be some areas of your property that are lower in elevation than others. These areas should be reserved for your hardiest fruits.

Cold air always travels downhill to the lowest point where it settles. Spring frosts will tend to collect in any low spots in your yard. These places are called *frost pockets* because they hold the cold air. Fruit plants, as a rule, should *not* be planted in places where their blossoms can be injured by frosts or late spring freezes. Do *not* plant fruits in frost pockets unless the plants are late blooming and extremely hardy.

Hillsites

You will be able to set out more fruits on a hilly terrain than on a flat piece of land the same size. But hilly sites offer some unusual problems. Soil erosion can become a major problem if fruit trees are planted without a sod (grass) cover. The grass helps to hold soils in place. If the soil is allowed to erode, the roots will become exposed and the trees will die.

With bush fruits or berry fruits, planting fruit in strips along the horizon of the slope can be an effective method of combatting soil erosion. These strips are called *terraces* and the process is known as *terracing.* Such terraces also help to prevent water runoff problems.

Fruit planted upon hillsites sometimes require more frequent watering than those planted on flat ground. It is advisable when planting to allow for a shallow depression around the base of each plant. This will help retain rainfall.

Space plants accordingly when setting them out on a hill or slope. Set the tallest ones lowest and the shortest ones higher up. This will keep the tall plants from shading the small ones. Keep those plants that blossom early in the spring, such as apricots, higher up than those fruit plants that flower later on in the season after the danger of frost is past.

SIZE OF YOUR GROWING AREA

Be sure you know the boundaries of your land before doing any planting. The size of your lot will give you an idea of how much room you will have for growing the fruits and help you determine selections for planting.

Dwarf Versus Standard

Dwarf fruit trees or semidwarfs are practical for most homeowners. Dwarfs are easier to take care of, require less pruning, and you will not need a ladder to pick the fruit. Dwarfs often bear fruit in two or three years after being set out. Standard-size trees can take from seven to nine years before they bear fruit; much depends upon the species and varieties.

Dwarfs outproduce standards. Many commercial growers are now planting the dwarf varieties because of their earlier bearing habit and higher yields of fruit. More fruit and many different kinds of fruit can be grown on a parcel of land using dwarfs. Three dwarf fruit trees can be set out in the same space as one standard-size tree.

Standard-size fruit trees are not recommended for the home grower. They will get too big to take care of and they require more pruning. With standards, you will be pruning for size control as well as for the other reasons you will prune. Standard trees grow bigger and require more space. They also require more fertilizer and water. The large size of your standard tree might shade other plants—creating problems. It will be harder to control pests on a large tree as compared to a dwarf and there are likely to be more pests to control. As a rule, it pays to spend the extra money to buy a dwarf fruit tree.

Hedgerows

If space is a problem, fruit plants can be trained to grow as hedgerows rather than as trees. For example, mulberries are well suited to this purpose. By growing a mulberry hedge, you will be able to fit this fruit into a small piece of property where the tree forms will not fit in. Hedgerows can be used to frame driveways, paths, or line borders or backyards. Unless you like sharing your fruits with your neighbor, plant the least desirable fruits along the border and the more desirable fruits in those areas of your yard where your neighbor will not have access to them.

An alternative to hedgerow planting is specimen planting. This involves growing fruits in their bush form—singly or in pairs. Because most fruits require cross-pollinators, it is advisable to grow at least a couple of bushes of two different varieties of the same species of fruit. These also can be planted in an attractive fashion. They can be used to frame entryways (one on each side of the door). You can border paths or plant bushes in a row. The bushes will grow larger and be more productive when grown as specimens instead of in hedges. You will receive more fruit on these larger plants.

If you want to grow a single specimen plant, you will need to set out a self-pollinating variety such as currants, gooseberries, or other similar fruits.

EXISTING TREES AND SHRUBS

Unless you are going to cut everything down, try to work out a harmonious arrangement with your present shrubs and trees. Do not cut down every tree you have. If a tree provides too much shade, you can usually reduce the amount of shade by trimming off a few branches. If you turn your yard into a desert, your new plants will have a more difficult time growing and you even *decrease* their chance for survival. Tree roots hold moisture in the soil in dry weather and help eliminate extra liquid in the rainy season. In addition, trees purify the air you breathe. Avoid the extra work and grief of cutting down beneficial trees.

Make A Map

Draw a rough map of your yard. On the map, sketch all present shrubbery; include trees, buildings, and any outbuildings present. Mark "T" for tall, "S" for small, and "M" for medium size to indicate the shade potential of each tree, building, or shrub. This will give you an idea as to where the sunny areas are and how much sun to expect in any given location. It will help you visualize where to put what.

By making a map prior to planting, you will be able to consider other variables such as form, shape, and color (foliage or blossom color). You will be able to keep in mind aesthetics when arranging your plantings. A map will also remind you to leave room for paths and play areas.

Natural Setting

If you plant your fruits in accordance with the natural existing surroundings, it should be quite efficient to maintain. If you try to remake over your entire land, you probably will require a great deal of time and expense, and the results might not be as attractive as those obtained by placing fruits within a more natural setting.

Most fruit plants have different pests than those that annoy other plants. There are exceptions so you should consult the appropriate chapters. By interplanting with nonfruits, the amount of insect pest buildup should be less than if the same fruits are planted in a solid block. The same is true for diseases.

YOUR TIME SCHEDULE

The time that you have available to devote to your garden is something that you will want to give serious consideration. If you want fruits without much effort, currants are among the easiest to grow. Plant them and forget about them. They will still produce! Of course, with a little care and love they should bear bumper crops. On the other hand, if you plant grapes you will need to spend a great deal of time with them. Grapes require almost constant attention.

It is a good idea to plan your time wisely. Do not plant three acres of strawberries if you only have one Sunday all summer to care for them. To some extent, the time you have for your fruits, will determine what you can plant.

Limited Time

Limited time is the usual problem with most people. The rush-a-day world of modern life can be quite taxing on human resources and energy. It can leave you very little time to care for your fruit plants. Unless you are growing fruit for a living, you probably will only have a limited amount of time to devote to it. Know what your time schedule is *before* you plant. You will want to select those fruits that will best fit into your time schedule. You will not be successful if you try to grow fruits that you can not take care of properly.

As a rule, the easier-to-grow fruits will take less time than the more difficult types. If a fruit requires a great deal of pruning, or has special cultural needs, it will certainly be more time consuming than a plant with few needs. If your available time is extremely limited, plant a fruit that will hardly require any care at all. Generally, small fruits such as strawberries are easier to grow than tree fruits. And dwarfs are less time consuming than standard-size trees.

Vacations

Do *not* set out your fruit plants this spring and go off for a summer vacation. When you return, your fruit plants will probably be dead. Newly set plants need regular care.

If you expect to go on a vacation and you will be gone longer than one week, try to get a trustworthy friend or neighbor to take care of your plants while you are away. Show them how to properly water your fruit plants (with a good soaking and not just a light sprinkling). If your friend does not mind weeding or mowing grass, demonstrate how they should do it so as not to injure your plants. Remember that strawberries are shallow rooted and they must be weeded carefully.

Only ask for help from a trusted friend. Somebody who promises to do you a favor but forgets is no help to you, and plants that have been recently set out can die from neglect. Your friend could also check to see that no one has burglarized your home while you are out of town. Have a good vacation, but plan ahead so that someone can take care of your fruit plants until you return.

BEST VARIETIES

Once you decide upon the fruits you want, always check out the best varieties for your particular region and needs. A good nursery catalog will provide most of this information. If you have additional questions, your county agent will probably have the necessary answers.

Plant only the fruits that you want and are willing to take care of. Do not plant something just because your neighbor has one. Grow the kinds of fruits that you and your family will enjoy eating.

It can not be stressed too many times: *check fruit hardiness.* Too many growers attempt to defy nature by planting fruits that are too tender for their area. They end up frustrated. Nursery catalogs will often offer hardy varieties of your favorite fruits or a worthy substitute. See Chapter 32.

Home growing of fruits and berries has many benefits. Many of the commercial varieties are not the best flavored. Part of the reason is that they are rarely sun ripened. They are usually picked green and ripened artificially. Another reason your own fruits will taste better than store-bought produce is that commercial varieties are selected in part for there capability of withstanding shipping. For the commercial grower who has to ship produce long distance, this is more important than flavor. The do-it-yourself grower can plant a fruit that might not be as firm or able to withstand shipping, but it will have a delectable flavor. Growing your own fruit also gives you a chance to grow the varieties that you like. These might or might not be the "popular" ones at the store.

You do not have to have a degree in horticulture to grow luscious strawberries, tasty apples, or other fruits compatible to your region. As long as conditions are not hostile, your fruits and berries should do reasonably well. The closer you can create conditions to meet the needs of your fruit selections, however, the better will be your chances for success in growing fruit. It is as easy as that.

Chapter 2

Nibblers, Gnawers, and Urchins

There are many potential threats to your fruit trees, bushes, and
vines. Aside from insects and diseases, these menaces include
rodents, deer, pets, children, adults, mechanical damage, and
weather.

RODENTS

Many species of mice like to feed upon the bark of fruit trees
and damage other fruit plants. Young trees (Fig. 2-1) with tender
bark are most susceptible to attacks by rodents. Rabbits and other
large rodents are a catastrophe when they are in your garden.
Rabbits will gnaw trunks, low limbs, and the exposed roots of your
fruit trees. Gnawing rodents can completely girdle trees by strip-
ping them of their bark.

Rodents are a common cause of injury and death to fruit plants.
Mice have the nasty habit of nibbling off runners and roots in
strawberry patches. Even your small fruits will need to be protected, but your tree fruits will be in most danger from rodents.

Mice are most noticeably active in the fall. They will build
nests and runways in the accumulated grass or weeds covering the
soil. Mouse droppings, chewed fruit, or the sightings of the mice
will indicate their presence. To detect mouse damage, remove
some of the soil away from the base of the tree. If mice are present,
you will find chewed roots and bark around the plant's crown (area
near the soil line). Mice will strip the bark off fruit trees.

Fig. 2-1. Young Apple Trees. Aluminum foil wrapped around the trunks and lower limbs will keep these young trees protected from injury by mice and other rodents. A wrap will also shield the tender bark from sunscald.

When trees are damaged severely, they will not survive. Death will occur in the spring shortly after new growth begins. Sometimes trees can live for a few years, but they will never be as productive; the quality of their fruit will be lower. Fruit trees rarely ever fully recover from rodent injury. Even when they survive, they are weakened and become more susceptible to other environmental stresses. Diseases, insects, drought and winter cold will all take a bigger toll from weakened fruit trees. Small fruits, such as strawberries, that have shallow roots can become stunted in growth and even die if too many of their feeder roots are nibbled off.

Protection

To protect your fruit plants from mice and rabbits, keep the grass mowed and weeds cut down. Mice especially like to hide in tall grass. Do not apply winter mulch until late in the fall. By that time, mice will have built themselves nests for the winter and they will not try to make a nest in your mulch. If you see any suspicious signs, check them out right away. Otherwise the mice will be feeding on your fruit plants all winter.

The fall is the best time to act—on those nice sunny days of Indian summer—when mice are most active. Protect small fruits, such as strawberries, by fencing around the entire patch. Use ¼-inch wire mesh to keep out mice and a taller and thicker wire mesh to keep out rabbits. Protect the trunks of your trees and bushes. You can construct a "mouse guard" by encircling the base of your fruit plants with ¼-inch mesh hardware cloth. Set this at least 3 inches into the ground and 2 feet above the ground. It should extend to the branches of the lower limbs.

Although mouse guards can endure for several years before they need to be replaced, it is a good idea to check them each year. They will not offer any protection against rabbits that are larger and can chew on lower branches. For protection against rabbits, you will need a *rabbit wrap*. Most rabbit wraps consist of expanded aluminum foil. They also offer your fruit trees protection from sunscald and mice. They are not as durable as wire mesh, but they are less expensive, and less work, and more practical for most people. You can save money by making your own wraps. The heavy-duty and extra-long aluminum foil that is used for broiling will work nicely. In a pinch, just regular aluminum foil will be better than nothing.

The shiny foil should cover the tree trunks and lower limbs. Wrap it tightly and tape it at the seams with adhesive tape to help it from being blown off in a gust of wind. Change foil each spring and fall. This will help to keep down any insects that might try to make a nest under the foil. It will also allow you to check the growth of healthy bark. If you find fungus growing on your bark, remove the foil, gently scrape off the fungus mold, and expose the trunk to sunlight and air for a few days. When it is dried off, dust it lightly with bourdeaux mixture, and then reapply the aluminum foil.

Plastic and treated crepe-paper wraps are sold commercially, but it is less expensive to use aluminum foil, and you will not have to worry about accidentally girdling your tree. Some wraps have to be loosened each year to allow for growth. Some companies sell chemical sprays that are supposed to repell rodents, but the reliability of these sprays should not be depended upon as the only means of protecting your fruit plants. Hungry rodents might eat the sprayed areas as well as the others.

Traps

Mouse traps can be an effective tool to reduce the mouse population. This is especially true if the traps are placed in strategic areas of mouse activity (such as in mouse runways). Traps for rabbits and other large rodents are also available. Many nurseries sell Havahart or similar traps. This kind of trap allows the fruit grower to capture the pest alive and remove it to another site several miles away.

There are other advantages to this kind of humane trap. It is less startling than to wake up in the middle of the night to the screams of an animal agonizing in a less humane trap. The neighbors are also less likely to turn you in to the humane society, if you use this type of trap, than if you run outside with a shotgun every time you see the "blasted varmints."

Poison

Poison baits should not be used in the home garden. Poisons are potentially dangerous and could accidentally kill family pets. Small children, who have a tendency to put things into their mouths, could easily fall prey to these poisons.

Natural Controls

Many birds and animals eat mice and small rodents. Hawks, owls, foxes, skunks, mink, weasels, and snakes are all among the natural predators of mice. Hawks and owls are no problem. Except for the threatening silhouette they make across the evening sky, hawks should not annoy you. Owls make hooting sounds at night that sometimes spook small children or house guests, but they are really quite harmless. The fox is not such a bad little creature; he's actually kind of cute. But he is not tame. People are rarely ever attacked by foxes, but a fox might bite if it is cornered and frightened. Rabie shots are very unpleasant. You should not get too close to a fox.

Skunks eat mice and small rodents. Unfortunately, when they are aroused or surprised skunks douse their victims with a strong, unpleasant odor. If you do not like surprises of this type, you might want to fence your yard to keep out skunks. You can let Fido chase the skunk off of your property, but be prepared to give him a good bath afterward (out in the yard). Mink and weasels are other wild animals you might encounter.

Most snakes are not poisonous. Nevertheless the sight of a snake slinking around in your fruit garden is not appealing.

Other conditions such as rugged weather and shortages of food will help reduce mouse populations. Your family dog can be effective in reducing the rabbit population. If you have a cat, they can be excellent mousers. Dogs will also chase mice.

DEER

If you live in an urban area, deer are probably the last thing you need to worry about. In rural areas, however, those statuesque animals will not seem as picturesque if they start nibbling on your fruit trees. Deer like to eat the tender shoots, branches, and leaves of young fruit trees. If deer are a problem in your area, a sturdy, high fence should keep them out. There are chemical sprays that are reputed to repell deer, but reliance upon them is not recommended.

Dogs are very territorial and they are a good defense against deer as well as other wild animals. Shooting at deer to scare them off is usually not a good idea. In most places where deer are a problem, there are game protectors who manage wildlife. There is no point in receiving a fine or going to jail. A cat will not do you much good when it comes to controlling deer. A dog that patrols your yard or a high fence will provide the best protection against possible deer damage to your fruit plants.

PETS

Teach your pets good garden habits or they will be a major nuisance. Fido or Tabby can wreck a strawberry patch. Your dog, especially puppies, will chew on your fruit branches or play with your tree wrap—causing serious injury to your plants. Keep your pets under control. They do not have to be on a leash, but they should not be allowed to play in your fruit garden or around your fruit plants. If your fruits are planted as part of your landscape, this will be of greater concern. You will have to keep your eyes open and catch the little rascals. If your fruit is grown in a special garden area, you can solve the problem by fencing off the entire area so that your pets will not be able to climb over, under, or through the barrier.

Animals that roam about the terrain, such as goats or cattle, can be a menace to your fruit plants. Do not let goats anywhere near your fruit trees. And your pet rabbit can be just as bad news as any wild rabbit when it comes to the safety and health of your fruit plants.

In case you have not guessed it already, a horse and an apple tree do not get along well. It might look cute to watch your pony eating apples from the tree, but he will eat more than just the apples. He will eat the leaves and nibble on the branches as well. The result is massive injury to your tree. Even if you have an intelligent horse, chances are he will not pick the apples properly.

Apples should always be picked when they are ripe or near ripe. At that time they will readily part from the branch with a gentle twist. If you pull the apple off, you can injure the fruiting spur. Next season's crop will come from this same fruiting spur. Any injury will result in lowered production for the next season.

Monkeys—oh aren't they cute? Not in your fruit garden! A monkey is like a cross between a child and a puppy dog. These hairy little primates are always into some kind of mischief. If you have a pet monkey, keep it away from your fruit plants. Monkeys love fruit and they will pick it whether it is ripe or not. After they eat to their fill, they use the fruit to play with. A "barrel of monkeys" can be a lot of fun, but not in your fruit garden. Keep all pets away from your fruit plants or at least train them to respect the plants.

CHILDREN

Young children, left unsupervised, will wreak havoc with your plants. Your fruit garden is not a playground. Keep children out of your garden and away from your fruit plants. Children get quite energetic in their play. They bump into things, knocking them over, get up, and laugh. The damage they can cause is no laughing matter. Keep your own children under supervision; provide a special part of your yard for them to play, if possible, and teach them respect for the fruit plants.

Keep your neigbors' children out of your yard except for short intervals when an adult (probably you) is available to supervise. Good fences make good neighbors. If you do not want to build a solid wall between your yard and your neighbors, try planting a hedge. Nice, thorny rose hedges can be attractive and give the appearance of being neighborly. They also will keep the neighborhood delinquents from ruining your yard. This is a more effective method than complaining.

Once you have made provisions for your own family and the neighbors, remember that company will occasionally drop by. When young visitors come, whether relatives or friends, they should not be left unattended. In just a few minutes, without the watchful eye of a guardian, children can do all sorts of damage. You cannot necessarily rely on parents to control their own children in your yard. Your own family will have to watch them. Perhaps one of the older kids will take the younger ones to a nearby park where they will be able to run as wild as they like.

ADULTS

Children are frequently careless, but adults know better. Right? Do not bet on that assumption. Grown-ups can be just as playful and wreckless as children. They may not climb your dwarf apple tree, but they might drive a snowmobile over your strawberry patch or ride dirt bikes between your fruit trees while using the trees as an obstacle course.

Your garden is not a playground. That is just as true for the children as it is for the grown-ups. Do not allow recreational vehicles in your fruit garden or around your fruit plants. Adults can be a bigger nuisance than children because it is not always as easy to discipline them. You must set the rules for your yard if you are to enjoy growing fruit.

MECHANICAL INJURIES TO FRUIT PLANTS

Even with the best of caution accidents occur. You can injure our plants while trying to tend to their needs. Mowing the lawn is often necessary during the summer. Fruit trees can be seriously injured if lawnmowers crash into them or scrape their bark. Use a hand grass shears under your fruit trees and bushes and around fruit vines. This will prevent major accidents from occurring.

Weeding is another time when injuries to plants will occur. Many small fruits, such as strawberries and currants, are very shallow-rooted. In yanking out weeds, it is very easy to remove healthy plants as well. Be sure to pull out only the weeds. Careful hand cultivation will cause fewer injuries than use of large tools that are awkward to work.

The blades of a hoe are sharp and they can go deep into the soil to cut feeder roots or scrape bark. Be very careful when cultivating for the control of weeds. You can accidentally nick your plant by swinging too hard with the hoe at a stubborn weed. As a rule, never use shovels for cultivating weeds. They can go too deep and uproot your plant or tree. If you are weeding a shallow-rooted plant, use only hand tools. You will have greater control over them.

Autumn raking is another time when injuries often occur. If you rake out strawberry plants from your patch, you will have a difficult time putting them back.

People seem to forget about their fruit plants during the winter when they are under a blanket of snow. Yet this is the time when many injuries happen. In areas that receive heavy snowfall, it is a common practice to use salt to melt ice and snow on pathways. Many people do not realize that this salt runs off of the pathways and leaches into the ground. Excessive levels of salt in the soil can kill your fruits. If you live where such practices are common, find a substitute for salt. A bucket of sand will help make walks less slippery and flame guns will melt ice.

Along with winter snows come drifts that can hide dwarf fruit trees. Your plants are more brittle during periods of extra cold. Take care that people or pets do not get to close to them while involved in outdoor activities.

WEATHER

Nature can be cruel on young, newly set plants. Sunlight, wind, and hail can cause considerable disruption in the life of your fruits.

Sunlight

All fruit trees should have their trunks protected with a tree wrap to prevent sunscald. The bark of young trees is thin and tender. In the winter, sunlight will cause the bark to warm up several degrees higher than the outside air if the bark is not shielded from the solar rays. When the sun goes down, there will be an abrupt temperature drop causing the bark to split. Winter bark injury is common when no measure of protection is afforded the young trees.

The Wind

The wind can sometimes cause trees to grow sideways. Colder winter temperatures are caused by the *windchill factor*. In the summer, winds worsen the results of drought by taking away moisture. If wind is a problem in your location, the setting out of a row of evergreen (pine) trees to serve as a windbreak will be desirable.

Hail

Hailstorms are one of the most damaging events of nature. Hailstones can ruin a strawberry bed or blemish fruits on trees. Hail can hurt the plants by causing tears in bark and breakage of smaller twigs. Any place where hail leaves an open wound in a plant there is always the possibility of infection. Fireblight, the leading killer of pear trees in the eastern half of the United States, is the most prevalent immediately following a hailstorm. If forewarned of an approaching hailstorm, cover your fruit plants with burlap bags to soften the blows of the hailstones. The plants might still receive some damage.

SAFETY IN THE GARDEN

Tools can become deadly weapons if left lying unattended in the yard. A rake with its spikes facing upward is painful to step on or have come flying up to hit you in the face. The same holds equally true for your hoe and shovel. Have a set place to store your tools when they are not in use.

Keep your tools away from where small children will have access to them. A pruning knife in small hands can mean loss of fingers—or worse. Pruning shears and other tools can inflict serious bodily injuries in the probing hands of the young. Your tools are not playthings. Do not let them fall into the wrong hands.

It is not always practical to keep watch on your tools at all times. Life is not like that. Sometimes you will be working in your yard and receive a telephone call or have unexpected visitors or other interruptions. It is best to be prepared. Be careful but be realistic. Do not take out more tools than you will need to do a specific job. Put away tools before you greet your guests.

Clean tools after each use. This will help them to last longer and work more efficiently. Garden manure and lime can be slightly corrosive. Wash off the metal blades of each tool and dry them with a clean rag. An occasional waxing of wooden handles will keep them in good shape.

A garage or tool shed is a good place to store tools. This is especially true if you have a closet that you can keep under lock and key. Do not leave tools out in the weather, or they will wear out faster and need to be replaced sooner.

With pruning tools, it is best to keep their blades clean. Oil the cutting parts with mineral oil. As a substitute for mineral oil you can use liquid vegetable oil. Do not use solid shortening. Your blades occasionally will need to be sharpened. This will inprove the performance of dull blades. Perhaps for a small fee you can have them sharpened at your local hardware store.

Wheelbarrows should be cleaned out after each use and turned upside down. That way rainwater will not collect in the tub and cause it to rust during the summer or allow ice formation in the winter that will expand and break the metal. Remember to take good care of your tools and they should serve you well.

Chapter 3

Soil Fertility

All fruits will grow better, faster, and bear younger when grown in a fertile well-drained soil. Sometimes people are fortunate to have a good soil, but most often they must work to improve their soil. It is necessary to successful fruit growing to work to maintain the fertility of your soil. If you want your fruit trees and bushes to stay alive and bear abundantly, you should understand the importance of organic matter and how composts and mulches can help you achieve your goals.

ORGANIC MATTER

Organic matter is one of the most important components of a good soil. The amount and type present influence the acidity (pH factor), amount and kind of minerals, and water-holding properties of the soil. Animal and plant remains in varying stages of decomposing make up this organic matter. It is called *humus* when it is in the soil.

Microorganisms such as fungi and bacteria feed upon humus in the soil. As they die they become part of the humus. Two things will affect the humans levels in the soil by speeding up the rate of decay. These are warm temperatures and the cultivation of the soil. Both tend to increase the activity of the fungi and bacteria. A soil rich in humus is ideal for growing fruits. Chemical fertilizers do not replace the loss of humus in the soil.

Composted organic matter is best. This includes animal manures as well as plant refuse. After manure is composted it is safe to use. A well-rotted manure will be nearly black and crumbly to the touch. It will have an earthy smell. On the other hand, fresh manure stinks and you will not want to touch it.

Although some people throw garbage into their compost piles, it is not recommended. Many canned foods have preservatives in them that slow down the process of decay. Some foods will spoil and attract insects. This is especially true for meat, milk, and sugar products. A clean compost does not include leftovers from the family dinner. Harsh detergents from the family wash should also be excluded.

Organic soil conditioners contain differing amounts of plant nutrients. Some will be able to supply a major portion of your plants' needs. Most will benefit from some supplemental fertilizers. The list of items that can be composted is practically endless. Some of the more common things are leaves, grass clippings, animal manures, and plant refuse.

Shredded newspaper is an item that you should not use in your compost pile. There are chemicals in the ink and paper that could affect the growth of your fruit plants. Until it starts to decompose, shredded paper tends to provide cozy housing for bugs. Be careful about using laundry detergents or other products that contain harsh chemicals. These chemicals will not readily biodegrade and you will have problems later.

Topsoil is often commercially available. It is usually better to purchase peat moss or composted manure and make your own topsoil by conditioning it. Otherwise you are paying in part for sand.

Leaves are usually available in the late fall and early spring. They are especially valuable. Remember the leaves of today are the soils of tomorrow. Either leave them on the ground to replenish your lawn fertility or put them into your compost pile. Ideally, leaves should be left on the ground where they fall to gradually become new soil. A compromise between the ideal and the practical seems the best solution. Rake lightly. "Hide" extra leaves under raspberry and nut bushes or beneath trees when possible. Use all "surplus" leaves, if any, in a compost pile, as a mulch, or bury them shallowly in the ground.

SOIL

Your soil's water-holding capacity—including drainage—and its natural fertility are the two prime factors to consider when judging its suitability for growing fruit.

Water-Holding Capacity

A sandy loam is best for most fruits. This type of soil holds enough water to nourish your plants, but still provides the necessary drainage to prevent waterlogging (which can kill your plants). If you know you have a good, sandy, loam soil, your next concern should be your soil's fertility.

If your soil remains unusually wet in the spring, it might mean you will have drainage problems. Soils containing much clay, heavy soils, or a layer of hardpan (rocks) below the topsoil can require special drainage procedures for you to efficiently grow fruits. Your county extension agent should be able to advise you on your soil if you have a question.

Just plain sandy (not loam) soil has the opposite problem. It drains too well. The water just passes through on its way to the water-well levels. Many people simply give up when they realize that they have sandy soil. It is not necessary for you to give up. You can get humus into your soil from such things as sphagnum moss or oak leaves you keep racking away and having hauled to the dump. Humus is exactly what your soil needs.

Most fruits absorb nutrients through tiny *root hairs*. Every time a plant is watered, it is also fed. Humus in the soil helps to release nutrients in a gradual way so that your little fruit trees or small fruits do not receive huge amounts of powerful fertilizers in a short period of time (which can kill them).

Many people have started with yards that were "barren deserts" and, through the burying of leaves in strategic areas, ended up with beautiful lilacs, roses, and fruiting shrubs.

Fertility

Good water drainage, aeration, and the water-holding capacity of your soil are more important than fertility because the fertility of your soil can be built up. Organic composts—including the leaves you have buried underground in your sandy soil and the mulches you apply to the surface—gradually leach fertile elements to your plants as they decay (and afterward). Well-rotted animal manures are an excellent source of nutrients and they also add organic matter to your soil. Commercial fertilizers are readily available to correct any deficiencies. Generally, the addition of commercial fertilizer or the heavy use of manure is not required until your fruits reach bearing (flowering/fruiting) age. There are timed-release fertilizers that can be added at the time of planting.

CAUTION!

☐ Do not add fertilizer unless the manufacturer says it is safe to do so.

☐ Follow directions carefully.

☐ If you are using animal manures, city sludge, human wastes, or other "natural" fertilizers along with your commercial packed products, you should use *less* commercial fertilizer than the manufacturer recommends.

☐ Do not use "green" (fresh) manure or human wastes.

☐ Even slightly rotted manures should not be permitted to touch any part of the plant, including the roots, because this can injure the plant.

Use a good topsoil or mix in peat moss and well-rotted manures to improve the fertility of the planting soil. Liquid manure is highly rich in nitrogen and very good for general plant growth and leafy growth. It does not, by itself, provide the nutrients required to produce blossoms and fruit.

It might be advisable to have your soil tested by your county agent before you begin planting. If your soil is very acidic, as evidenced by wild blueberries, the addition of lime in the areas surrounding your fruit can be very helpful. Although almost all fruits prefer a slightly acid soil, some fruits thrive on more acidity than others. Wood ashes are a good source of potash and they will temper an overly acidic soil.

Remember that your fruit plants, although amply nourished, must not be over fertilized.

COMPOST

The easiest way for the average home gardener to obtain inexpensive organic matter is to make it. To do this, you must build a compost pile. The best location is in an isolated corner of the yard where it will not offend the neighbors.

Compost is organic matter in the state of decay and not yet turned into humus. Most types of plant refuse make a good compost. Examples are fallen leaves or grass clippings. Diseased leaves or branches should not be used. Although some growers use garbage in their compost pile, I cannot recommend it. Certain items, such as meat or sweet puddings, especially attract flies and other insects. Raw nonsweet items such as potato peelings are less likely to attract pests, but they should still be buried in the pile.

During a period of from two to six weeks, the compost pile will reduce in size to about one-third of its original volume. What happens is that soil bacteria are working on it. Inside the pile, heat will build up to high enough levels to destroy harmful weed seeds and kill off any potential disease pathogens. To speed up the process, a layer of soil, no more than an inch deep, should be added to every layer of plant waste.

Special compost-making materials are commercially available; this includes compost bins and bacteria. Nevertheless, you will not need any fancy equipment to make good compost. All soil has bacteria in it that is capable of breaking down plant wastes. Nature has its own way of recycling.

When making compost, keep the pile moist but not drenched. Too much water will slow down the decay process because oxygen is needed by some of the microorganisms. To increase the nutrient level of your compost, add manure. Fresh manure will be sufficient, but cover it with a layer of sand to keep the gnats from breeding in it. If an alkaline compost is what you want, add lime to the pile. Each week turn the compost over as much as possible. This will help speed up the decay process and thoroughly mix the materials. If you are using a commercial compost bin, it will not be necessary to turn the pile. Just follow the manufacturer's instructions for use.

The time it takes for compost to form will depend upon many factors (mostly the temperature). The warmer the weather the faster the plant materials will decay. Do not use compost until it is thoroughly decayed. Do not try to rush the process; good compost takes time.

A handy way to make compost in small quantities is to use plastic garbage bags. Add the plant material, leaves or grass clippings, some garden soil, and water. Tie the bag and turn it every week. Set it out in a sunny location, but where the dog or other animals won't get to it. Do not add too much water; just moisten it. In a week or two, you might want to add a little more water. Be careful not to add too much water.

If you have a large yard and want to make quite a bit of compost, construct a compost bin. Concrete blocks or lumber will be all that is needed for basic building materials. Make the bins 3 feet wide by 4 feet long. They should be 4 feet high and open at one end to provide for easy access to the compost. If you prefer, place a door or gate at one end that can be fastened to keep out pets and small kids. A roof will not be necessary, but some gardeners prefer to keep out the rain so that they control moisture levels. It is up to the individual. If you do put on a roof, be sure to add windows for air circulation.

Decaying plants will produce methane gas. *Never* smoke while working in your compost bin. When ready, compost can be used in planting and also as a mulch.

MULCH

A mulch is organic or inorganic material placed around or near a plant. Mulches have four basic functions. They serve to:

☐ maintain soil temperatures.
☐ conserve soil moisture (reducing loss to evaporation).
☐ slow down or halt weed growth.
☐ help protect plants from winter injury.

In winter, the major concern is to protect plants from injury due to cold weather, fluctuating temperatures, and to conserve essential moisture. The roots of all tree fruits, small fruits, and vines all do better if covered with a mulch in the winter. There are two kinds of mulches: winter mulch and summer mulch. The main difference between the two is thickness and types of materials used. In the winter, you want a heavier mulch. A noncompacting mulch, such as straw or chopped hay, is preferable to a mulch that will compact and smother the plant. This is especially true for a plant like strawberries that will be entirely covered over with mulch during the winter months. Although some plants will do well with a sprinkling of mulch as a winter cover, in spring, summer, and fall mulches are used exclusively *between* plants.

Summer mulch serves to check weed growth, keep soils cool, and prevent moisture loss. In Northern climates (such as Wisconsin) summer mulches are ideally put down after the ground has warmed—usually in April or May.

Mulches are made from many different kinds of materials: grass clippings, leaves, sawdust, pine needles, composts, and others. A nitrogen deficiency will result if materials such as woodclips or sawdust are used without nitrogen from another source. If you are using an organic mulch, add a layer of composted manure. This will provide nitrogen to the soil bacteria and prevent the mulch from "robbing" nitrogen from the plant.

Some fruit growers use stones, gravel, or marble chips to mulch their plants. These are satisfactory. Check your mulch twice a year—in spring and in fall—for insect problems. If you use a stone mulch, the stones, gravel or marble chips should be carefully raked away from the base of the plant and washed off. The area underneath should be inspected for insects before the mulch is put back.

There are people who feel it is wrong to remove mulches. It is essential to remove the heavy winter coverings that would inhibit plant growth and keep the ground cold or frozen well into the spring. There is a school of thought that contends organic mulches should be allowed to decompose into new soil without being further disturbed. The mulch is raked lightly away from the fruit plant in a circle so that none of the material can touch the trunk. The area is then "dusted" with a light layer of soil (sand) or wood ashes. If you have any indication of an insect infestation, you will want to remove the old mulch entirely from the area.

If you do not make your own mulch from compost or have access to other sources such as chopped hay, there are commercial mulch preparations available. Mulches of shredded bark or white marble chips present a pleasing appearance. Bark would not be my choice because it tends to attract insects.

Plastic mulches can be used. They are quick and easy to put down, especially for strawberries, but are not as winter resistant as are the organic or stone mulches. Plastic has a tendency to tear and needs to be weighted down with rocks or dirt so that it does not blow away in the wind. There must be suitable slits put into the plastic to allow water to reach the roots of your fruit plants. Plastic mulches will not improve soil the way organic mulches do. If possible, choose to work with organic or stone mulches.

Chapter 4

Getting Started

There are many things that will help you to have a successful fruit garden. Most of these are simply common sense things. Some sound much more complicated than they are. Once you become familiar with growing your own fruits, you will not have to stop and analyze as much. Some of your activities will become almost automatic.

TOOLS

You will need some tools to help you grow fruit. Using a shovel obviously beats scooping out the dirt by handfuls. Most of the tools you need are basic items such as a long-handled shovel, a hoe, and sometimes a pitchfork will come in handy. Hand tools are acceptable substitutes if you have a really small garden. Such hand tools are about 12 inches long with a scoop, a claw, etc.

Grass shears are handy when you are growing fruit trees. They will enable you to cut grass growing under the trees with a minimal chance of causing injury to your tree. If you use a lawnmower, there is always the possibility of accidentally ramming into the tree.

Buy a good pruner. Pruning shears are easy to use and there will be less chance of cutting yourself or unintentionally hurting the tree than with a pruning knife. If you look at the hands of many professionals who use pruning knives, you will see that they are covered with little nicks and scars from accidental cuts. Some people wear thick gloves while pruning, but most find that awkward. Your safest bet is to use pruning shears. They have a little lock on them to keep the blades closed when they are not in use.

When your trees mature, the branches will be too thick (over ¼ inch in diameter) for pruning shears. Buy a pruning saw for such work. These saws are especially designed for pruning and they have very sharp cutting blades.

Tree paint or tree wound dressing is necessary for treating the cuts made after each pruning operation. This material will help prevent infection and insect pests from entering into the open wounds made by pruning cuts.

A wheelbarrow to help you haul composts, peat moss, manure, and other heavy items will be a real back-saver. Although having a wheelbarrow is a good idea, it might be possible to borrow one from your neighbor for only occasional use. Even your child's "little red wagon" can come in handy for some gardening chores.

POLLINATION

Pollination is a life process. It occurs when the pollen of one flower is transferred to another flower, either by insects (Fig. 4-1) or the wind. This *cross-pollination* is necessary for *fruit set* (fruit development to begin). All fruits require their flowers to be pollinated before they can bear fruit. Some fruits are capable of self-pollinating. They are called *self-fertile* or *self-fruitful*. Even fruits that are self-fertile will often bear larger crops when cross-pollinated with another variety nearby.

Most fruits require cross-pollination. This means that you must plant another variety of the same fruit species nearby for either plant to bear any fruit. To further complicate matters, there are some fruits that are *pollen incompatible* with other fruits. When planting these fruits, you will need to plant at least three fruits with the middle one providing the cross-pollination for the other two.

Pollen is transferred primarily by bees and by some other insects. It is important to understand the role of bees so that you do not start spraying to kill them off when you see them flitting around your blossoming fruits. You need bees to obtain fruit. Many commercial fruit growers also raise honeybees as a sideline and to help guarantee that they will receive heavy fruit set and bumper crops each year.

Because bees do not like to travel far, fruit trees should never be planted with more than 100 feet between them. The further you set your fruits from each other the more difficult it will be for the bees to transfer the pollen, and the less fruit set you will have.

Fig. 4-1. A bee pollinating an apple blossom. Pollen is transferred primarily by bees, and some other insects (courtesy USDA).

SHADE TOLERANCE

Unless your yard receives full sunlight, there are likely to be places that are semishady. Most fruits favor as much sunlight as they can obtain. Nevertheless, a few fruits will grow and produce well in those semishady areas of your yard or garden. Keep this in mind when you are laying out your plantings. When planning on where to plant what, consider the sunlight requirements of your fruit. By planting the more shade-tolerant species in those areas that are not as sunny, you will have more space to be able to grow more fruits in the same amount of room. An example of shade-tolerant fruits are sour cherries and currants.

UPON PLANT ARRIVAL

Upon arrival from the nursery, most fruit plants will be in their dormant stage. They will usually have a covering of damp wood shavings or sphagnum moss wrapped around their bare roots. This is to protect the roots from drying out during transportation. Unpack your fruit plants as soon as they arrive. You will want to plant them as soon as possible. Remove the protective packing material from around the roots and place the roots in a bucket of water.

If you have a very large fruit tree or several trees, place them in a clean garbage can filled with water. Be sure the garbage can is clean; rinse it out before you fill it with water. Let the roots soak at least two hours before planting. The tree will be able to obtain more moisture during these two hours of soaking than it will during a week in the ground. This will be a great help to the tree.

Do not soak strawberries. Soak other fruit plants for no longer than eight to 10 hours. If left in water for too long, they can become waterlogged and drown.

PLANTING FRUIT TREES

Tree fruits require different handling than bushes and vines. This is because they are deep-rooted and relatively large. They are more difficult for the beginner to grow than are small fruits.

If you cannot plant your fruit trees right away, store them in a cool, dry location. Protect them from freezing temperatures and heat. Check to see if the roots are damp. If not, add moisture but do not drench the plants. Keep the roots damp. Plant as soon as practical. Do not try to store plants for more than one week or they may weaken during storage. Fruit plants, although dormant, are alive and perishable.

Heeling In

Some people like to "heel in" plants if they arrive at an inconvenient time. To heel in plants, dig a shallow ditch and place the plant roots in it. Lay the plants horizontally along the ground and cover the roots with dirt. Protect the plants from the sun and wind. If the outdoors temperature is close to the point when the plants normally break dormancy, plan on planting them in a permanent location very soon. Do not let your pets dig up these plants. Use care when removing the dirt around their roots and transplanting them. Small fruits such as strawberries should not be heeled in. Store them in your refrigerator (not the freezer) until you are ready to plant.

Prepare a hole that is large enough to accommodate the roots of your tree without crowding. Never try to prune off the roots to fit the hole. A large, well-developed root system will be more important to future growth and development than a small root system with a large top. The root system serves two main purposes:

☐ Roots anchor a tree.
☐ Roots provide the tree with water and nutrients from the soil.

Although small fruits can be moved to different areas, it is not practical or wise to move trees once they have been planted and accumulated any size. It could stunt their growth, injure them, or even kill them.

To keep the tree upright when it is set in the planting hole, hold one hand on to the trunk while you put in soil. If you have a helper, have that person hold the tree while you fill in the hole. Try to keep the tree in as straight of a position as possible. Place topsoil near the roots. If you are using a loose organic matter, such as composted leaves, place in a shovelful of dirt over them so that they are not in direct contact with the roots. Tamp the soil down gently, but firmly to remove any air pockets that could injure tree roots.

Water the tree. Soak the ground thoroughly and water once a week after planting. Always soak the ground thoroughly when you water. On sandy soils, you will need to water more often. On clay soils, you can water less often. Newly set plants need water to help get them established. Work out a schedule.

Wrap Trees

The moment that your fruit tree is in the ground, wrap its trunk to protect it from sunscald, mice, rabbits, or other possible troubles. The bark of young fruit trees is thin and very tender. It will need some form of protection. Plastic tree guards are available commercially as are asphalt-treated crepe paper wraps. Some people use burlap cloth or rags. Aluminum foil is inexpensive and very effective. Do not use polyethelene plastic and do not tie the wrap too tight.

Stake Trees

Some trees, but not all, benefit from being staked. Trees are staked to secure them from the wind and prevent movement of their root systems. If trees are planted in a windy location or on very sandy soil, it is a good practice to stake them.

When staking trees, do not injure the tree roots with the stake poles. Tie the trees to the poles or stakes loosely enough so as not to girdle trees, but tightly enough so the tree will not move wildly in the wind. Use a soft string to tie trees to stakes; never use wire.

IT TAKES TIME

After planting, naturally you will be eager for your trees to break dormancy and leaf out. They will but it takes time. Sometimes it takes up to several weeks before the newly planted tree shows any sign of life. When plants are prepared for transplanting, they often lose many of their root hairs and fibrous roots (also known as the feeder roots). It takes time for the plant to recover from this loss. There is also a certain amount of shock because of the transplant operation. Shock is lessened with dormant plants. If a plant is in its active stages of growth, transplanting it can severely set it back or even kill it.

If your fruit plant does not show any signs of life after one month, you can test it for viability (life). Scratch an area of the bark with your thumbnail. If it is yellowish-green underneath, your tree is probably still alive. If it is brown underneath, you might have problems. If you suspect that your tree is dead or dying, get an expert opinion. Call your county agent for advice. If your tree is alive, be patient and just keep watering it. Sooner or later it will break dormancy and leaf out. If your tree is dead, get out your order papers that came from your nursery and check the replacement policy. For more information about guarantees, see Chapter 32.

PRUNING

There are three basic reasons for pruning. They are to:

☐ train your fruit plants to develop the form you want them to grow in.
☐ remove dead or broken branches.
☐ stimulate fruit production.

Each is a separate operation and each requires a different type of pruning. Prune only for a specific reason.

It is necessary to use the proper tools when pruning. With

small fruits or young trees, pruning shears will suffice. With larger trees you will need a pruning saw. Remember that every time you cut your plant you are leaving a wound. These wounds must be covered with tree paint or wound dressing to prevent the entry of disease or insects into them. Do not use ordinary paint; it could harm your tree.

Training Fruit Trees

Prior to bearing, all pruning will usually be for the sake of training the growth habit of the tree. Training should not be left up to chance. Neglected trees will require corrective pruning in later years that will be much more difficult than if they are trained when they are still young.

Fruit trees tend to develop according to different growth habits. Whenever possible, horticulturists prefer to train trees to follow the course of their natural growth habits. There are primarily three ways to train fruit trees. They are the:

☐ central leader system.
☐ modified leader system.
☐ open center system.

Pruning is one of the most difficult tasks for beginners. Mostly, this is because people forget to prune *only* for a specific reason. It is better to not prune than to prune without any goal in mind. People also fall into two categories when it comes to pruning: those who go "bananas" whenever they have a pruning shears in their hand and practically butcher their poor tree, and those who are afraid to make any cuts for fear of hurting the tree. Use common sense when pruning and the task will be greatly simplified.

The Central Leader System. This is a training method. The goal is to grow a tree with a roughly pyramidal shape—somewhat like a Christmas tree—and with wide crotch angles.

When properly pruned, the upper branches should be shorter than the lower limbs. This allows some sunlight to filter through to the lower parts. This shaping will be easy enough to do.

The leader is the branch that arises from the trunk and towers over the other branches. Any upper branches that compete with the leader should be eliminated. Cut them off so that only the leader arises from the top.

The angle of the branch refers to the area where the limb meets the trunk of the tree. This is called the crotch. Trees with narrow angles will not be as sturdy or able to bear as heavy loads of fruit as those with wide angles. The goal is to obtain branches with the widest possible angles. This can be achieved by selecting only those branches with wide angles and pruning off the other limbs. Sometimes if a branch is not growing properly you can correct its growth. Check with your county agent for assistance in correcting bad branch angles.

The central leader system is the method for training apple trees. Read it over again until you understand the goals. Once you feel that you know what you are after, then you will be ready to prune.

The Modified Leader System. The goals of this training method are essentially the same as for those for the central leader system—with one exception. A leader other than the one arising from the central trunk is to be selected and maintained. This is called a *modified leader* because it does not stem from the central trunk. The new leader will be the highest branch arising from the tree and it should grow in an upright fashion. All branches that compete with it should be cut off or trimmed back. The goal is to grow a tree with a roughly pyramidal shape—somewhat like a Christmas tree—with wide-angle crotches. This is the method for training pear trees. Make certain you understand what you want to accomplish before you begin to prune.

The Open Center System. The open center system, or *vase system,* was once used for all fruits. It now is only used on fruit trees such as peaches that tend to grow this way naturally. The tree will be shaped roughly like a vase. The goal of the open center system is to train a tree so that as much sunlight as possible can enter into the inside area of the tree.

Your major concern will be the thinning out of branches on the top and on the insides so that optimum sunlight can flow throughout the tree. Follow the natural growth habits of your tree and you should not have any problems. Do not train apples according to this method. The limbs will form weak crotch angles that can break under heavy loads of fruit.

Prune According to Age

Prune your tree in sections according to the age of that section *not* the trees age. When the tree has reached bearing age, you will use two types of cuts: *heading cuts* and *thinning cuts.* The heading cuts are made in one- to two-year-old sections to promote the growth of side branches. In 3-year and older sections, the pruning should be shifted to thinning cuts. These cuts reduce the number and length of branches and also serve to promote fruiting.

Preplanting Pruning

Most fruit trees will arrive pruned and ready for planting. Some nurseries do not provide this service or charge extra to do it. Most plants set out in grocery store parking lots are never repruned. If your nursery did not do this for you, you will want to prune your tree after you have planted it.

Cut every branch back by one-third. If your tree is unbranched (a *whip*), cut it back by one-third. This will encourage the development of vigorous wide-angled side branches. Select only the wide-angle branches to maintain and cut off all of the narrow-angled branches (unless they all have narrow angles). If all of your branch angles are narrow, you can put in braces to stretch them. Contact your county agent for assistance.

Carbohydrate/Nitrogen Balance

Experts talk of maintaining the *c/n ratio* of fruit plants. What they are referring to is the carbohydrate-nitrogen balance. It is not essential that you understand the chemical processes involved. Proper pruning will maintain this balance without any conscious effort on your part. This is important to fruit production. The goal is to try to achieve a balance between foliar (leaves) growth and the production of fruit buds.

If an imbalance occurs, you will experience problems. For example, sparse leaf production can result in heavy fruit set, but the quality of the fruits will suffer and next season's crop will be sparse. Certain apple varieties, such as Wealthy, lend themselves to biennial bearing (every other year they fruit) if left to themselves. By roper pruning to balance the leaf buds (which are slender and pointed) and the fruit buds (which are rounder and plump), you will be able to balance the fruiting habits so that you can receive an annual crop of fruit.

Caution. Pruning should be fairly light prior to bearing. Excessive pruning will delay bearing and have a dwarfing effect upon the tree.

FORCED BEARING

Sometimes trees grow to maturity and still do not bear any

fruit. To force mature trees into bearing, horticulturists use a practice called *ringing*. Never ring an immature tree.

Ringing is very easy to do, but it must be done with care so as not to injure the tree. A very sharp knife or razor blade is used. Rather than making one single cut all the way around the trunk, cut halfway around the trunk. About 1 inch lower, make a second cut halfway around the trunk on the other side that was not previously cut. The end of each cut should be in line with the previous cut. Be certain that the blade goes in deep so that you cut into the cambrium tissue (green inner bark). If you only scratch the bark, you will not accomplish the desired effect of forcing the tree to bear fruit.

If you have never performed this practice, and most people have not, you might want to have an expert do it for you. Getting somebody to do things for you for free is not easy, but it might be possible to persuade someone to do it. Your county agent or a horticulture professor at a nearby university might be willing to help you.

You can do the job yourself. Be bold of heart and keep a steady hand. Once you have made the initial cuts (and on old trees it will take more than a couple cuts to do it), wrap a loose cloth around the wounds. Do not treat these wounds or it might interfere with the effect you want to achieve. Ringing is a deliberate wounding of the tree. If it appears that fungi are attacking the tree, you can use a tree paint or wound dress, but only after you are certain that the ringing has worked.

Ring trees only in the spring before they leaf out. The tree must be dormant. Ringing might seem like a drastic measure, but if done properly it works. Do not ring trees that are newly set or not of bearing age. And be careful. Cause a controlled wound to your tree; do not just hack it up.

PHOTOPERIODISM

Photoperiodism is an unfamiliar word to most people, but don't let it scare you. It is really an easy concept to understand and it is necessary if you plan to grow fruit indoors under artificial lighting. Photoperiodism is the way plants respond to natural and artificial lighting. It is a genetic phenomenon. The light response determines the plants' growth habits—such as times of flowering. The strawberry is the most prominent example of a plant that is affected by photoperiodism.

The photoperiodic response of deciduous (leaf-falling) fruits is crucial not just for flowering, but for the plant's survival during the harsh winters that occur in many of the Northern areas of the temperate zone. *Photoperiods* (day lengths) give the plant its signals for growth. It tells the plant when it is time to prepare for winter dormancy. Short days are a cue to stop growth and "harden off." This hardening-off process causes stems to slightly thicken, become more rigid, and develop a covering of fine "hairs." The plant buds are very sensitive to photoperiods. When autumn comes, they will conserve moisture and the leaves change color and drop off. These measures help the plant to survive the cold winter months.

Many people are unaware that plants react to indoor lighting the same way they react to sunlight. The differences in lighting, which might not be noticeable to us, send signals to the plant affecting its growth habits. Whenever you are growing plants indoors in containers, it is a good idea to see that they receive sufficient lighting. A sunny room is preferable to one without any windows.

THE Q 10 FACTOR

Temperatures are another factor involved in the hardening-off process. Horticulturists speak of the Q 10 factor. This is merely a mathematical quotient to measure plant respiration. For every 10 degree rise in temperature, the respiration rate of a plant doubles. Conversely, as the temperatures drop the life activities slow down. Plants enter dormancy in a gradual manner. Once a plant is in a deep stage of dormancy, it requires a winter chill period before it breaks dormancy and resumes normal growth.

BOTANICAL NAMES

Latin is the universal language of the scientific community. Fruit species are given Latin names by horticulturists so that they can be readily identified in any country in the world. These are their botanical names. This practice of naming fruit species makes it easier for horticulturists around the world to exchange information and work together.

Fruit plants are actually given two names, both in Latin. The first name signifies the plant's genus (family). The second name is the species' name. For example, the Juneberry is called *Amelanchier alnifolia*. This is its botanical name. Its common name is Juneberry in the Midwest, Shadblow in New England, Serviceberry in other Eastern states, and Saskatoon Blueberry in the Northwest. So it is easy to see what confusion would arise if the plant were called by its common name; it has several!

Ordinarily, fruits can be safely called by their common names. Nevertheless, there are times, as in the case of the Juneberry, when knowing the scientific or botanical name would be helpful. Incidentally, the process of naming fruits is called *binomial nomenclature*. Binomial means "two names" and nomenclature means the science of naming.

Sometimes plants are given a third name that might or might not be in Latin. For example, the Russian mulberry has the botanical name of *Morus alba* var. *tartarica*. This distinguishes it from the White mulberry, its cousin, that is simply named *Morus alba*.

It can all become quite confusing. It is fairly easy for one person in another part of the country to grow the same fruit as another under a different common name and not know it because of the different names attributed to each fruit. That is when the Latin name comes in handy.

Part 2
Small Fruits

Chapter 5

Strawberries

Whether these red, juicy delights are grown for fresh or frozen use, strawberry shortcake, pies, preserves, or as a way to earn a little extra spending money, strawberries are the most popular fruit in the home garden. And there are good reasons why! If you do not want to wait years for your own fruit, strawberries are the answer. The strawberry will produce fruit (see Figs. 5-1 through 5-4) quicker than almost any other plant. They will often set fruit the very same year that they are planted. They are one of the easiest fruits to grow, outside in rows or in containers, and some varieties are trained for climbing on trellises.

The name *strawberry* comes from the Anglo-Saxons who called them strewberries because of the plant's growth habit. The runners strew or spread along the ground. Although strawberries were gathered from the wild, the development of the strawberry as a commodity didn't occur until the 1820s in England.

The strawberry has an interesting history. Although they grew wild in many parts of the world, the large, luscious strawberries of today (*Fragaria x ananassa*) are the result of hybridization. The commercial strawberry comes from the cross of two wild American strawberries: the Eastern Meadow Strawberry (*Fragaria virginiana*) and the Beach Strawberry (*Fragaria chiloensis*).

The Eastern Meadow Strawberry was taken by early tradesmen from Virginia and planted in the gardens of Europe as a novelty. In 1700, a French botanist named Frezier transplanted the Beach

Fig. 5-1. Stark Crimson King Strawberries. This strawberry will produce fruit quicker than almost any other. They will often set fruit the very same year they are planted (courtesy Stark Bro's Nurseries & Orchards Co.).

Strawberry from its native home, in Chile, to France. When the Beach and Eastern Meadow strawberries were planted in the same botanic garden, a natural cross occurred. The result was a new superior breed of strawberries that bore large delicious fruits. With rare exceptions, every commercial strawberry on the market today arose from the hybrid cross of these two wild types.

Fig. 5-2. The Junebearer is the most popular strawberry grown (courtesy USDA).

Fig. 5-3. Stark's Ozark Beauty Strawberry. The culture of the everbearer is different from that of the Junebearer due to its different growth habits (courtesy Stark Bro's Nurseries & Orchards Co.).

JUNEBEARERS AND EVERBEARERS

There are two basic types of strawberries: Junebearers and everbearers. The Junebearers are the most productive and best for the home garden. Junebearers are recommended because they usually bear fruits before the dry part of the summer. With everbearers, the summer dry spells often adversely affect the quality of the fruits. Sufficient water is crucial during all stages of fruit development. Inadequate water causes fruits to shrivel, become dry or become deformed. The fall crop from an everbearer usually is superior to its summer crop.

Everbearers tend to have more problems with insect pests. This is especially true if the plants are suffering from drought stress (insufficient water due to dry weather). Plants are weakened from lack of moisture. It seems to be a law of nature that anything weak or sickly is always a prime target for predators. These fruits become infested with picnic beetles and cannot defend themselves as well as healthy plants. Unless you are willing to invest a great deal of time and effort to their upkeep, everbearers do not fare as well as Junebearers. It is easier to grow everbearers in containers where you can be certain they receive the water they need to thrive.

The "climbing" strawberries that some nurseries offer are usually just everbearer varieties sold with instructions for tying them to trellises or other upright support systems. They are more costly then the same varieties sold elsewhere. If you have virtually no yard space for your berries or want to create a dramatic effect, this might be your answer. Otherwise, a regular patch will be easier and more productive for you. Growing strawberries in barrels or pyramids is not recommended.

With Junebearers, especially, and to some extent with everbearers also, the year following the initial planting will bring heavy crops. If you follow good cultural practices, expect nearly 1 quart of berries from each plant. Your plants will produce runners and "daughter plants" that also bear fruit.

CLIMATE

Strawberries are basically a cool-weather crop. Climate, however, is not as important in strawberry culture as is the photoperiod (the plants' response to light). The length and amount of daylight "tells" the plant when to blossom and when to produce runners. Because of the different regional conditions, varieties grown in Wisconsin are not suitable for growing in Florida (where strawberries are a winter crop).

Junebearers produce flowers under short days and runners during long days. Thus, Junebearers bloom in the spring and pro-

Fig. 5-4. Expect nearly a quart from each strawberry plant starting the year after planting (courtesy USDA).

45

duce runners in the summer. Everbearers have the opposite growth habit. They produce flowers during long days (in the summer) and runners during short days. Interestingly, when strawberries are grown on the equator they all act like everbearers except that they do not produce any runners.

SITE

Strawberries are not particularly fussy about soils. They grow on a wide range of soil types, but a sandy loam is best. Strawberries prefer a slightly acidic soil. For planting, choose a location with good water drainage. Strawberries will not tolerate "wet feet." If planted in an area where standing water appears on the soil surface well into the spring, there are likely to be problems with collar rot diseases.

Strawberries require full sunlight to do their best. They will grow in shade, but if the shade is too heavy they will produce very little or not bear any fruit at all.

Strawberries planted in rows do well on level ground. They are easy to care for. If you must plant them on a hill or slope, plant them horizontally along the side of the slope. Be certain there is room for paths. You will need to be able to reach your plants to take proper care of them. Strawberry plants set in vertical rows will likely be washed out or buried and your yard will become a muddy mess. Strawberries are very shallow rooted and are sensitive to the effects of soil erosion.

Never plant strawberries in sod (grass) or areas recently used to grow tomatoes, peppers, eggplants, or potatoes. These sites might contain verticillium wilt organisms (a disease that can attack strawberries) as well as grubs that will injure or kill your strawberry plants. Root-feeding insects, such as white grubs, can wipe out your entire patch in a very short time. If you must plant in sod, till it the previous fall. Let it stand idle over the winter and till it again in the spring before planting. This permits the grass to decompose and will reduce the insect population.

Avoid tight clay soils. If you have such soil, modify it by mixing in organic matter such as peat moss or compost to loosen it up. If noxious weeds are a problem in your yard, you will need to devote extra time to keeping your patch weeded or the weeds will take over and smother your strawberry bed.

PLANTING

Spring planting is best for strawberries in most parts of the country. In the south where strawberries are grown as a winter crop they should be planted in the fall. Do not plant until after the soil can be thoroughly worked in the spring. A slight frost probably will not kill your plants, but it could set them back. So if you plant early in the spring, be prepared to cover plants at night with a light mulch (such as straw) that can be removed during the day. Do not set out strawberry plants after the first of June. That is too late in the season to be planting. The roots of the plants need to be settled in before upper growth begins. The roots grow at cooler temperatures.

When your strawberries arrive, check the bundles. If necessary, moisten the roots but do not soak them. If you will not be able to set them out right away, for whatever reason, you can store them for awhile. They will keep in your refrigerator (not the freezer) for several weeks or until a more opportune time. Keep the plants in the plastic bags they come in. Fold the bags over loosely. Do not tie them; they need access to some air or they will die. Then place them on a shelf in the refrigerator where they will not be disturbed. Be sure the refrigerator is not set at near freezing.

Preferred Training Systems

To plant strawberries, you will need a long-handled shovel and a hoe. There are many training systems for planting strawberries. The preferred system used by commercial and home growers alike is the *matted-row system*. This is the most productive and easiest to maintain. Plants are set out in rows. These rows are about 2 feet in width with a 4-foot pathway space between rows. Usually the rows are double rowed, two close rows are planted together to form a single row. Within each row, the strawberries are spaced from 6 to 10 inches apart. No effort is made to limit the number of runner plants. They will soon fill the spaces forming a "mat" (hence the name matted row).

It is important to train runners so that they stay within the confines of the matted row, and not grow in the pathways. Occasional tilling of the pathways will help keep them free of runners and daughter plants. If ignored, the rows will fill in and become one giant unmanagable mess. Berry production will suffer under such circumstances and it will be especially difficult to harvest ripe berries.

Mulch pathways to keep down weed growth and to conserve soil moisture. A mulch of chopped hay or straw works nicely. It also keeps the dust down and the berries stay cleaner when there is a mulch. If berries get into direct contact with the soil, they can rot.

Black plastic is sometimes used for a mulch. While acceptable, it is more expensive than mulches made from organic materials. Also other mulches decay over time and add nutrients and humans to the soil. The black plastic does not.

Other Training Systems

In the *hill system* of training strawberries, the plants are set out in bunches or "hills." Set three or four strawberry plants to each hill. Place hills 12 or 15 inches apart within rows (if using rows) and 3 to 4 feet between rows. The hill system is best for everbearers. With a hill system, runner plants are pruned off to maintain hills. Some runners are allowed. The idea is that, although the hills swell in size, they are still definitely within limits. The pruning off of runners requires a great deal of time and labor to maintain the hill form.

In the *spaced runner* system, plants are set out 2 feet apart within rows, and 3 to 4 feet apart between rows. This is another system that is quite taxing on time and labor.

With the *staggered row* system, two rows of strawberries are planted with plants staggered in each row. The rows are spaced about 4 feet apart with a zig-zag appearance. A takeoff on this pattern is the *double row staggered system* in which staggered rows are planted in pairs. *Note:* Because strawberries are quite prolific in runner production, any row system will tend to form a matted row. If you are not growing everbearers or alpine types, the best way to grow strawberries is in the matted-row system. It will save you much time and work.

The Alpine strawberry *(Fràgaria moschata)* can be grown from seed and it will not produce runners. Its fruit is not the same high quality as the other types. It can be grown as a novelty, in containers, and it is excellent for lining paths.

CULTURE

The culture of the everbearer is different from that of the Junebearer due to its different growth habits. Basically, everbearers should be grown in hills or in containers. They need to be weeded, have runners pruned, and be watered on a weekly basis. Watering is required more often during periods of drought or on sandy soil.

The Junebearer is the most popular strawberry grown. It requires a summer mulch to control weeds and conserve soil moisture. Herbicides are not recommended for the home garden. Hand hoeing and shallow cultivation will get rid of most weeds. Hoe carefully! About 70 percent of a strawberry plant's roots are located within the top 3 inches of the soil and 90 percent of the roots are within the top 6 inches of the soil.

Shallow cultivation will reduce root damage and the risks of accidentally uprooting plants. The shallow root system of strawberries means that surface moisture is more important to their success than with many other fruits. Do not let the soil get too dry! While you do not want your patch to stand in water, you do not want it to suffer from drought stress either. Parched-looking leaves that are starting to curl indicate the plants are getting desperate for water. Use common sense in irrigating your patch. Sprinkler irrigation is good for strawberries, but it will encourage diseases of the leaves and cause fruits to rot if the plants are under a constant mist. Strawberries require about 1 inch of water every 10 days (more on sandy soils). This is only during the growing season. Never water strawberries in the winter.

Because of their shallow roots, frequent waterings of lesser amounts are best. A summer mulch, not thicker than 2 inches, helps to conserve soil moisture. Chopped hay, straw, or sawdust will do nicely. This type of mulch will add organic matter to your soil as the mulch decomposes. Mulch around the plants and on the pathways. Do not cover the strawberry plants with mulch. Leave room within rows for runners to develop and root. Apply mulches a few weeks after planting and do not disturb it after it has been put on. Avoid using materials that fly away easily. Leaves should be well composted before they are used as mulch. If they are used fresh, spread a layer of topsoil or well-rotted manure over them to help hold them in place. If sawdust is used for a mulch, it too will need a layer of well-rotted manure over it to keep it from "robbing" nitrogen from the strawberries.

Wood ashes, if available, are an excellent source of potash and will increase plant yields. The best mulching material is clean, seed-free straw or chopped hay. It is preferable to sawdust because it is easier to remove in the spring and less of a nitrogen robber.

Black plastic is now frequently used as a mulch for strawberries in many gardens. It is sold in row form and it is laid between rows. When using the hill system, slits are made into the black plastic. Runners can not take root in the plastic so it is effective in training everbearers. Plastic is light in weight and require some sort of weights be placed in strategic locations to hold it in place.

WINTER CARE

A winter mulch should be applied to your strawberries after the first hard frost. A light frost will not harm the plants, but they should be protected from hard freezes. If the mulch is applied too early, the plants will not become as winter hardy as they should and are liable to suffer during the coldest parts of winter. If applied too late, the plants will have already experiencd damage to their crowns and next year's fruit buds. When new leaves start to develop in the spring, fork off the winter mulch and place it between the rows in the pathways. Winter mulch will cover over the plants themselves. Clear off the mulch each spring or it will delay the growth.

The purpose of a winter mulch is to protect your plants from cold and against soil heaving due to fluctuating temperatures. The mulch should be at least 4 inches thick. Snow acts as a natural winter mulch that will insulate plants from the cold. Because snowfall is unreliable, it is better to use straw.

THE STRAWBERRY PLANT

Strawberry growth will start from the crown. This is the thick area in the center of the plant. Strawberry crowns are perennial (live year after year) but their roots are annual. Each year the strawberry plant sends out new roots from the crown. This means that after a few years the roots get higher and higher up on the crown. This is why older plants need to have soil added to them. Compost added between plants at least yearly gives a new, enriched, water-holding soil for the new roots. Constant raking of leaves that have fallen into the strawberry patch is more than a waste of time. The leaves will gradually form the new soil along with your compost. Only if you already have a bug infestation problem should you be concerned about leaf removal. Such a problem is unlikely unless the area has been constantly sprayed over time to eliminate natural predators that feed on harmful insects.

The growth rate of the strawberry—from flower to mature fruit—depends upon external temperatures; the higher the temperature the faster it grows. The growth slows down as the temperatures lower. Any temperature lower than 40 degrees Fahrenheit will cause the plant to go into a state that resembles dormancy.

Water is crucial to the strawberry during fruit formation and throughout fruit development and maturity. If there is not enough water, it will show in the lowered quality of the fruits. The water needed to "plumb up" the berry will go out of the berry and into the leaves and crown to keep the plant alive under hot and dry conditions. The fruits shrivel and probably never will regain their desired size. It is vital to have plenty of water during the period of final *fruit swell* (just before the berries get ripe).

Some growers advise the picking off of blossoms during the first year so that the plant puts all of its energy into its own growth instead of fruit production. This idea has not been substantiated. It is better to let the plants proceed with their normal life processes. If given water after fruiting, they should do well.

One advantage of growing your own strawberries is that they can be picked, at the peak of their perfection and eaten while ripe and at the highest levels of quality. Avoid picking berries when the plants are wet. And avoid picking wet berries. Let them dry off first. Pick as often as the need arises. That usually means every other day during harvest. Pick and remove any berries that are rotten or that are damaged by birds. Keep berries out of the hot sun after picking. Wash berries with the hull *on*. Remove the hull after washing. That way you will have less "bleeding" and mushing of fruits.

RENEWAL

Every three years you will need to renew your plantings. This is a process to stimulate the production of "new" young tissue growth that is more productive than the old plants. Renewal should take place shortly after harvest. When the last berry is picked, mow off the tops of the strawberry patch as close as possible to the ground without damaging the crowns. Do not set the lawnmower on the lower settings.

After the tops are mowed—and be very careful not to injure any of the crowns or kill them in the process—proceed to narrow the rows with a shovel or rotary tiller. The rows should be narrowed to widths of 10 inches. This is accomplished by tilling under both sides of the row or one side only, whatever you prefer.

While narrowing rows, work the mulch and humus into the soil. Fertilize the row with composted manure. Treat the renewed planting the same way you would a first-year planting.

For highest production, many growers will put in entirely new plants in a patch every few years. But good production can be continued by renewing of old beds. Renewal stimulates the production of runners that produce new daughter plants. These new plants are more productive than the old plants.

Do not apply fertilizer after August 1. Strawberries need a rest period to prepare for the cold months ahead. If they receive much fertilizer too late in the season, especially nitrogen, it will promote rapid succulent growth and hardening-off is delayed. The danger occurs when fall frosts come and the plant is not ready to meet it.

PEST CONTROL

Strawberries are relatively free from many insect and disease problems. They are probably one of the most rewarding plants in that respect. Nevertheless, they can have their troubles. You can avoid many headaches by selecting planting sites that are free of pests, using disease-free planting stock, and following good cultural habits. Remember that good pest control is based on trying to prevent problems rather than trying to overcome them.

Insect Pests. Insects should not be a major pest in your home garden. It is a good idea, however, to be aware of the common troublemakers.

Aphids. Aphids suck plant juices and spread viral diseases. They are usually most abundant in the early part of the season. Aphids cause a loss of vigor in plants and this results in decreased yields of fruit. Ladybugs, or lacewings, are natural predators of aphids and should be introduced into your garden.

Cutworms. Cutworms feed on leaves of fruit. They also cause damage of cutting off the plants at or below ground level. Cutworms come out at night to do their damage. They hide in the weeds and tall grass during the day. Do not plant strawberries in sod (grass). That automatically eliminates the cutworm problem.

Cyclamen Mites. These are microscopic-size pests. The damage they cause will certainly be evident. Affected plants become stunted and the new leaves will be thickened, small, and off color. Control the problem by yanking out infected plants and burning them. Follow up by using lacewings as a predator.

Flea Beetles. These pests will occur in weedy patches or if your patch is located near a weedy area. The beetles are metallic in color and very small (about 1/16 of an inch). They jump whenever disturbed. Control them by not allowing your patch to become a jumble of weeds.

Picnic Beetles. These are small black beetles with orange markings on their backs. They are attracted to sour odors such as those given off by overripe fruits. They will damage your ripe fruits. Control by removing rotten and overripe berries from your patch.

Leafhoppers. There are many kinds of leafhoppers; most are wedge-shaped. The adults fly away when disturbed. The young (nymphs) do not have wings. This insect has the peculiar habit of moving sideways. They feed on the underside of leaves. The leaves become stunted and curl because the leafhoppers inject a toxin into them while they are feeding so that they can extract more juice from them. Control leafhoppers by controlling weeds.

Spittlebugs. The adult spittlebug does not do much harm. The young ones do the damage. They produce a frothy mass found on strawberries in May and June. This foamy substance is called *spittle mass* and contains the yellow tiny insects that suck plant juices. Control the problem by removing the spittle mass whenever you see it.

Spider Mites. Many species of mites attack strawberries, but the two-spotted types are most common. Spider mites are very tiny (about 1/16 of an inch). They eat on the underside of leaves causing the leaves to turn bronze in color. Control them by introducing a predator insect such as lacewings.

White Grubs. Usually white grubs are only a problem when strawberries are planted in grass or if the patch has been allowed to become weedy. The grubs are white with brown heads and C-shaped bodies. White grubs feed on roots (killing or weakening the strawberry plants). The grubs have a three-year cycle so they can do a great deal of damage if not controlled. Control them by tilling your soil the fall before you plant your strawberries. Till the soil again in the spring before plants are set out. Keep weeds controlled in and around your strawberry patch.

Other Insects. You are not likely to have all of the possible insect pests that can attack strawberries—even if at times it may seem that way. Most often there will be only one or two major pests and they will do all of the damage. The pests that bother strawberries are mostly well documented and there is a great deal of research on them. If you are having serious problems, you should contact your county agent for assistance.

The agricultural extension service will be able to identify what the problem is and recommend treatment. If you are an organic grower, mention this to your agent and ask for natural (non-chemical) control techniques.

DISEASES

Diseases usually vary according to region. The first rule to controlling disease is to plant only disease-free stock. Healthy plants are better able to resist disease attacks. Select only adapted and, if possible, disease-resistant varieties for your area. Two practices that aid in controlling disease are rotation of crops and frequent renewal of plantings.

You can reduce the disease menace of a lightly infested patch by mowing off the tops (renewing) of the old plants. If you are using plants from an old bed, do not set out any plants that show symptoms or are suspected of being diseased.

Botrytis. This disease attacks the fruit and is very destructive. See Chapter 31. Botrytis forms a gray mold on the berry. The infection usually starts on flower blossoms and green fruits that were injured by frosts. The mold can also occur when a berry touches the ground, a dead leaf, or another decaying fruit. The disease is worsened by damp weather and the shading of the infected berry by foliage. Control by narrowing matted rows. Pick off leaves to allow sunlight to filter through. Do not strip your plants of leaves; just remove a few of those covering the fruits. Keep the rows mulched to protect the berries from direct contact with soil. Remove all infected fruit you see and destroy it.

Blackrot. This is a term used to identify a series of crown and root disorders that display similar symptoms. Bacteria, nematodes, fungi, winter injury, high water table, excessive fertilizer, insect damage, drought stress, and other problems can all contribute to this condition. Plants affected display darkened roots (part or all of which have died). To control blackrot, first identify the cause of the problem. If you are uncertain, contact your county agent. Once the cause is identified, you will be able to straighten out the situation so it is not likely to reoccur.

Leaf Spot and Leaf Scorch. These are fungus diseases and cause similar damage. See Chapter 31. Leaf spot occurs on the upperside of leaves as small purple spots with white centers. Leaf scorch produces small purple spots that are more irregular in shape. The spots can become so abundant that the entire leaf dries up— giving it a scorched appearance. Leaf diseases weaken plants and lower yields. Leaf scorch can also affect the runners and fruitstalks. Control the problem by narrowing matted rows and renewing plantings. Rake, very gently, or vacuum the old leaves away so that the disease will not spread. Rainy weather will help spread this disease. Whenever possible, use plant varieties that are resistant.

Red Stele. Stele is the name given to the central core of the feeder roots. When they are affected with this fungus disease, they turn a reddish color. You can identify this disease by pulling out a troubled plant and using a razor blade to expose its roots. Red stele usually does not invade the crown itself. Affected plants will still have a normal color on the outside of their roots. It is only when the stele is exposed that you find the disease. Leaf symptoms appear as the mature leaves turn yellow or red. The new leaves are a bluish-green color instead of the usual healthy, bright green.

Affected plants wilt before and during the early part of the fruiting period. Seriously ill plants die before the end of the fruiting season. Those with only a mild case will send out new roots to replace the dying ones. Usually these plants will not survive the winter. Those that do will be stunted and show symptoms the following spring. It is impossible to detect red stele except for about three weeks in the early part of the fruiting season. Control by planting in areas that are well-drained. Avoid heavy soils for planting and plant resistant varieties and renew plantings when needed. If the soil becomes infected, the only known control is to plant resistant varieties.

Verticillium Wilt. This is a soil-borne fungus disease. It attacks other plants as well as strawberries. The wilt fungus is most active in the early spring, during cool weather. In new plantings, you will see the signs of infection when runners start to form. With older plantings symptoms will show up around fruiting time. The outer leaves dry up and wilt. The affected leaves turn brown. New leaf growth stunts and new roots they grow from the crown will likely be short with blackened tips. When heavy infection occurs, plants collapse and die. Mild cases cause a drastic reduction in fruit yield. Such plants are also more susceptible to winterkill. Some plants will recover and produce new plants the next year. Usually the disease is not transmitted to the next generation of strawberry plants.

Control by not planting strawberries in areas where tomatoes, eggplants, peppers, or potatoes were previously grown. Give at least two years for the wilt to die out in the soil. Plant resistant varieties whenever possible.

Viruses. Most strawberry virus diseases are actually the result of a virus complex of two or more viruses affecting the same plant. The affected plants do not show obvious symptoms (as in the case of other diseases). Reduced yield and lower-quality fruit result.

Aphids spread most viruses from one plant to another during their feeding. Control aphids to control the spread of viruses. Lacewings and ladybugs can patrol your strawberry patch for aphids. In setting out new plants always use those that are virus free (when available). Virus-free plants will almost double your production and produce higher-quality berries.

Aster Yellows. This disease once was thought to be viral in origin. Now it is believed to be caused by mycoplasma found in the plant cells. It is spread by the aster leafhopper. The symptoms are dwarfed, yellowing plants. Often they have cupped leaves as well. Control this problem by controlling leafhoppers. Do not plant near aster flowers.

REDUCING LOSSES

There are several ways to reduce your losses to disease:

☐ Select varieties that are adapted to your locality and which will be resistant to known disease problems in your area.

☐ Buy only virus-free stock. Planting infected stock can help spread diseases and introduce diseases new to an area. Diseases tend to build up more rapidly on already diseased plants.

☐ Do not use plants from an old strawberry bed. They might be diseased.

☐ Do not start a new patch near an old patch or a wild patch.

☐ Renew plantings and rotate crops when planning to replace the bed entirely.

☐ Keep a summer mulch between rows to help keep dust down and dirt off the berries.

☐ Keep a heavy mulch over the berry patch in winter to protect the plants from winter injury. This is especially in areas where severe cold is a problem. Low temperatures often cause plants to decline and die.

As always, prevention is the best medicine. Everything that you do to prevent disease conditions from occurring—and the sooner you spot troubled plants and take care of them—the healthier and more productive your patch will be. "An ounce of prevention" is worth many pounds of strawberries.

BUYING PLANTS

How many plants should you buy? About 100 plants will keep the average family in fresh strawberries during the season. If your family members are heavy fruit eaters and if you have enough space, you will want more—to serve your visitors, for friends, or to sell. It takes about 5000 plants for an entire acre. This can be fairly flexible depending upon how close you plant them. If you have never grown anything before or if you are very busy, you might want to plan your buying over three years or so while adding to the patch with time. This way you won't have plant losses because you didn't have the time or inclination to care for them. And you will get the "feel" of handling strawberries. If after planting you do not like your location, you can arrange to put your new plants elsewhere. A buying plan might be 100 Ozark (everbearers) for fall berries and 200 Stark Crimson King (Junebearers). Or you might want to just purchase Junebearers. They will be easier to work with and maintain.

Always buy virus-free plants (when available). There is no obvious visual difference in looking at the plants as compared to plants that are not virus-free. The difference will show up in performance. Virus-free plants yield from 50 to 75 percent more berries than ordinary planting stock. The nursery company should state which plants are virus free. The word "REGISTERED" will appear on the bundle's label. All virus-free plants are grown under state supervision.

Another classification of plants grown under state supervision are *certified plants*. Certification indicates that the plants are free of most noxious diseases and insects (but they might carry a virus).

It is better to purchase planting stock from a reliable company than to get plants from your neighbor's patch. The strawberries should, however, be adapted to your region. Florida strawberry plants are not suited for Wisconsin, and vice versa (see Chapter 32).

You do not have to grow everbearers to have strawberries throughout most of the summer. You can extend the growing season by planting different varieties of Junebearers that ripen at different times. Some Junebearers ripen early, others ripen at midseason, and still others ripen late. The late-ripening strawberries usually are not as productive or as high quality as are the earlier ripening varieties. This is because their fruit starts to mature during the beginning of the summer dry periods.

CASH CROP

Because of their ability to produce fruit quickly, strawberries can be grown as a cash crop. Strawberries virtually always sell for a good price and they can be an excellent way to earn a little extra money. An acre in strawberries can net you over $1500 in returns. Naturally, the more land you have the more money you can make. If you have the time to devote to its care, it might be worth your effort to rent land. Those with less land or time can try selling strawberries to your neighbors, at a roadside stand, at a local farmers' market, or even to your grocer. Some grocery stores will buy fruit from you if the quality and the price are right.

Strawberries always sell. Home owner's should plant only smaller patches that are relatively easy to manage because strawberries require a lot of work to take care of properly. Small, well-cared-for plantings will usually be more successful than larger plantings that suffer from neglect. A patch should last up to three years before it needs to be renewed or have plants replaced.

PICK-YOUR-OWN OPERATIONS

If you have more than 2 acres to devote to growing strawberries, you might want to set up a pick-your-own operation. With this kind of business, you save on harvesting and transportation costs. The market is brought right into your yard and customers furnish labor. To ensure success, you need to plan your enterprise.

Location. Where do you live? Pick-your-own operations have best chance for success when they are located near population centers (towns or cities). This is because more potential customers are available in these areas. Rural areas close to tourist attractions also do well. Most of your customers will likely be people who live within a few miles of your home if you are not located on a main thoroughfare or paved road, you will need to put up signs to direct traffic to your land.

Advertising. Word of mouth is the best and least expensive advertising. To increase the number of customers, some advertising is useful. Signs can be beneficial. They must be easy to read and highly visible. Do not start posting signs along public highways before you check with your local county roads commission. They will inform you as to the regulations and fees required. Classified ads in newspapers or suburban shoppers are effective, low-cost methods of advertising. A number of 1-minute radio ads (about 30) will bring results. They are especially useful late in the season if you still have berries to sell.

Layout. The layout of your operation will depend upon the size of your field. If you will be growing varieties that ripen at different dates, it is advisable to have a small space between the plantings. This will keep customers from accidentally or prematurely picking the next bed of berries. Paths are necessary. Always use the matted-row system. It is the most productive. Footpaths must be at least 3 feet wide and crosspaths are needed every 200 feet or less. If rows are much longer, people will be trampling over the plants making their own "shortcuts."

Employees. Someone will have to supervise your operation. You need someone to assign customers to rows for picking, to keep people from "skimming" (just picking the biggest berries) or trampling, and someone to serve at the checkout stand to collect payment for berries picked.

You save money on labor costs when family members run the

operation. If your operation is too large or your family too small or unwilling to participate, you'll need to hire other people. Try to choose people who are friendly and outgoing. Good customer relations depend upon employee behavior. Your employees represent you to the customer. A quick-tempered or rude employee can lose customers, create bad feelings, and cost you money. People make or break a business. Be extra nice and make your customers want to come back next year. Remember that your best advertising is by word of mouth.

Some training is recommended for all employees (whether family or hired hands). This will keep operations flowing more smoothly. Each employee should be given a specific area of responsibility and understand the tasks and duties required. This is especially beneficial during peak periods. If you do not maintain some kind of order, things could become chaotic.

Be good to your employees. A good employee can actually draw in business. Remember that it gets hot out in the summer sun; your employees will appreciate a cool drink. You might even want to have a lemonade stand to sell your customers cold drinks and snacks.

Parking. Ample parking space is vital to a successful operation. Your neighbors will not appreciate it if your customers trample their lawns or block their driveways. Set aside an area for parking and make it easy to get to. The roadway that leads to your entrance and the parking area will make an impression on your customers. Parking areas do not have to be paved as long as they do not turn into mud when it rains. Grade roads to provide for good drainage. Post a speed limit sign of 15 mph (miles per hour) along roadways into the parking lot. This helps minimize dust and prevents accidents. Have someone greet customers and show them where to park. This will help you to maintain order and traffic flow. If you have a paved lot, make the parking stalls 10 feet wide and 20 feet long. Have at least 25 feet between rows to allow for back-up and turn-around areas.

Recreational Area. Many of your customers will bring small children. Be prepared by setting up a recreational area where children can play and where your strawberry patch will be spared the unnecessary destruction that would occur if used as a playground. If you have limited personnel, you might want to restrict picking to those over age 12. Try not to alienate people with young children. If you state the rules clearly and tactfully, problems will be held to a minimum.

Safety. You are held liable for any injury that occurs on your property. Check with your insurance representative about obtaining liability insurance for your operation. The cost of coverage will vary according to the scope of your enterprise. A first-aid kit should be readily available. Employees should wear clothing that identifies them as employees. Children should not be left unattended.

Checkout. A stand or checkout station should be available for collecting money and counting the berry cartons. There are three methods of measurement commonly used: volume, weight, and count. Strawberries are usually sold by volume (in quart or pint boxes). Quarts are the most popular size. This is the easiest way because people usually try to heap up their boxes as full as possible. When selling by the quart, it is a good idea to provide quart baskets for picking. Even if these baskets are later dumped into other containers, they provide a good system of accurate measurement. This will help you avoid unnecessary disagreements with customers over how much they owe.

When fruit is sold by its weight, you need a special scale that must be approved by the state division of weights and standards. This is not a practical way in most cases, but is gaining in popularity. A pound is slightly less than a quart. Most customers feel uneasy not knowing exactly what a pound of strawberries looks like. They are likely to mush them with too much handling. Strawberries are too small to sell by the count method (individual fruits).

Checkout stations can also sell refreshments if at least two people are working at them. The easier you make it for people to check out the smoother things will flow. Organize your checkout so that it moves in a one-way fashion. That helps lines to move faster and prevents arguments among customers as to who got there first.

Have enough change on hand and do not be afraid to accept personal checks. Allow checks to cover only the cost of the fruit purchased. This will protect you if a check does bounce and it will also enable you to have plenty of change on hand for cash-paying customers.

If you receive a bad check, allow the party to make good. Sometimes people accidentally overdraw on their accounts. If they fail to make good, record the customers name on a customer blacklist and be sure no employee will accept any more checks from them.

Pricing Policy. Keep abreast of the current retail prices for strawberries in your area. It is usually a good idea to price slightly under retail prices to encourage people to buy from you. If you charge the same price or more than stores, people will prefer to buy from the store instead of going through the chore of picking their own.

Keep your prices stable. Customers tend to be wary of places where prices fluctuate widely. Reducing the price at the end of the season to get rid of leftover berries or those of inferior quality is common practice. Do not price below your production costs. You must meet costs and make a profit; if you do not you are not operating a business. Add up your costs, fertilizer, hired help, advertising, and whatever other expenses you incur. Also keep in mind replacement costs because some of your plants will need to be replaced. The money you have left over when all expenses are paid, including taxes, is your profit—enjoy it.

Chapter 6

Raspberries

Always a favorite fruit—but so rare to find fresh and so expensive to buy in the store—the best way to enjoy raspberries is to grow your own. Although the red varieties (Fig. 6-1) are most popular, black, purple, and yellow varieties offer a rainbow of colorful fruits for summer parties and festive occasions. Try one—try them all, you will not regret planting raspberries.

Well-established, disease- and insect-free plantings are highly productive. They commonly produce yields of 1 to 2 quarts of berries on each plant. Raspberries involve more work than straw-berries, but they are not as difficult to grow as you might think.

The botanical names for raspberries are as follows. Red raspberries are named *Rubus idaeus* and black raspberries are named *Rubus occidentalis*. Purple raspberries are a hybrid of black and red varieties. Yellow fruited raspberries belong to the same species as the reds.

CLIMATE

Raspberries are a fairly hardy fruit. The red varieties are the hardiest (more so than the black and purple ones). Summer-fruiting red raspberry plants are tolerant of winter temperatures of minus 30 degrees Fahrenheit or lower when the plant is fully acclimated or hardened off.

The major problem is not cold as much as fluctuating hot and cold winter temperatures. This is especially a problem when below

Fig. 6-1. Red Raspberries. The best way to enjoy raspberries is to grow your own (courtesy Stark Bro's Nurseries & Orchards Co.).

zero temperatures follow above freezing temperatures after the middle of December. When warm temperatures occur in winter, the dark surface of the cane absorbs sunlight and becomes warmer than surface temperatures. This is especially noticeable when raspberries are planted on slopes facing south. Such a situation could cause the plant to suffer winter injury.

SITE

Raspberries are most productive when grown in full sunlight. They require good air circulation and a well-drained soil. To decrease the chance for disease and insect problems, always isolate cultivated raspberries from wild ones. Plant them in areas not previously occupied by wild raspberry or blackberry plants.

Raspberries prefer a sandy loam that is rich in organic matter. Unless you have access to an adequate supply of dependable water, it is best to avoid light, sandy soils as well as other types of soil that have a poor water-holding capacity. Some soils can be inproved with the addition of peat moss and compost (well rotted) when planting. A slightly acid soil is preferred over alkaline soils. If your soil is alkaline, the addition of peat moss will be of great benefit.

Raspberries should be planted on north slopes or on the north side of a building or windbreak where there is winter shade. The exception is for everbearer varieties. These should be planted on the south side or in a protected area to promote the rapid growth of the primocanes (one-year canes) early in the spring. Because everbearers will bear a crop the same year, you want them to get as early of a start as possible.

TYPES OF RASPBERRIES

The several kinds of raspberries include red, black, purple, and yellow fruiting varieties, as well as two types: the summer fruiting and the everbearers (also called fallbearers).

Red Rasberries

The red varieties are the most hardy and productive. They come in summer fruiting types and everbearers. The everbearers usually run into the same problem as do everbearing strawberries: summer droughts and insect pests. For this reason, everbearers are more work than the summer-fruiting varieties. If you grow everbearers, grow them for a fall crop and they will be easier to maintain.

Black and Purple Varities

These are not as winter hardy as are the reds. They also require more favorable growing conditions. If properly managed, the black and purple varieties can be more productive than the reds. In the home garden, however, this is not the case. Black raspberries have a distinctive flavor. The purple varieties are hybrids between black and red varieties. They grow in the same manner as do the blacks, but they are hardier and more vigorous growers. When properly maintained, they are capable of outyielding either black or red raspberries. Horticulturists attribute this extra productivity to *hybrid vigor.* This term is used to explain the superior performance of hybrid plants.

64

Yellow Raspberries

These fruits are similar to the reds in growing habits, but the color of the fruit is amber or yellow. Yellow raspberries can be grown as a novelty, but they are not usually as productive as are the red varieties. They are rarely grown for the commercial market.

PLANTING

To plant raspberries, you will need a long-handled shovel. Keep the plants out of the sun and wind while you are preparing the site for them. It is usually a good practice to allow the roots to soak in a tub of water for a couple of hours prior to planting.

Once you have determined an acceptable site for your raspberries, dig a hole for each plant, usually in a row with at least 3 feet between each hole. The hole must be large enough to hold the raspberry roots without bending them. If you have sandy soil, you should make an even larger hole and add leaves and peat moss to it (covering them over with topsoil) before you begin planting. This will help to hold soil moisture and improve your soil. The roots of the plant must touch only soil. Be sure to cover up any leaves that you add to the planting hole.

Most raspberry plants have thorns. It is a very good idea to put on a pair of thick work gloves while handling the plants. This will help to avoid getting pricked. Plant each plant with care. Hold the plant upright with one hand and shovel in topsoil with the other. Tamp down the soil gently to eliminate any air pockets near the roots. Soak each plant with water, and water once a week thereafter, soaking each plant thoroughly when so doing.

Raspberry plants should have their canes tied to a support system. This will help to prevent cane breakage in high winds. It will make the crop easier to manage and it will be easier to control pests. A plant that is staked is easier to pick come harvest time. It is also easier to keep sanitary. Most raspberries, except for the black and purple varieties, tend to *sucker* (send up canes from the root). Your plants will form a briar patch if left to themselves or if pruning off of the suckers is neglected.

Never plant black raspberries near red ones. A mosaic disease that occurs in red raspberries is fatal to black varieties.

THE RASPBERRY PLANT

Raspberries have perennial roots and crowns, but their above-ground canes are biennial (they live for only two years). The first year they send up the *primocane* (the first year cane). This is nonfruiting except in the case of everbearers. During the second year, they send up new primocanes and last years canes become *floricanes* (two-year-old canes). These are the canes that bear flowers and fruit. After they fruit they die. Once the ripe fruit has been picked, the floricanes will have finished their life's purpose and should be removed.

TRAINING

If you train the growth habits of your raspberry plants, it will make picking easier and you will achieve higher yields. The two common methods used to train raspberries are the hill system and hedgerows.

The Hill System

When using the hill system, set a stake in the center of each hill. One plant will be sufficient per hill as they multiply. The stake should be metal or treated wood. It must be tall enough—at least 4 feet—so that you can tie the canes to it. Tie the canes loosely with a rugged twine; do not use wire. The top of the canes, after pruning, should be held closely to the stake. Do not tie them so tight as to cause injury to the cane or so loosely that the canes can whip in the wind. If canes are allowed to whip in the wind, you will suffer breakage of canes and decreased yields. Do not tie the young shoots or suckers to the cane until late fall.

Hedgerow

When planting in a hedgerow, use a trellis or fence to keep the canes upright. The trellis will make it easier to pick crops and maintain the plants. This system is best for people who have more room than those who would use the hill system. To build a permanent trellis, set up support posts at reasonable intervals along the row. Stretch wire between the posts. You can use a galvanized or aluminum wire. Use a heavy-gauge wire. Your hardware dealer can tell you what kind is acceptable. Probably #10 gauge wire is best. Some people prefer to use two wires, set at different heights, to achieve greater control over the canes. Place the canes between the wires. Use metal hooks to keep wires together if they spread. You will be able to move these hooks along the wire easily to where they are needed. Tie the canes loosely to the wires after pruning. Use twine and wear gloves to protect your hands.

A temporary trellis can be made if you prefer. Use stakes and binder twine. Set heavy stakes in the row at 15-foot intervals. Less space is needed in smaller yards. Tie the binder twine to the end stake and fasten it to each stake in the row. Repeat this procedure on the opposite side of the row. You can use a second support line at a lower level if you want more support for the canes. Tie canes loosely to the twine. The twine must be taut (tight so it does not sag). If it sags, your plants will blow in the wind. This could loosen them from the support system. Remember that a support system must provide support; that is the whole purpose.

Before you build a trellis or fence to support your raspberries, you might want to check out others in the neighborhood so you have some idea as what the completed system should look like. If it seems too complicated, you can substitute a chain link fence or a split rail fence. Such fences are quite effective and they are really the safest bet for a beginner.

The dimensions of your raspberry support system will vary according to how many plants need support and how big of an operation you are planning. Once you have this in mind, you will have a good idea of how much fencing materials you will need. A split-rail fence makes an extremely attractive support system for training raspberries.

CULTURE

Water, weed control, and fertilizer are the three keys to successful raspberry culture. Water is the primary need. During the stages of fruit development on through maturity, it is crucial that your raspberry plants receive adequate water. The period just before the raspberries turn ripe is known as *fruit swell*. During that time, the raspberries reach their final size. If they do not receive enough water, they never will reach the size they should and the quality of the fruit will suffer. Fruits will be shriveled, deformed and not taste as good—with dry flesh. Be sure to water plants during dry periods.

Weeds must be controlled around your raspberry plants so that they do not compete for moisture and nutrients. Weeds can be removed by shallow cultivation. A summer mulch around plants for controlling weeds is also recommended. This will save you much of the work of weeding because the mulch smothers most weeds and prevents their growth. Grass around the base of your raspberries should also be removed. It is better to keep an area around the base of each plant free of grass. The same mulch used to control weeds will also help keep grass down.

Fertilize your plants each spring. Raspberries are heavy feeders and a circle of manure around the base of each plant in the spring is effective. If you are using fresh manure, be sure that it does not touch the plant itself. Also toss a few shovelfuls of dirt over the manure to keep gnats from breeding in it. It is not pleasant to work in the garden with gnats after you.

Do not fertilize plants after August 1 or you will interfere with the hardening-off process. The plants will need this period in the late summer and early fall to prepare for winter. To do this they must slow or stop growth and harden off. Heavy application of fertilizer late in the season delays hardening off and could leave your plants subject to winter injuries.

PRUNING

Summer-Fruiting Red and Yellow Raspberries. Prune to the ground all canes that have borne fruit. Do this right away after harvest. These canes have served their life's purpose and will shortly die. If you prune them out right away, they will not be able to attract diseases and insects. Remove all cuttings from your raspberry patch. This pruning out of the old canes will give new room for the young canes to grow. Thin out these new canes. Leave only three or four of the sturdiest ones for each 4 feet of row. If you are using the hill system, leave six or eight canes per hill.

Do not cut back the cane tips until the following spring. Then you are able to observe winter damage and dieback that might have occurred on each cane. The dead parts should always be removed.

Spring pruning is done while plants are still dormant early in the spring. Spring is a good time to assess what needs to be pruned because there will be no leaves in the way. Pruning must be done after the danger of winter injury is past and no more subzero weather is expected. It should also be done before new growth starts so the plant is not setback during its active stages of growth. If you did not get around to pruning out the old canes and thinning out the new ones last fall, now is the time to do it.

Cut back side branches on the fruiting canes that remain after you have pruned out the others. Prune off the tips of the fruiting canes slightly. This is called *tipping.* It is done to prevent canes from becoming top heavy with fruits. Be careful not to cut off too much or you will reduce the size of the crop. Never cut off more than one-fourth the length of the cane.

Red and Yellow Everbearers. Everbearers produce their largest crop in the fall (on the primocanes). To increase production, you will want to increase the vigor and number of primocanes. Prune down all canes in the late fall after the plants are dormant. Be careful not to injure the crowns. In the spring, new growth (primocanes) will develop. These canes will produce fruit in the fall of the same season.

Fruit continues to ripen until frost. You can extend the harvest season by using sprinkler irrigation for frost protection in the fall. Using this method of training, everbearers are extremely easy to grow and are most productive. The main advantage of using this method is to increase fall crops. You also will have fruits ripen slightly earlier. The disadvantage is that you will receive no summer crop because summer crops are always borne on floricanes and you never have floricanes with this type of pruning. In essence, you are raising your raspberries like an annual—for a large fall crop.

This pruning system does NOT work for summer-fruiting varieties—only for everbearers. The summer-fruiting types produce canes one year and flower and fruit the next year. Everbearers bear fruit on primocanes so they can be grown either way. Pruning them like the summer fruiting varieties will give you a small crop as well. It is easier, however, to prune them for their fall crop.

Because this technique is so simple, everbearers are the easiest to grow of the raspberries (when grown for fall production). Another advantage of fall pruning is that you will have fewer insect and disease pests. There should be less problems with rodent damage as well. Mulch thoroughly in the winter to protect crowns and roots of your raspberries.

Black Raspberries. There are two times to prune black raspberries; summer and spring. Spring pruning is called *dormant pruning* because the time to prune the plants is while they are still dormant. In the summer, when the primocanes are about 2 feet tigh, pinch off the tip of each cane. This causes canes to produce side branches. Do not confuse your pruning practices. When pruning red raspberries, you prune off the side branches. With black raspberries, you encourage the production of side branches. Right after harvest, prune off all canes that bore fruit down to the ground level. Remove these cuttings from your patch and destroy them.

During spring pruning, cut back all side branches to about 12 inches. Select five of the sturdiest canes and prune out all others. Be certain to remove the cuttings from the patch. If you forgot to prune out the old fruiting wood after harvest last year, do so now.

Purple Raspberries. In the summer, pinch off the tops when the primocanes are about 30 inches tall. This encourages the canes to form branches. After the canes have borne fruit, prune them down to ground level and dispose of the cuttings.

In the spring, purple raspberries can be pruned somewhat similar to black raspberries. Select the five biggest canes and prune out the rest. Prune side branches to about 18 inches. Secure the canes to the support system. If you did not remove last year's fruiting canes, do so now.

INSECT PESTS

There are several insects that annoy raspberries. Usually insect pests will be minimized by following good cultural practices such as sanitation and weed control. Sometimes a few pests will get out of hand and more drastic measures may be needed. Do not plant raspberries near wild raspberries because they may host insect and disease pests.

Red-Necked Cane Borer. The red-necked cane borer is a bluish-black beetle about ¼ inch long in its adult stage. It makes its appearance in late May or June. The beetle is easy to recognize by its coppery red neck. The adult female lays her eggs in the cane and the larvae bore beneath the bark. Boring larvae cause the stems to swell several inches along the cane. By late fall, the swellings will contain white-colored grubs, about ½-inch long. Control them by fall pruning. Prune out and burn all canes with these abnormal swellings.

Raspberry Cane Borer. The adult female beetle is slender, black with yellow stripes, about ½ inch long, and they have long antennae. The grubs (young bugs that look like fat worms) bore into the cane to hibernate for winter. When spring arrives, the grubs bore downward inside the cane, killing it. Whenever this insect is present it makes characteristic markings on the cane. There will be a double row of punctures around the stem tip. These holes will cause the cane tips to wilt and die. Prune out wilted canes at least 6 inches below the wilted area. Burn these cuttings to kill the insects inside.

Raspberry Fruitworm. This grub is about ¼ inch long, slender, and white. It feeds inside the buds or developing fruit and causes the fruit to drop prematurely. The larvae drop to the ground with the fruit and overwinter in the soil. The next spring it will emerge as a beetle. The beetles are light brown, ⅛ inch long, and sort of hairy. They feed on young leaves and lay their eggs near the buds and green fruits. Control them by cultivating the soil underneath the plants in the fall. This breaks up the pupal cases (overwintering stages) of the pests.

Raspberry Crown Borer. The borer is 1 inch long with a white body and brown head. It feeds at the base of the plant in the larger roots and crown. The insect causes the leaves to turn red prematurely and the canes to wilt in late summer. The adult is a moth. It looks like a "yellow jacket" and appears in late summer or early fall. The female moth lays her eggs on the leaves, the larvae crawl to the crown, and they overwinter under the bark just beneath the soil surface. In the spring, the larvae attack new cane buds. They take two years to develop into moths. Control them by pulling up infested plants and burning them.

Raspberry Cane Maggots. The adult is a small grayish fly that is a little smaller than the common housefly. The flies appear early in the spring and lay their eggs in the shoot tips or new buds. The maggots (which look like little worms and are the young stages of the fly) gridle stems by their feeding habits. The damage usually appears in late spring. The cane tips wilt or break off and the base turns purple. Where the stems are broken off it will look as if cut by a knife. The maggots move downward into the stems below the break point and overwinter within the stems. Examine your raspberry patch in May or June for signs of damage. If you find broken cane tips, prune off several inches below the break point and burn these cuttings. In late fall, check again to see if you missed any. Pruning can give you near total control of this pest as they rarely attack more than a few canes in a patch.

Raspberry Sawfly. The adult is a wasp that is black with yellow and red markings. The larvae bothers the leaves. These worm-like creatures are pale and thin. They feed along leaf edges and eat until only the veins remain. These are difficult to control. Use of a predator insect, such as lacewing, is recommended. Flypaper can also trap adults, but it is messy to work with.

Tree Crickets. The adult female causes the injury. She bores a number of tiny holes into the canes and lays an egg in each hole. The holes are usually lined up in a single row. The cane area above the holes usually dies. The insects overwinter in the egg stage. In spring the eggs hatch. Tree crickets do not normally feed upon raspberry plants, but they sometimes will eat leaves or ripe fruits. Most often they feed upon aphids and slow-moving pests. They do injure the plant by their egg-laying habits. The adults are pale green, 1 inch long, and they have long antennae. Examine canes in the fall for egg-laying punctures. Prune out and burn these cuttings. That will destroy the overwintering eggs.

Spider Mites. Spider mites are very tiny creatures that are not ordinarily visible to the naked eye. They feed on the undersurface of leaves. The leaves become spotted with brown or white spots. If there is a high population of mites, the leaves will fall off and the fruits will dry up. Mites are mostly a problem during periods of drought. Control them by use of a predator insect such as lacewings. They can be controlled to some degree with ordinary soap (not detergent) and water. On thorny plants such as raspberries, this is not practical.

DISEASES

Diseases reduce yields and lower fruit quality. Here are some general cultural practices that help. Plant only disease-free stock. Do not plant near wild raspberries. Yank out and burn diseased plants that occur in established plantings. Prune fruiting canes immediately after harvest. Control weeds. Maintain good air circulation in the patch and keep it open to plenty of sunlight because high moisture conditions favor disease development.

Spur Blight. This is a fungus that is especially bothersome to red raspberry plants. The symptoms first appear in early summer on the young canes. Purple or brown discoloration occurs usually near the area of leaf attachment. The areas enlarge up to 2 or more inches. When these infected canes start fruiting the next year, the branches that grow from these diseased areas will be weak with yellow leaves. The affected area turns gray in the fall the bark splits and small pimples form. These pimples contain the fungus spores (seeds). Berries borne on diseased plants are small, dry, and seedy. Control this disease by removing fruiting canes after they have fruited, thin out the rows, and keep the weeds down.

Anthracnose. This is another fungus that grows on all raspberries. The black and purple varieties are the most susceptible. Small, purplish spots occur on young canes. They enlarge and become slightly sunken with buff-colored centers and purple borders (forming large spots on the canes). As heavily infected canes mature, they crack along the length because of drying out. The berries they bear are small, dry, and seedy.

If the infection occurs late in the season, the spots will be larger and merge to form a condition known as *gray bark*. This is the same disease. Control the problem by not planting black raspberries near red ones, and by spraying with a copper-sulfate fungicide such as bourdeaux mixture.

Cane Blight. This fungus disease causes canes to wilt at just about the time the raspberries start to ripen. Cankers (wounds) appear at the base of infected plants. Control the problem by pruning (especially before a rain). Rain helps spread the disease. Remove and burn all cuttings and keep weeds under control.

Yellow Leaf Rust. This fungus disease attacks mostly red raspberries. It causes leaves to turn yellow and drop. The earliest symptoms are when little yellow blisters appear on the leaves. Brown or black spots will appear on the underside of leaves in the fall. This disease is easily mistaken for orange rust. Control by pruning out the fruiting canes after harvest.

Orange Rust. This fungus disease occurs only on black and purple raspberries. Reddish-orange blisters first appear on the underside of leaves, usually in the spring. Canes bearing the infected leaves will look spindly and weak. Do not grow raspberries near wild raspberry or blackberry plantings. Use only disease-free stock when planting. Remove infected plants from established plantings and burn them.

Leaf Spot. This fungus disease attacks leaves. It causes greenish-black spots that turn gray as the leaves mature. Infected tissue will drop out and leave holes in the leaves. Control leaf spot with a copper-sulfate fungicide such as bourdeaux mixture.

Powdery Mildew. Red raspberries, especially Latham, are very susceptible to powdery mildew. Mildew infection leaves a grayish-white coating over the leaves. Damp, muggy weather and heavy dews encourage the development of mildew. Control mildew by pruning to encourage good air circulation and sunlight penetration. Use copper-sulfate fungicide, such as bourdeaux mixture, for guaranteed control.

Verticillium Wilt. This is a soil-borne fungus disease that infects the plant through its root system. The symptoms vary as to the season, temperature and whether red or black raspberries are involved. Control by planting only disease-free stock. Do not plant in an area where tomatoes, peppers, eggplants, potatoes, or strawberries were previously grown. Also avoid planting near pine trees.

Late Raspberry Rust. This fungus disease does not develop until late in the summer, usually around July or August. It will cause leaves to drop off earlier than they normally do. Small, yellow blisters develop on the underside of infected leaves. It can also attack canes. Control this disease by pruning out infected areas and burning them. Also prune out all fruiting wood immediately after harvest.

Mosaic. This is one of the most common viruses. Aphids transmit this disease. It causes some leaf mottling early in the season or it will cause rough blistered mottling, stunt plant growth, and even cause afflicted parts to decay. If there is only a slight affliction, the disease reveals itself through low fruit yield and low quality fruits.

To control mosaic, prune all plants displaying symptoms. If more than 20 percent of the plants are infected, tear out the infected plants and burn them.

Before replacing the plants with new ones, it will be necessary to control aphids. Use a predator insect such as lacewings for aphid control. This will help prevent the spread of the disease if there are any traces left where you did not spot it.

Leaf Curl. This is also a virus transmitted by aphids. If this is a known problem in your area, plant only resistant varieties. If you already have the disease, treat it the same way as mosaic. Remove infected plants. They are identifiable by the downward curling of their leaves. Introduce lacewings to the patch to control aphids.

Crown Gall. This is a bacterial disease. The symptoms are wartlike dark swellings around the crown area of the plant or along roots that have broken off during cultivation. Control by planting only disease-free stock. Be careful not to injure plants when cultivating around them.

Chapter 7

Blackberries and Dewberries

The blackberry (Fig. 7-1) has great versatility. It can be enjoyed ripe and fresh right off the bush or made into mouth-watering jam, a robust juice, wine, and they make for a scrumptious pie. In the past, the blackberry has not been as popular with home growers as other small fruits, primarily because of its thorns. It is a good idea to wear gloves and a long-sleeved shirt or blouse when working in the blackberry patch. Otherwise, you can get scratched up quite badly.

With the new thornless varieties available, there is no reason that most people can't enjoy growing their own blackberries. The thornless varieties take the agony out of working in the blackberry patch. Although they are not usually as winter hardy as the varieties with thorns, some are quite hardy. If you have any question about hardiness, consult your nursery.

Some varieties of blackberry require cross-pollination, but others do not. Check with your nursery company about the pollination requirements of the blackberries you order. Sometimes even those fruits that are capable of self-pollinating, will bear bigger crops when they are cross-pollinated with another variety. Remember that you will have the greatest success in growing blackberries when you choose varieties that are adapted to your area.

The American blackberry (*Rubus ursinus*) was not cultivated in the home garden much prior to the Civil War. When people wanted blackberries they simply went off "blackberrying" (gather-

Fig. 7-1. Blackberry plants. It is a wise idea to wear a good pair of gloves and a long-sleeved shirt or blouse when working in the blackberry patch.

ing fruits from wild patches). Blackberries grew in many wooded areas and before the urbanization of America, people would simply harvest what they needed from these native stands.

In some rural areas this custom still exists. With the diminishing wilderness and the easy culture of new hybrids it is more practical to grow your own blackberries.

Botanists sometimes classify blackberries and dewberries as separate fruits. There are physical differences in the fruit structure and growth habits. Nevertheless, most horticulturists simply classify them as two types within the blackberry family.

BLACKBERRIES

Blackberries are relatively hardy, but they might not endure the rugged winters of the Great Plains or Mountain states. The new smoothstem varieties are even less hardy than the thorny types.

The most important consideration when setting out blackberries is the availability of water. While the fruit is growing and during its stages of ripening, the blackberry requires a large amount of water.

In areas with severe winters, the slope of the planting must be considered. Blackberries planted on hillsides are in less danger of winter injury and spring frosts than are those planted in frost pockets (low-lying areas). In windy areas, it is advantageous to have a windbreak (row of trees or shrubs) nearby to protect the plants from the elements. Winds can cause severe damage to blackberry plants by whipping and breaking the canes.

Blackberries do well on most types of soil. They prefer a well-drained soil with access to ample moisture. If your soil is very sandy, you will need to add large quantities of organic matter to improve its water-holding capacity. Sandy soils are poor blackberry soils. The blackberry plant is very sensitive to drought stress and will require additional waterings during summer dry spells.

Avoid heavy clay soils where water stands on the soil surface well into the spring. During the winter, such soils hold too much water and can damage roots. Never plant blackberries in an area that was in tomatoes, peppers, eggplants, potatoes, strawberries, or raspberries the previous season. This way you should be able to avoid problems with verticillium wilt.

Planting

Do not let the roots dry out before or during the planting operation. Plant your blackberries as soon as possible. If you cannot plant them right away, heel in the roots. Do this by digging a shallow trench, out of direct sunlight, and place the roots into this trench. Lay the plants on one side so that they do not stand upright. Pour a bucket of water over the roots and then cover them with moist dirt. Be sure that all of the roots are covered and that the plants will not be exposed to direct sunlight. Plant the blackberries as soon as you can. This is only a temporary method to keep plants alive until they are set out in their permanent location.

If you are able to set plants out right away, let the roots soak in a tub of water for a couple of hours. In good soil, blackberries can be planted without much effort. Cut a slit in the soil with the blade of your shovel. Press the handle forward to open the slit. Put in the root of the blackberry plant. Withdraw your shovel and pack the soil down firmly with your feet. On ordinary soil dig a regular hole. Add peat moss and good topsoil when refilling the hole.

The distance you space plants depends upon the growing conditions in your area, if you have good soil, and how much land you have. Most plants do better when they are not spaced as far apart as many people recommend. Plants are most productive when grown in hedgerows. Space them 3 feet apart within rows and 5 to 9 feet apart between rows. Blackberries perform best when they receive full sunlight. The more sunlight they receive the better they perform (provided they are also receiving adequate water and nutrition).

Some growers contend that by arranging rows in an east to west fashion they can get a slightly higher percentage of sunlight on their berries than if they were planted from north to south. Either way, as long as they have access to plenty of sunshine, they should do well.

Training

The hardest part of growing blackberries will be their training. This process is worst with the thorny varieties because they are not as much fun to work with. Wear the proper clothing. This includes something to protect your arms and hands from scratches.

Blackberries have erect or semierect canes. Most will grow without a support system. Nevertheless, they are easier to take care of and more productive when trained to a support system. Canes break if they are left to whip freely in the wind. They will also suffer from accidental injuries when people are working around them.

Poles, fences or trellises are the common systems for training blackberries. If you have only a few plants and want to disperse them throughout your yard—or achieve a special landscape effect—they can be tied to poles. The preferred method is to train them to trellises.

Construct a trellis for your blackberries by placing a heavy-gauge steel wire between two poles. The poles can be metal or wood as long as they are solid. If you are using wood, it is best to use a treated wood that will not decay. The wire must be taut (tight, not flexible). It should be straight and must not sag in the middle. If it does sag, pull it tighter so that it straightens up. The poles should be at least 4 feet high and the wire should be set at about 2½ feet above the ground.

The canes should be tied to the wire. They should be tied somewhat loosely so as to not cut off their circulation (but they must be secure). Use a soft string and tie each cane separately (not in bunches). This allows for better sunlight penetration and air circulation to help reduce the incidence of fungus and mildew diseases. By allowing for greater sunlight penetration, you increase the productivity of the fruiting canes.

If you do not want to build your own trellis, chain-link fences or split-rail fences are excellent substitutes. They are probably the safest bet for beginners.

Pruning

The crowns of the blackberry plant are perennial; new canes arise from them every year. The canes are biennial (they live for only two years). The first-year canes are called primocanes. The second year these same canes are called floricanes. It is in the second year that canes bear flowers and fruit.

The primocanes are devoted to vegetative growth, sending out laterals (side branches), and gaining height. The floricanes produce the fruiting buds. After they fruit the floricanes die. They have served their life's purpose and do not fruit but once. Shortly after harvest the old floricanes should be pruned out to ground level. This is a good sanitation practice. Old and dying canes will attract insects and diseases or serve as a nesting area for pests. Pruning them out will open up room for the growth of new canes.

Laterals (side branches) should be pruned each year in the spring. Fruit from pruned laterals will be larger and of higher quality than that from unpruned ones. In some areas where winters are harsh, there will be a natural tip dieback as tips of the canes die from winter injury. Prune this dieback and about one-half inch more (unless the dieback is severe). If dieback is severe, prune only the dieback area.

Before growth starts in the spring, prune the side branches to about 12 inches in length. This might seem hard to do at first. Many people are reluctant to do any pruning for fears of hurting the plant. Nevertheless, it will be good for the plant, increase production, and provide better-quality fruit.

Blackberries are quite prolific and many varieties send up shoots from the roots. These shoots are called suckers. Prune these suckers to the ground each spring. If they are not kept under control, the natural tendency for the plant is to form a thicket. This is not a desirable condition because such growth is difficult to manage and harvest fruits from.

Some people prefer to pull our suckers rather than prune them out. If you do this, be careful not to injure your plant. These suckers can be transplanted to other areas where you want blackberries to grow or they can be given to friends who want to start their own blackberry patch.

Tipping

When canes reach a height of 3 feet, prune off the tips. This will encourage side branches to develop. These branches will bear the fruits. Tipped canes are more stout and better able to support a heavy load of fruit. If canes are not tipped, they will be leaner, taller, and not as strong. They will not bear as much fruit. Sometimes they will break off under the weight strain.

Thinning

After harvest and all floricanes are removed, some of the new canes should be thinned out. Leave only three or four canes. Select the largest of the new canes to stay and prune out the weakest-looking canes. This makes for easier management. If you let suckers form within the rows, thin them to about five or six canes per lineal foot of row.

In areas of the South where anthracnose and rosette pose serious disease problems, pruning should be more severe. Prune down all canes, both old and new, after harvest. Then fertilize to promote the growth of replacement canes for the production of next year's crop. A well-rotted manure is an excellent fertilizer. Do not fertilize any plant after August 1. If you are using a commercial fertilizer, use a well-balanced formula such as 10-10-10.

Weed Control

Keep your blackberry patch free of weeds. If weeds are allowed to grow, they will be difficult to control and will compete with the blackberries for nutrients and moisture. Start cultivating in spring and cultivate as needed to control weeds. To avoid hurting any shallow roots, do not cultivate deeper than 3 inches near the plant. That will be deep enough to stop most weeds. If necessary, you can yank out deeper weeds by the root. In pathways in between rows, you can cultivate mechanically (with a rototiller) if you prefer. Around the plants, a simple hoe or hand tools will be best. Discontinue cultivation about one month before freezing weather normally begins.

Mulch

Some people like to use a summer mulch around their blackberry plantings. This will help somewhat to keep down weeds. It also helps to conserve soil moisture. Any organic mulch adds nutrients to the soil as it slowly decomposes. A winter mulch should be about 4 inches thick. Chopped hay or straw are easy to work with.

Harvest

There is nothing like picking blackberries from your own

patch. It is an activity that the whole family will enjoy. And probably the whole neighborhood unless you have a good fence.

Pick the fruit when it is ripe. It will have a sweet flavor and good color. Pick often because the fruit won't all ripen at once. Plan on harvesting berries about every other day. The fruit should be picked early in the morning before temperatures get too hot. Blackberries will not spoil as quickly if they are picked in the morning as they do when picked in the afternoon. When picking, place the fruits gently into small containers. Be careful not to crush or bruise the berries. Use of small containers is preferable to large containers. Quart- or pint-size baskets do nicely.

After the baskets have been filled, place them in a shady spot while filling up your other baskets. Do not let them set out in the hot sunlight. If you are using metal pails to pick berries, cool the pails first and store the berries in smaller containers. They keep better that way.

Only pick ripe berries. Those that are not quite ripe yet should be spared until they are fully ripe. They have a better flavor when ripe. Berries that are overripe or decaying should not be placed in the same containers as the fruits you plant to eat. To do so will lower the quality of the other berries.

Berries picked when properly ripe, handled carefully, and stored in a cool place or in a refrigerator will stay in good condition for several days. Berries that are overripe or injured spoil quickly.

DEWBERRIES

Dewberries are essentially "trailing blackberries." They are sometimes classified as separate fruits because of a few differences. If it sounds confusing, that is because there are two schools of thought on the subject. Botanists generally want to classify them separately, but many horticulturists combine them.

The fruit of the dewberry differs from the fruit of the blackberry. Dewberry clusters are usually more open, ripen earlier, and will be larger in size. The dewberry is often sweeter than blackberries. Some examples of dewberries are boysenberries, loganberries, and youngberries.

Dewberry canes have a trailing habit that is similar to grapes. They are not erect and these canes *must* be tied to some kind of support system in order for the plant to stand up. Blackberry canes, in contrast, are tied in culture but are capable of standing by themselves; dewberry canes are not.

Because of this different cane growth habit, dewberries have different cultural and pruning requirements than the blackberry. The climatic requirements of dewberries are similar to those required of blackberries. Dewberries are not quite as hardy as blackberries as a rule. They cannot be recommended for areas where winter cold injury is normally a problem.

Site

The best site for planting dewberries is a place in the sun. They perform best when exposed to optimum sunlight levels. Sometimes you will be able to increase the level of sunlight that reaches plants by pruning off the lower branches of shade trees, instead of removing the entire tree. Northern locations in the yard are not usually the best sites to locate your dewberry plants.

Avoid planting dewberries in frost pockets (low-lying areas). They need a somewhat sheltered location. Dewberries are considered a tender plant so the care you take in selecting a site will pay off.

Dewberries prefer a rich loam soil. It must be well-drained, but needs to have a high water-holding capacity. Sandy soils or soils that get very dry during hot periods in the summer should be avoided. Water is crucial to the dewberry and especially during fruit growth and swell (final formation of the fruits before they ripen). Plants that do not receive sufficient water will likely be stunted and produce inferior fruits.

The same rules apply to dewberries as to blackberries. Do not plant them in an area previously occupied by a solanaceous crop (such as tomatoes, potatoes, peppers, and eggplants). The addition of organic matter to the soil, whether in the form of peat moss or compost, will improve the textures of most soils.

Planting

Soak the roots of your dewberries for a few hours before setting them out. Do not let them soak overnight or the roots will become waterlogged. Dewberries need a support system. This should be up prior to setting out the plants. If the plants are set out before there is a support system for them, it will be harder to train them. Some people like to use an old grape arbor or rose arbor for this purpose. You can do this, but it is better to build a trellis or to use a split-rail fence.

Dewberry vines grow profusely. They require a trellis of their own. They should not be grown alongside your grapes or other plants. The two fruits are likely to compete and the grape leaves will shade out the dewberries. Dewberries will sprawl all over the place if they are not trained.

You can construct a trellis for dewberries by setting up one similar to that used for blackberries. With dewberries you should stretch two steel wires between the poles, one above the other, by about a foot. Tie the canes to the wires so that they grow in a horizontal position along the wire. Use soft string to tie canes. A split-rail fence makes an easy and attractive support system for dewberries.

Dewberries are heavy feeders and should be given a circle of manure around the base of the plant in the spring. Do not touch the plant with manure. If you are using fresh manure, cover it up with a few shovelfuls of dirt to keep the gnat population down.

Plant dewberries the same way you plant blackberries.

Culture

The three main things to remember in dewberry culture are: weeding, watering, and fertilizing. Weeds must be kept down. Dewberries are fast growers and they need all the water and nutrients they can get. They should not have to compete with weeds. Weeds also can harbor insect pests. Cut out any weeds from around your dewberries. Grass should not be allowed to grow under your plants. Keep the area cultivated for best results.

Water your plants after planting and once a week thereafter. Always soak each plant thoroughly when watering. On sandy soils, you will need to water more often. On heavy soils, less watering will be required. Be sure that your dewberries are watered during dry periods and during the fruiting season. If they fail to get adequate water, the fruits will suffer in quality.

Fertilize your plants each spring. Manure or wood ashes are good fertilizers. If you use a commercial fertilizer, use a complete formula such as 10-10-10.

A summer mulch will help conserve soil moisture and keep weeds down to a minimum. In winter, a mulch is necessary. This is especially true for those who live in areas where the dewberry is marginally hardy. The winter mulch should maintain soil temperatures so that the soil does not heave and uproot the plants. It also will keep the roots protected from cold injury. Do not plant dewberries if winters in your area regularly have temperatures that drop below zero.

Pruning

After the berries are harvested, prune old canes and burn them. Do not prune the primocanes; they will produce next year's crop. Thin out the new canes. Leave about 12 of the largest ones. These will be the best and most vigorous canes. They should be tied to the trellis wires or support system as soon as they are large enough.

Occasionally you might have to prune for broken canes or disease control. Remember that the floricanes bear fruit. Do not cut them back too heavily if you can avoid it or you will reduce your yield of dewberries.

INSECT PESTS

Blackberry and dewberry plants are subject to attacks by the same insect pests that bother the raspberry. See Chapter 6. The best way to minimize damage is to follow good cultural practices. Keep the weeds cut down and the area around your fruit plants clean. Remove old canes after harvest and prune out any problem canes. Remove all prunings and burn them.

DISEASES

Possible disease injury to blackberry plants and dewberry plants is preventable with conscientious effort. Choose disease-resistant varieties whenever a problem is known to your area. Pick up windfallen fruits. Keep old canes removed after they have fruited. Isolate new plantings from old plantings or wild patches.

Verticillium Wilt. This soil-borne fungus infects the roots of susceptible varieties. Boysenberry and youngberry are very susceptible to verticillium wilt. Canes turn yellow and die in midsummer. This is a common disease in many parts of the country. If you live in the Southeast, it might not be much of a problem. Never set plants out in an area that was previously planted to solanaceous crops (tomatoes, peppers, potatoes, eggplants, etc.). Whenever possible plant resistant varieties.

Gall. Two types of gall affect blackberries and dewberries: cane gall and crown gall. These are bacterial diseases that live in the soil. They enter the plant through wounds that can occur during cultivation or pruning operations. These diseases are widespread throughout the United States. Wartlike sores develop on infected crowns and canes. This weakens the plant. Control by planting disease-free stock in soil not previously used to grow brambles (blackberries, dewberries, or raspberries).

Leaf and Cane Spot. This is a fungus disease common to the Southeastern states and the Pacific Northwest. Purple spots with white centers appear on the leaves and canes of infected plants. Often the disease results in the weakening of canes and can cause defoliation to occur prematurely. Control leaf and cane spot by pruning out infected canes. Remove and burn all diseased canewood.

Orange Rust. This is a fungus disease common to the Eastern half of the United States. This disease establishes itself internally in the crown area of the plant. When the new buds open in the spring on infected plants, they develop orange blisters filled with the spores of this fungus. Plants with orange rust are weak and often barren of fruit. This disease can not be controlled by sprays. Control the problem by planting disease-free stock in areas free of infected plants.

Double Blossom Rosette. This fungus disease is most prevalent in the Southeast. It attacks flowerbuds and causes them to swell up and produce reddish flowers with twisted petals. This gives the appearance that the flowers are double. These flowers will not produce fruit. Plants with this disease can develop broomlike shoots of growth. Control double blossom rosette by pruning out old canes after harvest. Remove prunings and burn them.

Fruit Rot. Several fungi invade the fruit itself. These are collectively termed *fruit rot.* They attack fruits before or after harvest. Infected fruits develop a gray or cottony mold over them. The overripe or damaged berries are most susceptible. Remove rotting berries from your good fruits to prevent the spread. Refrigeration inhibits, but does not control, fruit-rot organisms.

Sterility. This is a virus disease that causes plants to produce sterile flowers. It is most prevalent in the East. Sterile plants grow vigorously until fruiting time. Control sterility by planting disease-free stock and eradicating any sterile plants that are present.

Chapter 8

Grapes

Grapes are extremely difficult fruit for beginners to grow. This is mostly because of the complicated pruning system that is required If not properly pruned, grapevines do not yield or grow well. If this is the only fruit you plan on planting, you might want to reconsider. It might be a good idea to plant an easier fruit to grow such as strawberries. If you still want to grow grapes, you could also plant an easy-to-grow fruit. If you are not successful at growing grapes, it should not altogether discourage you from growing fruit.

Do not let anyone kid you into thinking it will be easy to grow grapes. Growing grapes is not easy. It is time consuming and a great deal of attention must be paid to specific details in grape culture— especially pruning.

There are four species of grapes that are commonly grown in the United States, these are: the European grape, *(Vitis vinifera)*; the Eastern Fox grape, *(Vitis labrusca)*; the Muscadine grape, *(Vitis roundifolia)*; and the Riverbank grape, *(Vitis riparia)*. Other types grown are mostly hybrids of European and Eastern Fox types. The French hybrids are what you will want if you intend on making homemade wines. The European grapes are primarily confined to California, the Muscadines to the South, the Riverbank for the Far North (it is also used for rootstock), and Eastern Fox for the rest of the country.

SITE

A sunny location is required; grapes do not perform well under shady conditions. Sunlight increases yields. Quality. Grapes that receive full sunlight develop a superior aroma and flavor over those receiving insufficient sunlight.

Grapes need a well-drained soil and good air circulation. Air circulation is helpful in preventing problems with mildew. Although grapes are not especially particular about soils, a sandy loam is best.

Grapes are sensitive to photoperiod (daylength). For the best results, plant only those varieties adapted to your area. See Figs. 8-1 through 8-4.

PLANTING

A shovel is the only tool needed to plant your grapes. Once set

Fig. 8-1. Himrod Grapes. Grapes are an extremely difficult fruit for beginners to grow. Mostly this is because of its complicated pruning system (courtesy Stark Bro's Nurseries & Orchards Co.).

Fig. 8-2. A grape arbor should be constructed before planting.

in the ground, grapes should not be moved. They develop a deep root system that can go down to 100 feet when mature. They should be planted in a permanent location.

Dig a hole for each vine. Do not try to cram several vines in one hole. Be sure that the hole is large enough to hold the roots without cramming them.

Grapes need a support system. A grape arbor should be constructed before planting. The vines will be tied to this arbor. Buy an arbor already made or use a spit-rail fence if you have any qualms about building one yourself. To construct a grape support system the easiest way—other than buying a prebuilt one—is to use two fence posts. They should be at least 8 feet high. Set each post in line with each other about 6 feet apart. String up two steel wires between each post. The first wire should be 3 feet from the ground and the second wire should be 5 feet or 6 feet above the ground. The wire must be taut.

While planting grapes, be sure to keep the plants out of direct sunlight and the wind, and keep their roots damp. Soaking the roots in a tub of water for three or four hours before planting is recommended. The planting holes should be rich in humus. Add peat moss or compost if necessary. Once the grapes are set in their permanent location, they should not be disturbed.

Fig. 8-3. Glenora Grapes (courtesy Stark Bro's Nurseries & Orchards Co.).

Fig. 8-4. Canadice Grapes (courtesy Stark Bro's Nurseries & Orchards Co.).

CULTURE

Weeds must be controlled. The area around the base of each plant should be free of vegetation of any kind. Cultivate shallowly so as not to injure plants. A mulch around each plant is recommended. This helps to conserve soil moisture and control weeds.

Spring applications of manure help to provide your plants with a rich source of fertilizer. If you are using fresh manure, do not let it touch the plant. Cover it with a few shovelfuls of dirt so that gnats do not breed in it. The manure should be spread evenly in a circle under each plant. Water plants thoroughly once a week.

TRAINING SYSTEMS

There are several training systems for growing grapes; they are also pruning systems. Different systems are used for each species.

The Four-Caned Kniffen System

This method is used for Eastern Fox grapes such as Concord. The training process takes about three years and becomes a pruning system after that. The first year the plant is set it should be pruned to 5 or 6 inches in height and contain two or three good buds. The good buds are the fat ones. This encourages root development. After that operation, which is done in the spring, allow the vines to grow as they like.

During the second year, you must limit the vine to a single trunk. This is important. Multistemmed vines are not as productive. Choose the vine that grew the best the previous year and tie it to the support system (fence or trellis). Prune all of the other vines. As the season progresses, allow only four of the side branches to grow, two in each direction (two on top and two on bottom). All other buds should be pinched off. At the end of the second year, your vines should be taking shape nicely. Tie branches to the wires with soft string. Do not tie them too tightly or you will injure them. Tie them tight enough so that they do not blow wildly in the wind.

The third year the grapes come into bearing. During that same year, allow four other side branches to grow parallel to the other branches. These are necessary for the next year's crop and will replace the fruiting branches after harvest. Prune all other growth except for the fruiting vines and their replacements.

A mature vine will produce 30 or more bunches a year when trained to the four-caned kniffen system. The vines will produce for almost a lifetime if given proper care.

Note: Reread these instructions. Be sure that you fully understand what you are trying to achieve before you begin. Remember that grapes are borne on 1-year-old wood; once a cane has fruited it will not bear again. The best fruiting canes are pencil-sized canes. The purpose in pruning grapes is two-fold: first to train the vine to a single trunk, second to maximize fruit production. Encourage the growth of fruiting canes near the trunk. This places the canes nearer to the root system; this is vital for large yields. The farther the fruiting canes are away from the roots, the less productive they are.

Be extremely attentive to what you are doing anytime you prune. During the first two years it is imperative to train growth so that you develop a single trunk. Remember that pruning is half science and half art. You will probably never really get the hang of it from any textbook. It is something that will come from practice.

The Geneva Double-Curtain System

The purpose of this training system is to maximize sunlight input. Regular systems typically provide two areas where light is available, the front and the back. With the Geneva double-curtain system, the vines are opened up in the center to expose four sides.

Therefore, you obtain the most sunlight possible on the leaves and fruit. This system also allows for better air circulation and lessens problems with grape diseases such as mildew.

To use the Geneva double-curtain system, build a Y-shaped arbor. Two parallel wires separated by 3 feet should be between each post. Train the vine to develop a single trunk the first two years. Then train branches by tying them to each wire. This will open them up and expose four sides.

With this system during the second year, allow only two of the side branches to grow; prune all others. Tie these branches with soft string (one to each wire). The mature vine will form a Y-shape when viewed from the side. Each branch will divert from the trunk to the support wires. This system is ideal for light penetration and productivity.

Do not use string or cheap plastic in your arbor. They will not provide a permanent support system; neither does clothesline. Remember that it is easier to have the supports up in place come planting time rather than to try to build them afterward.

Muscadine Grapes

Muscadine grapes need to get off to a good start. The first years of their growth are crucial. Plenty of water and weed control are important steps in aiding their success. The vine should be trained roughly to the four-cane kniffen system. It will consist of a trunk, four arms, and fruiting spurs.

The first couple of years are devoted to training the trunk and arms. Each spring the vine produces about four shoots. When the shoots are about a foot in length, select the best and remove the others. Tie them to the supports. When the tip of the cane reaches the wire, it should have its top cut off. This removes the terminal bud and breaks what is called *terminal* dominancy. This causes the shoot to branch out. Train these branches along the wire to form the arm of the plant on each side.

Pruning European Grapes

With European grapes as with other types, the important thing is to maintain a single trunk for the basic framework of your plant. These grapes are pruned according to the *spur system*. This is used only for Thompson seedless grapes and similar California-grown grapes. Do not use the spur system on other grapes. They have different fruiting habits.

With spur pruning, you do not allow "arms" to form. Instead you cut back to the nodes at least 3 inches from the trunk, but not to the trunk itself. This will stimulate the production of fruiting spurs.

You might need help from your county agent if you are in doubt about what you are doing. Remember that to prune correctly you must understand the growth and fruiting habits of your grapevine.

HARVEST

Grapes should be harvested when they are fully ripe. Do not pick the fruit berry by berry. Clip the bunches and gently place them in a basket or pail. Small containers are best. Pick grapes when the weather is dry. Never pick grapes after a rain or during one. Morning pickings are preferable to afternoon pickings when the weather might be hot. The grapes should be kept dry. Fruit rot is likely to attack wet grapes.

Do not wash the grapes until you are ready to use them. Be sure dirt and bugs are off of the grapes before you refrigerate them. Grapes must be refrigerated to be kept for any length of time. Do not freeze grapes or they will be soggy when they thaw.

DISEASES

There are three major grape diseases. They are downy mildew, powdery mildew, and blackrot.

Downy Mildew. This is a fungus disease. It is the worst disease of grapes. Downy mildew is one of the reasons the European grapes cannot be grown in the Eastern half of the United States. This fungus attacks the leaves, young fruits, and fruit clusters about the time grapes are pea size. Downy mildew likes hot and humid conditions. The spores overwinter on the old leaves. The first symptom appears as a white powdery substance covers the underside of leaves. The leaves turn brown as the disease penetrates leaf tissue. If it is on the leaves, it can also attack the fruit clusters. It will cause them to curl and the berries will be stunted and then rot. Control the problem by removal of old leaves after they have fallen in autumn.

Powdery Mildew. Akin to downy mildew, powdery mildew first appears on the upper surface of leaves as a chalk-like powder. This disease can also be controlled by the same measures used to control downy mildew.

Blackrot. This fungus disease attacks leaves, blossoms, shoots, and fruit. Young, tender tissue is most susceptible. The fungus causes lesions to appear on the leaves or fruit. The rotting of berries will start as light brownish spots develop. This disease overwinters on old leaves. Control blackrot by removing old leaves from your grape site.

INSECT PESTS

Damage by insects varies according to the region of the country and type of grapes grown. Some pests will be quite common.

Grape Mealybug. The adults are ¼ inch long with a cottony white coat. The young are crawlers. They make their presence known in the spring and later on in the summer. The mealybug secretes "honeydew" on which a sooty mold develops. They weaken grapevines by sucking plant juices, and ruin the appearance of fruit and leaves by leaving a trail of honeydew and sooty mold wherever they go. Control mealybugs by introducing a natural predator. The ladybug is an effective way to get rid of mealybugs.

Grape Phylloxera. The grape phylloxera resembles an aphid. This is an insect that limits the production of European grapes in this country. The young attack leaves and roots. Grape phylloxera form galls (swellings) on leaves and suck juices from roots. Vines become stunted and sometimes die. Control by planting resistant varieties. With European grapes, they can be grafted on to resistant rootstocks. Infested leaves should be removed and burned.

Gall Makers. These are an assortment of insects and mites that live inside galls on leaves and stems. They are very small. Gall makers weaken plants by sucking juices. They also cause unattractive galls to appear. Control them by pruning infested leaves and canes and burning them.

Grape Flea Beetle. The adult is a shiny, dark greenish-blue jumping beetle about ¼ inch long. The larvae are light brown grubs with black spots, up to ⅜ of an inch long.

The grape flea beetle feeds on new leaves and buds. The adult beetle causes the worst damage by feeding on buds that are just starting to open. When weather permits, each beetle can destroy several buds. This results in an enormous loss of potential fruit production.

Control the problem by shaking the vines so that beetles drop into a bucket of kerosene or onto sheets saturated with motor oil. The best time to get this pest is on bright sunny days when they are most active. The beetle is hard to find on cold or rainy days. When disturbed, the beetles feign death at the slightest jar. They do the most damage to grapes grown near woodlots or wasteland in which they hibernate. Whenever practical, the elimination of their hibernating sites will greatly reduce their numbers.

Grape Rootworm. The adult is a hairy brown beetle, about ¼ inch long. The larva is white with a brown head; it is curved and hairy. The adult damages leaves by making a chain-like pattern of holes in them. The larvae eat small roots and form pits in larger roots. A heavy infestation can kill a grapevine.

Control rootworms by cultivating the soil to eliminate the pupal (overwintering) stage of grape rootworms. It is easier to control grape rootworms when vines are healthy, well pruned, and fertilized. Neglected plants do not have the vigor to combat these pests. If the adult beetle is a problem, it can be collected and dropped into a bucket of kerosene.

Grape Leafhopper. Leafhoppers are likely to be a problem with grapes. They are small, wedge-shaped creatures. The adults fly away quickly when disturbed, but the young cannot fly. They have the peculiar habit of moving sideways. New growth is most seriously affected by leafhopper feeding. Leaves crinkle and turn yellow.

Control should be aimed at the young. Use a mild solution of soap (not detergent) and water. A mild soap such as Ivory is effective. Avoid harsh soaps or detergents that can injure your plants. Use 1 pound of soap for every 8 gallons of water.

GRAPE CLASSIFICATIONS

Grapes are used in jellies, in pies, for fresh juice, or for wine. Grapes are classified into three categories for use: table grapes, wine grapes, and wine and table grapes.

The table grapes are those eaten fresh for desserts. The wine grapes are those that make the best wine, and the wine and table varieties can be used for either purpose.

No matter what purpose grape you are growing, the quality of the ripe fruit is dependent upon many factors. The most important factor is sunlight. The quality factors in grapes are the sugars, flavors, and aromas. The more sunlight your grapes receive the higher the sugar development, and the better the flavor and aroma of the ripe grapes.

Unless you live in California, the wine grapes you grow will likely be French hybrids or Concord. These produce quality, vintage wines that rival those of Europe. People who live in California have greater choice in selecting the varieties they prefer to grow.

Incidentally, there are many wineries located in that state. If you have the chance to visit California you might want to take a public tour of a winery.

Although wine can be made from any grape, certain varieties produce distinctly superior wine. If you are interested in home wine making, it is worthwhile to select the best varieties for that purpose.

If you are interested in growing grapes for table use, some varieties are better than others for that purpose. Thompson seedless is the standard of table grape excellence. Unfortunately, it is limited to California as an area where it can be grown. Those who live in the Eastern half of the United States will do better to plant a cultivar (variety) such as Interlaken or Himrod. Both are excellent table grapes, (white varieties) with quality comparable to the Thompson seedless. Both are also seedless varieties.

The concord was once the favorite table grape in this country, but it has lost ground over the years. Part of the reason is that concord grapes have seeds that consumers find a nuisance. Concords also have slip-skins (which readily separate from the pulp). If you do not mind spitting out seeds or having messy fingers, the concord is an excellent-flavored table grape. And there are now seedless selections of concord available for those who prefer a seedless table grape.

Table grapes must be kept under refrigeration to maintain their best quality. Concord grapes are especially quick to perish—a few hours out in the sun at a picnic or whatever—and there will be a rapid deterioration of their quality.

Keep in mind that when you are considering a grape for table selection the seedless types are preferred. They are easier to eat and offer to your company than are the seeded varieties. Otherwise be prepared with several spitoons handy.

CULTIVARS

Listed below are some general recommendations for cultivars of grapes classified by use. Your local nursery company might offer a wider selection. Read their catalog carefully and be sure to select only those grapes that are hardy enough to grow in your area. If you are interested in wine-making, your public library or local bookstore should have books on home wine making.

Wine Grapes

De Chaunac (red wine).

Foch (burgundy wine).

Chambourcin (red wine).

Seyval (white wine).

Baco Noir (burgundy wine).

Catawba (champagne).

Delaware (champagne).

Hunt (muscadine grape). Bronze wine.

Concord (blue wine).

Table Grapes

Concord (blue grape).

Concord seedless (blue grape). This is a seedless type of concord with the same excellent flavor.

Fredonia (blue grape).

Duchess (white grape).

Thompson seedless (white grape for California).

Interlaken seedless (white grape). A good substitute for Thompson seedless.

Suffolk Red (red seedless grape).

Romulus (white seedless grape).

Steuben (blue grape).

Scuppernong (bronze muscadine grape for the south).

Wine and Table Grapes

Concord.

Aurora.

Delaware.

Niagra.

Chapter 9

Gooseberries and Currants

The main limiting factor in the home production of currants (Fig. 9-1) and gooseberries is not the climate—it is the law! These fruits can be the alternate host to a disease called white pine blister rust that is deadly to white pine trees. It is illegal to grow currants or gooseberries in some parts of the country. Before planting any currants or gooseberries, you must make certain it is legal to do so in your area. Check with your county agricultural extension agent.

Gooseberries are not as popular in the United States as they are in England where gooseberry pie is a favorite dessert. Actually, some people pick the fruit too ripe. The greener, hard fruits will make a tastier pie. Toss in a few ripe fruits, especially of the pink and red varieties to add color.

VARIETAL SELECTION

There are many varieties to choose from. Old standards and new cultivars offer an attractive selection of plants to choose from. The following is a list of some of the most popular types. Not all nurseries offer currants and gooseberries.

Red Lake. This currant is an introduction from the University of Minnesota. It is a late-ripening variety. The plants are hardy, vigorous, and quite productive—yielding good-quality berries.

Wilder. This is another popular red currant. The fruit is larger than red lake and clings more to the bushes when ripe. The berries have a mild flavor.

Fig. 9-1. Currant bush. The main limiting factor in the home production of currants and gooseberries is not the climate—it's the law!

White Grape. This is the most popular white currant variety. The berries are amber, large, and they have a mild flavor.

Downing. This is a green-fruited gooseberry. It is very hardy and productive but the quality is somewhat poor—yielding small, pale green fruits.

Poorman. This is a red-fruited gooseberry. The plants do well on heavy soils. These bushes are not as thorny as are some varieties. The fruit is of good quality and medium in size.

Pixwell. This is a pink-fruited gooseberry. The fruit ripens in clusters with an attractive pink color. The canes do not have as many thorns as some varieties.

If you want fruit without much effort on your part, currants are among the easiest fruits to grow. Plant them and forget about them. They will still produce! Gooseberries are almost equally easy to grow. Almost anyone will be able to grow currants or gooseberries. They are among the hardiest fruits and can withstand temperatures down to minus 40 degrees Fahrenheit. This is a fruit that even grows in Alaska. If you thought you were too far north to grow fruit, try growing a currant or gooseberry bush.

SITE

Currants and gooseberries prefer a cool, moist location with good air circulation around them. Shady areas are favored over those with full sunlight. Here is a fruit you can plant in those areas of your yard where your other fruits will not thrive.

Plant in rich, fertile soil that is high in organic matter. The soil must be well drained and all perennial weeds must be removed. Buy only 1-year-old plants. These are the easiest to work with. It is best to plant these fruits in the spring. Each is capable of self-pollinating so you need plant only one of each. If you will be planting several, space them from 3 to 4 feet between each planting so that they have plenty of room to grow.

To plant currants or gooseberries, all you need is a shovel. A long-handled shovel with a pointed blade is easiest to work with. A pitchfork might come in handy for moving piles of rotting leaves, but you do not have to go out and buy one for the occasion.

Dig a hole large enough to contain the roots of your bush without crowding. Currants and gooseberries are very shallow-rooted. Add plenty of humus to the soil. Dig a larger hole than you need. Toss in leaves and alternate with layers of dirt, peat moss, and composted manure. Do not use fresh manure.

Set the bush into the hole and fill in the rest of the hole with a mix of one part each of topsoil, peat moss, and composted manure. Soak the planting well and water it once a week thereafter. Always soak the plant when you water it; never use light sprinkling. The soil should be damp to the touch, but it should not be drenched or have water standing on the surface for prolonged periods. A mulch can be used to conserve moisture and keep down weeds.

CULTURE

Weeds must be kept under control around your currant and gooseberry plants. Both plants are shallow-rooted and they do not compete well with weeds. Cultivate carefully around the bushes with hand tools. These instruments are available in an assortment of styles resembling miniature hoes, rakes, and shovels. They are inexpensive to buy and they are thoroughly effective and best for use around shallow-rooted shrubs. They offer less chance of injury to your fruit plants. You can also pull out weeds by hand. When doing so, be careful not to injure the roots of your bushes.

A mulch keeps weeds under control. If you are using an organic mulch, such as sawdust or woodchips, it is a good practice to add extra nitrogen to the soil to keep the mulch from robbing nitrogen from your plants. Fertilize each spring with a layer of manure in a circle around the base of each plant. The manure should not touch the bush, but it should extend under the branch areas. If you are using fresh manure, add a few shovelfuls of dirt over the top to discourage gnats from breeding in the manure.

Whenever you are working around your bushes, remember that they are very shallow-rooted—even more so than strawberries. If you dig more than ¼ of an inch around the base of your plants, you can cause injury.

Currants and gooseberries grow well with practically no care. With proper attention, however, they always yield bumper crops.

PRUNING

Currants and gooseberries are perennial bushes. They should be pruned after the fourth year to make them more productive. The younger wood bears more fruit. The purpose of pruning these fruits is to stimulate fruit production. The type of pruning process used is called *renewal pruning*. This method encourages the production of young wood.

Fruit is borne on short spurs at the base of last season's growth. The fruiting wood that is most productive is 2-year-old wood. The 1-year-old wood is not very fruitful and 4-year-old wood hardly bears any fruits at all. The goal of the pruning program for these fruits is to maintain a large supply of fruiting spurs in the 2-year-old range. The older the wood gets the less fruitful it becomes.

This sounds complicated, but here is how you do it. During the spring of the first year after planting, prune all but the four strongest canes. These will be the biggest and tallest canes. All other canes should be cut out. Each cane will branch out and additional canes will form.

The following spring, select four canes from the previous season plus four canes from the planting year to maintain. This leaves you with a total of eight canes. Always select the most vigorous canes and cut out the others.

The next spring you will have four 3-year-old canes, four 2-year-old canes, and four 1-year-old canes. Repeat this cycle through the next season until you have a total of 16 canes (four for each of the four years). Your fruit will have reached bearing age by now and you should be harvesting large crops.

In the spring of the fifth year, remove the 4-year-old canes. Continue thereafter each spring by removing the four oldest canes (after each cane has reached the age of five). At the same time, reduce the number of new canes each year to four.

DISEASES

There are several diseases that attack currants and gooseberries, but most are fairly easy to control. There are exceptions.

White Pine Blister Rust. This is a fungus disease and it is *the* limiting factor for the home production of currants and gooseberries in the United States and Canada. Black currants are no longer grown in this country. Most of the wild gooseberries were eradicated in campaigns headed by the lumber industry in the early part of this century. The white pine is an important tree in the commercial production of lumber. Because even cultured plants can host this disease, all currants and gooseberries are banned in some localities. Check with your local county agent to find out what the law is before you do any planting.

The first symptoms of this disease show up in the spring as small yellow spots on the underside of leaves. By late summer, brown thread-like growths will have developed from these same areas. They contain *teliospores* that germinate and produce *sporidia* that infect the white pine in the fall. Control with a copper-sulfate fungicide such as bourdeaux mixture.

Powdery Mildew. Gooseberries have more problems with mildew than do currants. White powdery patches of the fungus appear on the leaves of infected plants. The progressing fungus also attacks shoots and fruits. The entire surface will become covered with a thin coating that turns brown. Black dots that contain the spores will appear. Heavy deposits of mildew, stunt and dry the leaves, weaken plants, and lower production of fruits. Infected berries will be neither edible nor desirable. Control powdery mildew by pruning to improve air circulation.

Anthracnose. This fungus disease first appears as black spots on the leaves. The infection occurs anytime during the growing season. The spots enlarge and leaves will take on a purplish margin. Leaves soon turn yellow and fall from the tree. Plants are weakened. Fruits are small and of poor quality. Control by pruning to increase air circulation.

Leaf Spot. This fungus disease resembles anthracnose, but there will be tiny specks that cover leaf surfaces. These contain the disease spores. Diseased leaves turn yellow and fall off. Control leaf spot by pruning to increase air circulation. Leaf spot and anthracnose can be treated with a copper-sulfate fungicide such as bourdeaux mixture.

Caneblight. This fungus disease causes canes to suddenly wilt and die. It usually occurs shortly before harvest. Control with bourdeaux mixture.

Cluster Cup Rust. This disease usually occurs only in neglected home gardens. The rust can affect the entire plant, but it usually confines itself to just the leaves. Do not plant currants or gooseberries near sedge plants. These are alternate host for the disease.

Botrytis. This occurs in areas with poor air circulation or during periods of excessive humidity and moisture. Botrytis affects the tips of canes causing them to dieback. It produces a gray mold that consumes the berries. Control botrytis by removing moldy berries and pruning to improve air circulation.

Currant Mosaic. This is a virus disease that causes the leaves to turn two-tone with light and dark areas. It almost gives the appearance of an iron deficiency. Plant only virus-free stock and keep new bushes away from old plantings or wild bushes.

INSECT PESTS

The pests of the currant are also the pests of the gooseberry. Keep this in mind when planting either species. Do not plant near wild bushes.

Currant Borer. This creature has a name like some people you might meet at parties—but it is no relation. The first symptoms of currant borer infestation are yellowing foliage on individual canes. Usually this occurs in the late spring. The adult is a clear-winged moth somewhat wasp-like in appearance. In early June, the female moths deposit eggs on the canes. The larvae (which is the borer stage and does the damage on the plants) is pale yellow. They tunnel into the canes where they overwinter. Red currants are especially susceptible to this pest. The infested canes most often die. Control by pruning infested canes and burning them.

Currant Aphid. Aphids annoy the currant bush and do the same kind of damage that they do to other plants. They suck juices and transmit viruses. Damage appears in the form of crinkled leaves with red areas between the veins on the upper surface. On the underside you find small, green aphids. They remove sap, distort growth, and cause leaves to blacken as sooty mold grows on the excrement that the aphids leave.

Control the problem with lacewings or ladybugs. These are predator insects that eat the aphids. Incidentally, ants harvest aphids and eat their secretions of honeydew. Controlling ants will help control your aphid population.

Currant Stem Girdler. This insect damages the stems. The adults are sawflies. They injure stems by puncturing holes in which they lay their eggs. The plant will start to droop and new shoots wilt in the spring. The larvae tunnel into the canes. Do not plant currants or gooseberry trees near poplar or willow trees. These are favorite feeding hosts for this pest. This bug is especially bothersome on gooseberries. Control by pruning the infested canes at the first indication of drooping. Burn all cuttings.

Gooseberry Fruitworm. This fruitworm attacks both gooseberries and currants, damaging the fruits. You are not likely to spot many of these bugs in one place as it only takes a few to eat a large amount of fruit. The larvae are green with dark stripes along their sides. Control by hand removal and drop them into a bucket of kerosene. It is best to wear gloves when doing this messy chore.

Four-lined Plant Bug. This insect is usually only a pest in the wild or in areas such as vacant lots or old railway tracks. It is not likely to attack your home garden unless your garden is neglected and slovenly. The bug causes spots to appear on leaves, shortly thereafter the leaves mishapen and turn brown. Control by hand removal and drop them into a bucket of kerosene.

Imported Currant Worm. As though we did not have enough insect pests in this country without importing them, this is the worst insect pest you can have unless, of course, you already have all of the others. These bugs will strip foliage in just a few days. The larvae are spotted caterpillars and they do most of the damage. The adults are sawflies about the size of regular houseflies. The adults come in spring and lay their eggs. A second outbreak is usually later on in the summer. The insects are especially fond of gooseberry plants. Control by hand removal and the old kerosene bucket.

Currant Fruitfly. Berries drop prematurely and have dark spots on them whenever this pest is present. In the dropped fruit will be small, white maggots (the larval stage of flies). They seem to show a preference for the late maturing varieites. Control by keeping windfallen fruit picked up.

Chapter 10

Elderberries

They sometimes grow wild along the roadside. The low bushes have thick clusters of purple berries. They aren't much to nibble on raw, but the jelly is delicious. Elderberries are a delightful addition to any garden. The fruit is too perishable to be bought in the store and you can't count on collecting the berries from the wild anymore.

The fruit is highly perishable and does not keep long—even under refrigeration. Elderberries can be used to make pie or to flavor other fruit pies. The seeds are large and hard and can become somewhat annoying because they tend to get stuck in your teeth.

The common garden elderberry in the United States is the Sweet Elder *(Sambucus canadensis)*. It is a vigorous grower. In moist areas, it will reach about 6 to 8 feet tall and almost as wide.

In olden England the elderberry was used to make wine and medicine. Many monasteries grew elderberries for this purpose. The monks found that elderberries were easier to grow than grapes for wine making and that elderberries produce a high-quality wine. They also discovered that the berries seemed to have medicinal value.

The secret of the medicinal value of elderberries probably lies in the fact that they are a rich source of vitamin C. In the days when there was not much variety in the foods people ate and a well-balanced diet was a luxury of the rich, some shortages of essential nutrients, such as vitamin C, were common.

SITE

Elderberries are not fussy about where you plant them as long as they are given plenty of water and some sunlight. The elderberry does not require full sunlight, but it is best to avoid heavy shade. Another thing to remember when selecting a site for your elderberries is that they rapidly grow into large shrubs. Be sure to leave plenty of room for their growth. Elderberries perform best when another variety is nearby for cross-pollination. Plan on setting out two plants.

Elderberries favor a rich loam. The one thing elderberries do not tolerate is drought. If you have sandy soil, or soil with a low water-holding capacity, it should be improved before planting elderberries in it. Add plenty of peat moss to the planting hole and water newly set plants with some frequency. Do not let elderberry soils dry up or get crusty. To do so will have an adverse effect upon fruit production. The elderberry is already a small berry. If it suffers from drought stress, the fruits will become shriveled and the quality of the fruits will be lowered. If you live in an area with a high water table be certain that you can provide adequate soil drainage.

PLANTING

Follow the directions for planting your elderberry bush that arrive with your order from your nursery. Plant elderberries in the spring as early as the ground can be worked. In the South, they can be set out in the fall as well.

Take a long-handled shovel with a pointed blade and dig a hole. A wheelbarrow will come in handy for hauling peat moss and composted manure. The hole must be large enough so that the roots of the elderberry bush can fit in without crowding. If it is not large enough, dig it out until it is before you plant your elderberry bush.

Elderberries are usually planted in pairs for cross-pollination. Handle each plant separately. Dig two separate holes no closer than 7 feet between them or farther than 20 feet between them. If plants are set out too far apart, it makes it more difficult for the bees to cross-pollinate them. You probably will want to dig a large hole and add alternating layers of leaves and topsoil before planting. This will increase the organic composition of the soil.

Some nurseries provide a wooden or bamboo stake for tieing your elderberry after it has been planted. This is not necessary because elderberries grow best as a bush. Nevertheless, you can stake your plants if you prefer.

CULTURE

Elderberries require very little care. Weeds should be kept down; this is especially important around newly set bushes. Water your plants at least once a week (more often on sandy soil). When watering, thoroughly soak the area under the branch spread. Do not just water at the base of the plant. Water under the "wingspread" of the branches. This helps promote better root growth.

To weed you can use a hoe. This makes it easier than trying to do it all by hand. Always hoe carefully around the base of the plant so you will not injure the roots or bark. Uproot the weeds if possible. If you only chop off the tops, the weeds will come back up.

Mulch to control weeds. Place in a circle any good mulch material around the base of the elderberry bush. It is best to not touch the truck of the bush with the mulch material. Composted leaves, sawdust, or any number of things can be used for mulch. If you use sawdust or other organic mulches, it is a good idea to sprinkle on some manure to add extra nitrogen. The mulch will rob your plant of nitrogen if you do not add nitrogen. If fresh manure is used, cover it with a shovelful of dirt. Be wary of using leaves that are not composted. They might compact and prevent your bush from receiving enough water.

Elderberries are rapid growers and they benefit from a regular fertilizing program. Add manure in a circle around the base of each plant in the spring. Be generous because these plants are heavy feeders. If you are using a commercial fertilizer, a complete formula such as 10-10-10 is better than just applying nitrogen.

PRUNING

Elderberries require pruning to maintain size and shape. They spread from rhizomes on the root and become quite dense if they are left uncontrolled. From a landscape viewpoint, this is necessary to keep in mind when setting out your elderberry plants.

Very little pruning is done for training the plant's early growth habits. Most pruning will be to stimulate the production of fruiting wood. This process is called *renewal pruning* because the goal is to "renew" the plant each season to encourage the production of new growth. Some pruning will be necessary to maintain size and keep the bush from becoming too "leggy." This condition is where growth is sparse on the lower parts except for the older nonfruiting wood.

Fruit is always borne on 1-year-old wood. The elderberry bush produces a branch the first year and bears fruit on that branch the second year. It is easiest to prune in the fall after the crop has been harvested. That way you will not accidentally cut out next year's fruiting wood. There might be some winter injury involved. This might especially be true in the far north where fall pruning is not ordinarily a good practice. If you wait until spring to do your pruning, however, you might not remember which parts need to be cut off. Therefore, you should prune your elderberries immediately after harvest.

Prune all branches that bore fruit. These will not fruit again. If there is new growth on these branches, do not remove it. This is new wood that will bear next season's crop. The more fruiting wood you have the bigger of a crop you can expect to harvest. All cuttings should be removed to your compost pile along with your other organic debris.

HARVEST

The berries are best when used for jelly, juice, or wine. They do not taste good fresh. They are too "puckery." If made into juice, you will need to strain out the seeds and add sugar to sweeten it. Also it is better when chilled. Elderberries are rich in vitamin C.

Elderberries crush easily and the juice stains your hands and clothes. Although the berries are used as a natural food coloring, it does not look so attractive on the hands and clothing (purple stains rarely do). Growers are advised to harvest the fruit wearing an old work shirt and rubber gloves.

The berries are too small to pick one by one. If you try to pick them by the handful, you will smash them. A neat way to harvest elderberries is to pick the entire cluster by cutting the stem with a jacknife. There is much less damage to the fruits when they are harvested in this fashion.

Chapter 11

Rhubarb

Rhubarb matures in late spring before any other fruits are ready. Rhubarb is commonly called the pie plant, and a real treat of a pie can be made from your own plants.

Rhubarb *(Rheum rhaponticum)* grows best in the northern half of the United States. It is a cool-weather perennial (Figs. 11-1 and 11-2). Rhubarb does not thrive in areas where the average summer temperatures are much above 75 degrees Fahrenheit or where the average winter temperatures stay much above 40 degrees Fahrenheit. A temperature below 50 degrees Fahrenheit is needed by the plants so that they can break dormancy. Because of its winter chill requirement, rhubarb is not recommended for the South. In the Deep South, it will only survive a few months.

FRUIT OR VEGETABLE?

Rhubarb is a difficult plant to classify. Its situation is somewhat similar to the tomato. The tomato is an annual and a fruit, but it is used as a vegetable. Tomatoes are usually dealt with when discussing vegetable culture. Rhubarb is the opposite. It is a perennial vegetable, but it is used as a fruit. This might not be horticulturally correct, but it is in line with the popular sentiment.

The part of the plant that is eaten is the stalk. These are pulled in late spring or early summer. *Never* eat the leaves. Rhubarb leaves contain oxalic acid and oxallates. Sometimes these elements are in large enough dosage to cause *fatal* poisoning.

Fig. 11-1. A row of rhubarb ready for harvest (courtesy Paul & Alvalina Nandory).

SITE

Rhubarb grows best planted under full sunlight and cool, moist conditions. It is very hardy and holds up under spring frosts quite well. Leaves might turn brown around the edges, but they are not eaten anyway and no damage is done to the stalks.

Most people plant rhubarb on the border of their vegetable garden. In that location, the plants are likely to be safe when the rest of the garden is being tilled. Rhubarbs are a perennial and they should not be disturbed once they are planted. Although they can be moved, it is not recommended because it interferes with their growth. Every time a plant is moved it suffers from some shock and takes time for it to get adjusted to its new site.

Rhubarb is not especially ornamental so you probably will not want to grow it in isolated plantings throughout your yard. It is usually grown in rows and it makes an effective lining for a garden path.

Rhubarb grows in almost any type of soil as long as it is well-drained soil. It grows best in rich, loam soils that are high in organic matter and fertility. The rhubarb plant is a heavy feeder so annual application of fertilizers is a good idea. Animal manures or a balanced commercial fertilizer will do nicely. Animal manures are best because they add humus to the soil as they decay.

When preparing the soil prior to planting, work in plenty of composted manure. The richer the soil the better the growth will be. Fresh manure should not be used at planting time because it will burn the plant. It can be planted along the sides of rows provided it does not touch the plant.

PLANTING

To grow large stalks of rhubarb, plant them in good soil. Rhubarb requires good drainage, but it needs plenty of water to produce the most tender stalks. Plant rhubarb by digging an extra-large hole. Add composted manure to the hole. Be certain to use only composted manure. The crown of the rhubarb (some nurseries also call them eyes) should be planted no deeper than 2 inches below

Fig. 11-2. Strawberries in a matted row system. Some people like to grow strawberries along side their rhubarb.

the surface. They should be set out about 3 feet apart in rows that are 5 feet apart.

Water the plant thoroughly after planting and each week thereafter. Do not plant rhubarb in grass. Cultivate an area for your plants. Grass will compete with the rhubarb for water and nutrients and grass is faster growing than the rhubarb plant. All perennial weeds should be removed from the area. If you think you will have difficulty remembering where you planted the rhubarb, because it will be underground once it has been set out, mark the area with a stake or some other marker. Do not cover up the plant with a rock or other heavy object that will impede the growth of the plant.

CULTURE

Do not pull any rhubarb during the first two years of growth. Otherwise you could severely weaken the plant. It is also a good idea to cut off the seed heads before they go to seed. If you allow the plant to go to seed, you weaken it because it puts all of its energy into seed production. By cutting off the seed head, it will put energy into growing a larger plant. That is exactly what you want.

Once established, you will have to remove small stems from the plants early in the season. This helps to promote the growth of the big stalks. Trim the rhubarb plant if it gets too thick. This will allow for good air circulation.

The area around the base of your plants should be kept free of weeds and grass. A hoe can be used to cultivate the area. If you use a rototiller, be careful not to get too close to the plant or you will injure the roots. Water should not be allowed to stand on the soil surface around your rhubarb for prolonged periods (such as several days). If standing water persists around the collar of the plant, the plants might develop rot organisms. Well drained soils will not have that problem.

If you are having an unusually dry period during the time of your rhubarb development, be sure to add extra water to your plants. If they do not receive sufficient water, they will be more "stringy" and the quality of the stalks will suffer.

Fertilize your plantings heavily each spring. Circle each plant with manure. If you use fresh manure, toss a few shovelfuls of dirt over it. If you use a commercial fertilizer, use a balanced formula such as 10-10-10.

MULCH

To control weeds and conserve moisture, use of a mulch is

advised. Be careful not to cover the plant when you mulch. Just spread the mulching materials around the sides in a circle. Chopped hay or straw makes a good mulch and so does manure. Rhubarb will benefit from the addition of manure so use it generously.

A winter mulch is necessary to protect the plant from cold and fluctuating temperatures that can cause soil heaving. The winter mulch should be heavier than the summer mulch. It can cover the entire plant. The mulch must be removed in spring before growth starts. Take it off and work it into the soil between the rows. If you leave a heavy mulch over the plants, it will delay the sun's warming of the soil and inhibit the early growth of the rhubarb.

REPRODUCING PLANTS

It is best to buy the plants you need from your nursery. Rhubarb should not be reproduced from seed. The seed will not reproduce true to type and will not retain the desirable characteristics of the parent plant.

Older, well-established plantings can be reproduced by crown division. Do not try to reproduce by dividing young plants. The crowns should be at least three or four years old. Dig the dormant crowns early in the spring *before* growth has started. Split them between the large buds or eyes and leave as large of a piece of storage root as possible with each eye. Each crown will produce between four and eight pieces.

Plant the new pieces the same way you would those that arrive from the nursery. Eyes must face upward.

HARVEST

The harvest season for rhubarb is only a few weeks in late spring and early summer. The stalks will get dry and stringy later on in the summer. They should not be picked at that stage. They should be allowed to produce for next year's crop.

Do not pull leafstalks from newly set plants. Harvest only from plants that are three years old. Pull only the best and biggest stalks. The stalks separate from the crown. Grasp them near the base and pull them slightly to one side to harvest them. Pull in the direction that the stalk is growing. Always pull rhubarb from the socket; do not cut it.

Cut off leaves as soon as the stalk is pulled. The poisons in the leaves can travel down the stem if they are left on too long. Cut off the leaves in the field and use them for mulch.

The smaller stalks should be thinned to permit better development of the remaining stalks. Do not pull all of the stalks. Some stalks should be left on the plant so that it will grow and produce for next year.

Rhubarb is a heavy producer once established. If you are a heavy user of rhubarb, you will want to set out more than one plant.

After harvesting, let the plants grow. Cut off seedstalks as soon as they appear. A heavy crop of rhubarb depends upon the leaf growth of the previous season. After the last harvest (you will not want to pick rhubarb after July 1), fertilize and water your plantings. Do not fertilize your plants after August 1.

VARIETAL SELECTION

There are many excellent cultivars of rhubarb and the red ones are usually preferred. They are sweeter than the green rhubarb so they take less sugar when made into pies or sauce. The red kind make a more attractive pie with a bright pink to red color. The red varieties are less bitter as well. Some red selections are Canada Red, Valentine, and Crimson Wine. Your nursery might offer others. The leading green variety is Victoria.

Rhubarb is rarely eaten fresh. It is high in malic acid and not very sweet. Some people will occasionally chomp on a stalk after adding sugar or salt to it.

If you grow the green variety, you might want to plant a few of the red. By mixing the two in cooking, you can create more colorful and appealing desserts. Once you have tasted the red varieties, you will notice the difference—a less bitter flavor. Strawberries are sometimes added to rhubarb pie or jam.

DISEASES

The rhubarb will not have many disease problems as long as the plants receive proper care.

Phytophthora Crown Rot. Also known as foot rot, this is the most serious disease affecting rhubarb. Slightly depressed lesions develop at the base of leaf stalks infected with crown rot. These grow rapidly to cause the collapse of the entire stalk. This disease spreads most rapidly under warm and moist conditions. The disease can spread and kill the entire plant. There is no effective control for foot rot, but planting on a well-drained soil with good air circulation helps.

INSECT PESTS

Insects rarely do much damage to rhubarb. In part, this is

because rhubarb manufactures its own insecticide. The leaves are not only deadly to people, but to insects as well. With proper sanitation and by keeping weeds down, the home grower should have few problems.

Rhubarb Curculio. An insect called the rhubarb curculio can become a nuisance. It is a snout beetle about ¾ of an inch long. It bores into the stalks, crowns, and roots. It also attacks coarse weeds such as wild dock. Control them by burning infested plants and destroying any wild dock in the vicinity. This is most effective in July after the beetles have laid their eggs.

FORCING FOR INDOOR GROWTH

Forcing refers to the growth of a plant indoors for winter production. Rhubarb stalks can be grown from large crowns taken indoors and kept at suitable temperatures with ample moisture and humidity. If you are growing them to sell, you would probably grow them in a greenhouse. Otherwise, you can grow them in a basement or cellar. Six good crowns will produce enough stalks for the average family.

A major problem you will encounter when growing rhubarb indoors will be trying to maintain high enough humidity. Proper temperatures will not be difficult to provide, but the humidity of most modern heated basements is likely to be too low. You could place a humidifier in the basement to add moisture to the air.

The crowns you select for forcing should be good producers. The growth of the plants in the field are a good indicator of which plants will be the best producers. The crowns selected should be at least two years old. Large crowns with a few big buds are preferable to small crowns with small buds. Do not try to force plants that have been harvested during the summer. They will be worn out from producing the summer crop and they will yield poorly.

Chill Before Forcing

When the top growth of the rhubarb stops in autumn, usually after the first frost, the buds on the crown will enter into a rest period. This rest period lasts for several weeks. Do not try to force the stalks into production until they have completed their rest period and received a period of chill. A few hard freezes in the field is not sufficient to bring the plants out of their rest. They require at least six weeks of temperatures of 28 degrees Fahrenheit or below to give good yields. If you live in an area where you are afraid the snow will come and cover the plants before you can dig them up, you can give the crowns the chill they need by putting them on a shelf in your refrigerator (not the freezer) and let them set for six weeks. Keep the crowns from getting excessively wet, but do not allow them to dry out either. They will need to set there for at least six weeks before you can place them in your forcing bed or pans.

Rhubarb will begin growing, after it has received sufficient chill, once it has been returned to the warm temperatures again. The best yields are obtained when forcing temperatures are maintained around 56 degrees Fahrenheit. That is a bit chilly in the house, but you will not want to try to force rhubarb in your living room anyway. Lower temperatures will add more of a pink color to stalks, but they also grow slower. Any temperature below 50 degrees Fahrenheit will decrease yields. Temperatures much above 60 degrees Fahrenheit will result in faster growth, but also lower yield. As the plants move toward the end of their forcing period, they will lose color until the crown becomes exhausted.

Water to keep the forcing pan or bed moist, but do not overwater. The soil should be damp to the touch, but it must not be drenching wet. Adequate moisture is needed to promote succulent growth. Production will drop off severely if the plants do not receive enough water.

Varieties for Forcing

Some varieties take to forcing better than others. The best varieties for indoor production are, Victoria, Sutton's seedless, and Strawberry.

Harvesting Forced Crops

Usually it takes 1½ months after plants are planted before they are ready to harvest. The duration of harvest time depends upon a number of variables such as variety, crown vigor, and forcing temperature. You can extend the period of harvest over a longer period when you grow rhubarb indoors than you are able to when it is grown outdoors. Pick the largest stalks first and continue to do so until the plant is exhausted. After the roots are forced, they should be discarded. Forcing drains too much out of the plant; it will never fruit again. Do not bother trying to save the root for setting out in the garden in the spring. Buy new plants.

Part 3
Tree Fruits

Chapter 12

Apples

Apples are America's favorite temperate-zone fruit and the preferred fruit for the home garden (Fig. 12-1). Apples are not an easy fruit to grow because they attract more insect pests than any other fruit. Raising apples that are blemish free will require a great deal of attention and hard work. You will need to develop a rigorous control program or you could lose every apple on your tree to insect pests.

Apple trees will provide you with a great deal of satisfaction with both their fruits and their delicately scented blossoms. Remember that they will require care for several years before they begin to bloom or bear fruit. So you will probably want to plant strawberries or some other rapid producer at the same time. Otherwise, you are likely to get impatient while waiting for your apples.

Apples are among the hardiest of fruits. Some varieties can withstand severe cold and are best adapted for the North. Most apples do not grow well in the South. Southern winters are not sufficiently cold enough to meet the chill requirements. If you live in an area where insufficient winter chill is a problem, check with your nursery for apples that are better adapted for Southern growing. Examples of such cultivars are Ein Shemer or Beverly Hills.

Remember that unless you live south of Missouri your major concern will be winter hardiness rather than sufficient winter chill. Check with your nursery to see which varieties are best for your area. See Fig. 12-2.

Fig. 12-1. Apples are America's favorite temperate-zone fruit (courtesy Paul & Alvalina Nandory).

The apple *(Malus pumila)* is one of the oldest fruits in cultivation. Archaeologists have discovered the remains of apples among the relics in prehistoric lake dwellings in Switzerland. Apples were grown during the days of the Roman Empire. Pomona was the Roman Goddess of fruit trees. Pomum is the Latin word for apple. Today the science of growing fruit is called pomology.

The apple has left its mark on many cultures. In France, potatoes are referred to as "apples of the earth." In Spain, tomatoes were called "love apples" because they were thought to have an aphrodiasiatic effect upon people. In these United States, the phrase "apple pie" often is used to denote wholesomeness. New York City calls itself the Big Apple, and more recently Minneapolis, Min-

Fig. 12-2. The Ein Shemer apple is an apple for low-chill conditions (courtesy Stark Bro's Nurseries & Orchards Co.).

nesota has started calling itself "Minneapple" as a take-off on New York's nickname.

Despite its popularity, the apple is sometimes maligned as the fruit that Eve took a bite out of in the Garden of Eden. Horticulturists protest that this can not be so. Many fruits were called apples in ancient times, but the true apple is a temperate-zone fruit. It seems more likely that Eve bit into a fig.

Although apples have been grown throughout most of civilization, the apples we usually think of today are relatively new introductions of the last century or two. They are the result of selecting superior strains and propagating them by grafting. Hybridization and controlled plant breeding are now used to develop new types.

Apples probably first came to America with Dutch settlers who brought apple seeds with them. Apples were growing in Massachusetts as early as 1630. We are all familiar with childhood tales of Johnny Appleseed. This man really existed, but Johnny Appleseed was only his nickname. His real name was John Chapman and he came from Massachusetts. He was a preacher remembered for the planting of apple seeds throughout Ohio, Indiana, and Illinois. Books, poems, and songs have been written about Johnny Appleseed.

As with other fruits, certain apples are better than others for different uses. For example, some apples are best eaten fresh as a dessert. There are apples that must be baked to be appreciated.

Other apples are best suited for sauce or cider. However you like to eat your apples, there is a type for every purpose. When you plan on growing apples, do not limit yourself to only the popular varieties or you will be missing something. The major apples of commerce are: Red and Golden Delicious, McIntosh, Winesap, Jonathan, and Rome Beauty.

SITE

Apples need a location with good air drainage. Throughout much of the United States, spring frosts before, during, or after bloom wreak havoc with fruiting. Select a site where the dangers of frost injury to your flower blossoms will be at a minimum. Trouble spots are easy to locate. Cold air is heavier than warm air and it will always travel downward, settling in low spots in your yard. These are called frost pockets. If at all possible, try to avoid planting apples in these undesirable locations.

Apple trees should be sheltered against high winds. Such winds can interfere with pollination or blow fruits off of the tree. In the winter, these winds increase the chances of cold injury. When protecting trees from winds, be careful not to shade them. Apples perform best in full sunlight. If they are shaded, it will lower production and quality.

PLANTING

Follow the directions for planting that come with your apple tree. The only tool you need to plant apple trees is a shovel. A long-handled shovel with a slightly curved blade is easiest for most people. A pitchfork will be handy in moving large clumps of leaves. If you do not have a pitchfork, you can lift leaves with your hands. With clay or sandy soils, leaves or compost should be added. For sandy soils, it will improve their water-holding capacity; for clay soils it will improve aeration.

The hole must be large enough to contain the roots of the tree without bending or crowding them. If it is not large enough, dig it out until there is plenty of room. If the hole becomes too large, fill in part of it with good topsoil. With sandy or poor soils, dig a deeper hole and add alternating layers of leaves and dirt. Compost or peat moss can be used as a substitute or in combination with the leaves. Cover the last layer of leaves with plenty of good topsoil before setting the tree in the hole. The roots must not come in contact with any leaves or compost. Pack dirt firmly around roots and tamp down to eliminate any air pockets.

Keep the roots out of wind and sunlight during the planting operation. Cover them with a wet cloth or soak them in a tub of water just before you place them into the planting hole. Do not let them dry out. It is best to plant in the early morning or evening rather than during the hottest parts of the day.

If you have clay soil, a layer of gravel should be placed at the bottom of your planting hole. This should be covered with dirt that is followed by a layer of leaves and topsoil.

Set the tree into the hole with the roots spread out evenly so that they go out in all directions. Be sure that you hold the tree upright in the hole. If you have a helper, let that person hold the tree while you fill the hole. If you are alone, use one hand to hold the tree by the base of the trunk and use the other hand to fill in the hole. Adjust the tree from time to time to make certain that it is not crooked.

The entire hole should be filled in before you water the newly set tree. Tamp down the soil so that it is firmly packed. Be gentle enough so that you do not injure any roots. Water the tree by soaking it with water. Water should be visible on the surface of the soil for a few minutes. After that water has soaked in, fill in any gaps with soil. Tamp the soil down and water again. Keep the soil moist until growth starts. Frequent light waterings should be avoided because they will encourage shallow rooting. Water heavily once a week and more often on sandy soil, but less often on clay.

PRUNING

Some nurseries will prune the tops of your apple tree for you. This will be evident from looking at the trees. You will be able to tell if a tree has been cut or not. The trees that are sold in outdoor shopping malls seldom have tops pruned. People are more impressed at the size of the trees that are not pruned than the ones that have been properly pruned. Before you do any cutting, check to see if your tree looks like it needs pruning.

If your tree has arrived unpruned, the tops will need to be cut back to provide for balanced growth. Pruning the top will help the tree get over the initial shock of being transplanted. Many of the roots will have been broken off or cut during the digging of the tree, especially the more fibrous feeder roots. By reducing top growth, the roots will get off to a better start. This reduces the number of branches and leaves that the root system has to supply with moisture and nutrients during the first growing season.

Your local nursery company will usually include instructions for pruning back the tops of your apple trees. Follow their instructions. Do not prune roots. The roots should be allowed to grow. If roots are damaged or broken, they can be cut—but be careful. It is best to not do much trimming of the roots or you will weaken or kill the tree.

Prune trees after they are set out and not before. It will be easier to see what you are doing if the tree is already in the ground. It also gives you a better idea as to what the tree will look like (whether or not the branches are balanced) if you prune after planting. Select the most vigorous branches, with wide crotch angles, and cut them back by half. The weaker branches should be eliminated. Cut them out completely.

Training

It is not necessary to have a lot of special equipment for pruning. You should be able to pick up either an anvil-type pruner (pruning shears) or a pruning saw at your local hardware store. The anvil-type pruner (which roughly resembles a pair of pliers or wire cutters) can be used to snip off branches that are under ½ inch in diameter. A pruning saw should be used for branches that are over ½ inch in diameter. It is possible to use a plain handsaw, but a pruning saw will be easier to use and it will probably be sharper. You will find it much easier to use pruning shears on your small trees than any kind of saw.

When you are trimming a side branch from a tree limb, make the cuts as close as possible to that limb. Ordinarily, you will be holding the branch with one hand and cutting with the other hand. If you will be trimming off a branch where it is attached to the tree, cut as close to the tree as possible (leaving a small stub if any). Make sure that you do not cut into the tree. This could cause serious damage.

You will want your apple tree to have a strong central leader (where the trunk is taller than the side branches). This will undoubtedly mean that you will have to prune your tree during the first couple of years to develop its proper shape. Prune the tree to shape the branches so that the upper limbs are shorter than the lower limbs (sort of like a Christmas tree). After a few years, if you want to keep the tree from getting too tall, it is possible to shorten the leader and some of the high central branches by merely cutting them off at the desired length.

Cut out branches that cross each other. Thin out parts of the middle area of the tree where branches get too thick. The goal is to get as much sunlight as possible through to the apples.

Apples are always borne on short, stubby little spurs along branches. Be careful not to cut off these fruiting spurs or you will not have any fruit. Pruning trees is an art. Part of the purpose in the early years is to build the "framework" of the tree. Pruning does have a purpose. Do not cut without a specific reason for doing so. A good rule of thumb is not to overprune—especially in the early years. Overpruning will delay bearing of fruit.

Water Sprouts

Some apples produce suckers that come up from the roots of the tree. These should be pruned. Apples will also produce *water sprouts*. These are rapid-growing shoots (Fig. 12-3) that sap the

Fig. 12-3. Watersprouts. The three sprouts shooting straight up from the branch should be pruned (courtesy Paul & Alvalina Nandory).

Fig. 12-4. Stark's Golden Delicious is a good pollinator (courtesy Stark Bro's Nurseries & Orchards Co.).

energy of the tree and do not produce fruit. Water sprouts will appear on some of the branches or at the base of the tree. They are easy to recognize because they look a little different in color from the rest of the branches and they shoot straight upright in their growth. Prune water sprouts whenever you notice them.

POLLINATION

Apples require cross-pollination. Plan on planting at least two varieties for this purpose. See Figs. 12-4 through 12-6. They should not be planted farther than 50 feet away from each other (preferably closer). If planted over 100 feet away, the bees that carry and transfer pollen from one tree to another will not do their job. Bees do not like to travel great distances.

Some varieties of trees will produce partial crops without cross-pollination with another variety. But even these trees produce more fruit when provisions for cross-pollination are made. If the varieties selected are both good pollinators, two trees will be all you need to plant. Some varieties are poor pollinators. Examples are winesap and Rhode Island greening. When planting these trees, it is a good idea to plant at least one good pollinator, such as golden delicious, to insure adequate fruit set.

Fig. 12-5. The Starkspur Rome Apple is a good pie apple (courtesy Stark Bro's Nurseries & Orchards Co.).

Flowering crabapple trees are excellent sources of pollen. If you or a neighbor have such trees, they will help to pollinate your apples. Some new cultivars of flowering crabs, such as profusion, are better pollinators than other crabapples. Remember that the disease of crabapple trees will also attack apple trees. Hopa crabs are hosts to a wide range of diseases and so are hawthorne trees. Avoid planting apple trees near hopa crabapples or hawthorne trees.

Varietal differences occur in bloom time. Some apple trees bloom earlier than others. Usually the bloom periods will overlap and cross-pollination will occur. If possible, however, plant two varieties with similar blooming habits (two early bloomers or two late bloomers). Weather conditions can also interfere with fruit set. Problems can occur if it's too cold for bee activity or if it is very windy. And surprise spring frosts and freezes do occur.

DWARF TREES

Dwarf trees are generally superior for the home fruit grower than standard-size trees. They bear quicker (three years instead of seven to nine), they are easier to prune and harvest, and they take up less space so you can plant several—at least three dwarf trees for each standard-size tree.

Dwarf trees are usually produced by the grafting of a cultivar to a specific dwarf rootstock. There are a number of rootstocks available to dwarf apple trees; each has its own characteristics. When ordering your apple trees, you will find that some nurseries will offer you the choice of choosing your dwarf rootstock as well (some make this selection for you). There are several types of size-controlling rootstocks; most of them come from England. Reputable nurseries will tag each tree with the cultivar name and the rootstock used. An example is Red Delicious/M26.

When selecting rootstocks, some consideration should be made as to the size of tree you want. Some dwarfs will be smaller than others. Listed below are six of the most common rootstocks used to control the size of apples and some of their characteristics.

☐ M2 produces a tree two-thirds or more of the standard size. It is well anchored and does best on well-drained soil. Often used for

Fig. 12-6. The Starkspur McIntosh apple is a hardy apple for the North (courtesy Stark Bro's Nurseries & Orchards Co.).

less vigorous apples, trees grown on M2 can be maintained at 14 to 18 feet.

☐ M7 develops a tree about one-half of standard size. It will need support the first year or so because it is not anchored well. It often produces suckers from the root that require pruning. This rootstock is used for vigorous cultivars, but is not recommended for golden delicious. Trees grown on M7 can be maintained at 12 to 15 feet.

☐ M9 produces the smallest tree. It requires staking to help anchor the tree. Trees on M9 have brittle roots and these break quite easily if not secured to protect the tree from moving in the winds. These trees require good soil. Trees grown on M9 can be maintained at 8 to 10 feet.

☐ M26 produces a bigger, higher-yielding tree than apples grown on M9. These trees also should be staked. They develop a dwarf tree that can be kept at 10 to 12 feet.

☐ MM3 will produce a tree about one-half the size of M2. It is drought resistant and an early and heavy producer. Trees grown on MM3 can be maintained at 14 to 18 feet.

☐ MM106 will grow a tree slightly larger than M7. This rootstock produces a sturdy root system, it is resistant to wooly aphids, and it does not sucker. It can be maintained at 12 to 16 feet.

Be sure that, if you are given a choice in rootstock selection for your dwarf tree, you choose one that best meets your needs. When planting dwarfs, be sure that the graft union is above the ground at least 2 inches. It is better for the tree to be planted slightly too high than too deep. If the graft union is covered with dirt, the top *(scion)* of your tree will develop roots and the tree will grow to full size.

Dwarf trees should be spaced closer together than standard size-trees. About 8 feet between them is usually sufficient room for each tree to develop.

CULTURE

Keep weeds down, especially around your newly set trees, because weeds will compete for moisture and nutrients. Tall weeds can even shade young trees and provide harboring places for insects and disease pests. You can grow your trees in sod—right on your lawn. When growing trees in sod culture, extra water and nutrients will be needed because the grass will rob some from your tree. Do not let the grass grow too tall under the tree or it will be a convenient hideout for mice. When cutting this grass, a grass shears is better to use than a lawnmower because it involves less risk of accidentally injuring the tree.

Some people prefer to keep the area around the base of the tree free of weeds or grass. This is the usual practice. Metal grass stops are commercially available for this purpose and they are very effective. On occasion, additional weeding might be necessary, but it will be no major task.

Water your apple trees about once a week. Give them a thorough soaking each time you water. Maintain a regular fertilizer program. Although fertilizer is not usually necessary prior to the tree's bearing, it is a good practice to maintain the fertility of the soil. An annual application of manure in the spring, spread in a circle under the branchspan of the tree, is effective in promoting good growth. If you are using fresh manure, toss a few shovelfuls of dirt over it so that gnats do not breed in the manure piles. Be generous with the application of manure; spread it under the tree fairly evenly. Do not allow fresh manure to touch the trunk or any other exposed part of the tree. A fall application of woodashes will supply the tree with needed potash. Test your soil for its pH to see if it needs to be limed.

Mow grass and weeds around your apple trees to remove possible nesting areas for mice, rabbits, and other pests. Keep windfallen fruits picked up and dispose of them as soon as you see them. These decaying fruits tend to attract insects that later annoy other fruits on the tree.

APPLE INSECT PESTS

Growing apples will be something of a challenge. Apple pests are worse than the pests for many other kinds of fruit. This is true not only because there are so many, but because the fruit itself is the target of much of the damage they do. The most difficult insects to control when growing apples are the codling moth and apple maggot.

Codling Moths. The adult is a grayish-brown moth with wingspans that spread just under 1 inch. The larvae (young worm-like stage) will be white or pinkish with a brown head and up to ¼ of an inch long. The codling moth overwinters in its larval stage in cocoons under bark scales, debris, or ground litter. Larvae can be found in windfallen fruit, (usually) near the core area.

The codling moth is the main cause of the "wormy apple" (the so-called worms are the larval stage of the moth). These moths can also blemish and stain the apple peel. The codling moth is the worst and most destructive pest of apples. It is also one of the most difficult to control. Close to 100 percent of the apples on your tree can become infested with this horrid little creature. Codling moths will also attack other fruits such as pears and peaches. They reproduce at a remarkable rate; often there are several generations within a single year.

The larvae hibernate in tough cocoons under loose pieces of bark, in tree crevices, or in other sheltered areas. Codling moths lay eggs on the leaves and sometimes on the fruit and branches.

Control will be difficult. Release a predator insect, such as trichogramma wasps, in two-week intervals. These tiny wasps parasitize the eggs of the codling moth. These wasps are quite tiny and do not sting people. In the fall, look for cocoons; remove them and burn them. Scrape away loose bark on trees, but be careful not to injure trees while you are doing this. Use a dull instrument, such as a butterknife, to remove the bark. Collect debris from the ground as well as windfallen fruits.

If you still are having troubles, more drastic measures might be required. Remember that you will have some losses of fruits to insects no matter what means of control you employ.

Apple Maggots. The adult is a black fly with white bands on the abdomen. It is about ¼ inch long. The female fly lays her eggs in developing apples. The eggs hatch into maggots (which is the larval stage of the fly). The maggots are pale yellow, wormlike creatures up to ⅜ of an inch long.

Apple maggots cause damage by tunneling into fruit. This distorts developing fruits and causes them to rot and drop prematurely. The apple maggot is a serious pest. They either destroy the fruit or make it too unappetizing to eat. The fruit will become a rotted mess filled with maggots in the case of heavy infestation. When fruit is only slightly infested, the damage might not be apparent. As the fruit ripens, the burrows made by the maggots will show up as little dark lines under the apple peel.

The maggot overwinters in the soil as a small brown puparium about ¼ inch long. In spring, it changes into the adult fly. Unlike many insects, the timing of their appearance as adults is somewhat unpredictable and can occur at any time during the summer. Adults mate soon after they emerge. The female starts to lay her eggs about two weeks later. The apple maggot can cause fruit to drop before it has reached full size. Larvae in these fallen fruits can grow up and reinfest the fruit on trees.

Control by keeping all fallen fruit picked up. Remove these fruits from your yard and destroy them. If you see evidence of apple maggot infestation on fruits on the tree, thin out these fruits to prevent the maggots from infesting other apples.

Leafrollers. The adult moths are brown with light markings on their wings. They have a wingspan of ¾ of an inch. The larvae are greenish with brown or black heads. They reach ¾ of an inch long. The larvae feed upon the buds, fruit, and leaves. They web leaves together and eat irregular holes in them. Folded leaves might indicate their presence.

Control with the introduction of natural predators such as toads and birds. Pick off the affected (folded) leaves, remove them from the area, and destroy them. For those who are stout of heart, you can squish the creepy things in the folded leaves. Wear gloves if you do it because it is a messy job. The more you can do to reduce the population early in the season the fewer subsequent generations will have to be dealt with later on.

Tent Caterpillars. The adults are white or brown moths. They are active at nights in the summer. The larvae are hairy caterpillars that are 1 to 2 inches long. They construct "tents" of webbing on branches, feed off the leaves of the fruit trees, and sometimes defoliate a tree.

Control tent caterpillars by removing webbed tents with the caterpillars inside. Be careful not to break the tent open or it will allow some of the bugs a chance to escape. Sometimes people prune an entire branch and remove the whole thing to where it can be burned or in some other fashion destroyed. Do not just knock it to the ground. Do not try to burn the tent while it is still attached to the tree or serious injury might occur. Your apple tree is alive and fire hurts living things.

The tent caterpillar lays its eggs on the twigs of the tree during the summer. The eggs are laid in bands and covered with a foamy secretion that dries to a brown color that makes it look like an enlargement of the twig. The larvae start to develop inside of the egg, but do not hatch until spring. Control caterpillars by removing these egg masses from the branches and destroying them before they hatch.

Apple Red Bug. The adult is orange-red with darker markings. It reaches up to ¼ of an inch long. A nymph is bright red and smaller than the adult. The apple red bug punctures fruit and causes spots and deformation. The bug overwinters in the egg stage. These eggs are located in the bark of branches and bark pores. They hatch early in the spring. Control them with dormant oil spray.

Apple Skeletonizer. The adult is a small, dark brown moth. This is also its overwintering stage. The larvae are caterpillars that feed upon the leaves and weave them together. Control by hand removal. Apple Skeletonizers will not become a problem if picked off and dropped into a bucket of kerosene when they are first noticed.

Cankerworms. The adult male is a grayish moth. The females are gray but without wings. The larvae are wormlike creatures that are brown with yellow stripes on each side. The female lays her eggs on branches or twigs. The larvae feed on leaves for about a month. Then they drop to the ground and pupate. They overwinter as eggs or pupae. The primary damage they do is to cause defoliation by their chewing of leaves. The loss of leaves weakens your apple tree and makes it more susceptible to other stresses. Cankerworms usually occur in cycles. They will be a major nuisance for three to five years before natural predators and climatic conditions reduce their numbers.

Birds are the best control for cankerworms. Cultivate around the tree in the middle of summer to expose pupae that live in cocoons near the soil surface. This helps the birds to find them. The wingless females will try to crawl up the trunks of apple trees to lay their eggs. Sticky bands around the trunks will trap these bugs. Removable bands are the most effective.

Climbing Cutworms. The adult is a dark gray moth. It has markings on its front wings and lighter markings on its back wings. They are attracted to light. The larvae are round and reach up to 1¼ inches long. They feed at night. Climbing cutworms curl up into a tight ball when disturbed. The major damage they cause is from their feeding upon the buds before the leaves form. Control them by using sticky bands around the tree trunk.

Green Fruitworms. These are pale green caterpillars that resemble climbing cutworms. They are 1¼ inches long. The larvae will have a white or yellow stripe on each side. The green fruitworm does most of its damage to young fruits in May (when they are most prevalent). Some fruitworms continue to do damage to about the middle of June. They eat large holes in developing fruit and cause the fruit to develop misshappened.

Most of the caterpillars attain their growth during the first week of June. At this time, they burrow into the soil under the trees, going from 1 to 3 inches deep where they construct a cell. Around mid-September, the moths emerge from these cells and hibernate in sheltered areas. Some of the pupae will not develop into moths until the following spring.

Control by handpicking caterpillars that will be large and easy to spot. Wearing gloves is advisable. Carry a bucket filled with kerosene so you can pick off and dispose of several caterpillars at once. To reduce the number of pupae in the soil, cultivate under the tree to a depth of 4 inches. This will destroy the caterpillars in their earthen cells. Cultivation reduces the number of emerging adult moths as well.

Eye-Spotted Bud Moth. The adult is a gray moth with a beige band on its front wings. The larvae is brown with a black head and up to ½ inch long. The larvae eat buds, blossoms, and leaves (spinning webs around them). They will injure *terminal shoots* (end branches) and cause a bushy type of growth. Fruit production will decline.

Look for bud damage in May. Dead brown leaves might indicate the presence of the eye-spotted bud moth. Control by removing the nests from the tree. Introduce a natural predator such as trichogramma wasps. Releases of trichogramma wasps at two-week intervals will do much to reduce the number of bud moths.

Leafhoppers. The adults come in many colors; most are wedged-shaped up to ⅛ inch long. They fly away quickly when disturbed. The nymphs are similar to the adults, but they do not fly and they are smaller. Leafhoppers have the peculiar habit of moving sideways. Young apple trees are most seriously bothered by this pest. The insects like to suck juices on the underside of leaves. This causes leaves to crinkle, yellow, or brown.

Control should be aimed at the nymphs that cannot fly. Use soap and water and give your tree a bath. Do not use detergent. Use a gentle bar soap such as Ivory.

Tree Hoppers. Similar in appearance to leafhoppers, these insects are a little bigger. The adults grow to ⅜ of an inch. They do their damage by laying eggs in twigs and branches. This roughens the bark and stunts the growth of the branches. Tree hoppers are especially abundant in areas where weeds, grass, or fields of alfalfa grow near apple trees.

Control tree hoppers by keeping weeds and grass mowed. Dormant oil sprays will kill the overwintering stages of the tree hopper.

Rust Mites. These creatures are very tiny. Rust mites cause blisters to appear on the apple, lowering its quality. They also produce brownish blisters on the underside of leaves. They can turn fruit buds brown and make them flare open during the winter. Mites enter bud scales in late summer and early fall, where they overwinter. Their burrowing under the fruit-bud-scales, produces weak flowers and emaciated fruit. Control by dormant oil sprays.

Appletree Borers. There are a number of different borer species that bother apple trees. The adults can be beetles or sometimes moths. The damage occurs as the larvae feed upon the growing tissue of the trunk, limbs, and roots. Gum or insect debris will likely be present at the hole of entry. The tree weakens and might die.

Control by removing broken, diseased, or dead limbs. Treat all wounds promptly. Crushed mothballs on the soil surface encircling around the trunk will repell borers. Do not come closer than 1 inch to the trunk.

DISEASES

There are many disease organisms that attack apples. Some infect the tree and others infect the fruit itself (sometimes both). Check with your county agent to see if you have a diseased tree *before* you try to treat it. All diseases are not present in all parts of the country. Two common diseases are apple scab and cedar apple rust.

Apple Scab. Apple scab is a fungus disease that is easy to recognize. On leaves, the infected area shows up as faint spots that gradually darken. They will soon be covered with a greenish-black growth. As the disease progresses, the lesion area forms bulges. This will cause the leaf to curl. Young leaves will become stunted in their growth. The scab cells remain on the leaf for the life of the leaf. Usually all tissue will not be killed, but the area the scab covers will die. The result is dead areas in the leaf. The dead areas are easy to detect because they will be off color, usually brown.

When apple scab invades the fruit, it produces the same spotted areas as on the leaves. Heavily infected fruit will crack or drop off the tree before it turns ripe. If the fruit gets apple scab while still young and in its developing stage, it will never develop properly, forming odd-shaped fruits.

Apple scab overwinters on old leaves and reinfects new leaves as they open in spring. Severe outbreaks occur when rainfalls and warm temperatures combine to make conditions favorable for the growth of the fungus. Already infected plant parts help spread the disease by producing new spores. Control apple scab by removing old leaves after they have fallen in autumn and burn them.

Cedar Apple Rust. This fungus disease attacks apples, haw- thornes, crabapples—and to a lesser degree—pears, Juneberries, and some ornamental trees and shrubs. On apple trees, the rust will invade the leaves and sometimes twigs and fruit. When it attacks the leaves, small yellow spots appear on the upper leaf surface—usually in the spring. These enlarge and darken to orange. A black spot forms in the middle. The number of these lesions varies. Infected leaves will be smaller. Their growth will be stunted by the disease. As the rust fungus progresses, the leaves will fall. Severe defolia- tion can occur. This is especially true if the weather is dry.

Infected twigs develop a swollen section about 1 inch long. This only occurs on new growth.

The lesions on apples will be similar to those on leaves, only larger. They are often located toward the bottom of the fruit. The apple skin will become rough and raised. If developing apples are attacked, the fruit will not form properly. Whole fruits can be lost to this disease.

The loss of leaves also has a detrimental effect upon fruit production. It lowers yield and quality. If the disease is allowed to persist for several years, it will weaken trees and can result in barren apple trees.

The cedar apple rust fungus has a two-year life cycle and needs both the apple tree and the cedar or juniper to host the disease. Control by not planting near cedar or junipers. This might not be practical because your next-door neighbor might grow junipers and they are not likely to appreciate your digging them up or setting them ablaze. An alternative means of control is to plant the disease-resistant trees whenever possible.

Chapter 13

Pears

The pear (*Pyrus communis*) is not one of the easiest fruits for the home gardener to grow. In the Western half of the United States, you will have an easier time growing pears than in the Eastern half of the country. The major limiting factor to pear production is a disease called fireblight. To avoid this problem, plant only varieties that are resistant to fireblight. If you spot this disease, your only recourse is to prune out the infected parts immediately. The symptoms are very obvious. The tree will look as if its branches have been singed with fire.

CLIMATE

Winter hardiness might present a problem to the home grower in some parts of the North. The hardiest varieties will not tolerate temperatures that drop much below minus 15 degrees Fahrenheit. If you live in an area with severe winters, you might consider ruling out pears from your choice of fruits to grow.

Some varieties of pear can be grown as far south as the Florida Panhandle. In the Deep South, however, there are likely to be problems with insufficient winter chill. For best results, always select a pear that is suitable for your area. Contact your nursery or county agent for a list of varieties from which to choose.

SITE

Pears bloom earlier. Therefore, spring frosts pose a greater hazard to pears. If trees are planted on a slope or hill, they can sometimes escape spring frosts. Do not plant pears on windswept hilltops. Frost pockets should also be avoided. Spring frosts can kill blossoms and prevent fruit set. Although pears will grow in partial shade, it is generally recommended that they be set out in fully sunlit areas where they can receive the maximum amount of sunshine.

Almost all pears require another variety growing nearby for cross-pollination. Keep this in mind when you are selecting a site. If your yard is small, you might prefer to plant dwarf trees. They are easier to manage and maintain.

Do not hide your pear trees. Show them off. The pear in blossom is very ornamental with its large white showy flowers. It is a lovely accent to any landscape. Use it where it will be most stunning.

Pears prefer a fertile, well-drained soil. A loam type is best. They will grow on sandy soils, but pear trees will require additional and more frequent watering when grown on such soils.

Pears can be directly planted in sod (grass). This is something you must not do with most other fruits. It is acceptable with pears because you do not want rapid growth. The goal in growing pears is to maintain only moderate growth each season. Hence pears should not be fertilized prior to fruit bearing. This will discourage rapid, succulent growth. Such growth would be very tender and susceptible to fireblight. Moderately growing trees have a better chance of recovery if attacked by fireblight. Unless you live in one of the dry regions of the West, such as in California, fireblight should be the main concern in the back of your mind whenever you are working around your pears.

PLANTING

Plant pear trees in the spring. Fall planting is not advisable in most areas because of the danger of winter cold injury to the newly set trees. In the South or places like California, you have the option of fall planting.

Keep roots out of direct sunlight and drying winds during planting. Soak the roots in a tub of water for two or three hours to get them off to a good start. The pear tree will absorb more water soaking in that tub for a few hours than they will during a week in the soil. Be sure that the planting hole is ready. If you must, you can store the tree in your basement (provided that it is cool down there). Do not store dormant trees near a heater or they might break dormancy and you could have problems.

Some people like to heel-in their pear trees when they do not have the time to plant them right away. This can be accomplished in one of two ways. The first is to dig a hole in a shady spot in your garden, stick in the tree, and cover its roots with moist soil. The second way is to dig a trench in the garden, again find a shady spot, and lay the entire plant in the trench—covering the roots with moist soil. The advantage of the second method is that there is less danger of winds knocking the tree around and injuring its roots.

As soon as you can, try to get the tree planted. Trees keep a few days in a cool basement provided their roots are kept moist. But if kept in storage too long, they will lose their vigor.

The planting hole should be deep enough and wide enough so that all of the roots will fit in without crowding. If you are growing a dwarf tree, be careful that you keep the grafted area at least 2 inches above the soil line. This area is at the base of the trunk where the tree's bark will show a change in color. If you do not keep this area above the soil line, the top of the tree will set out roots and the tree will revert to standard size.

Remove all labels and tags that come attached to the tree and any string that could bind roots or branches. If left on, these could girdle the tree once it starts growth.

Use the best soil when filling in the planting hole and pack it down firmly to prevent air pockets from forming in the soil. Be careful not to injure the roots when you are tamping down the soil. Do this a couple of times before you add the final fill. That will make it easier to get the soil firmly packed in. Water thoroughly, let it sink in, and then water again.

CULTURE

Pears do not require much care the years prior to bearing. If you fertilize them, do so only lightly to maintain moderate growth. Do not prune them except to shape them or remove injured wood. Fertilizer and pruning are growth stimulants. A fast-growing pear tree is more susceptible to fireblight than a tree growing at only a moderate rate.

Weeds and tall grasses should be controlled. Be especially careful to not injure the tree when hoeing weeds. Any cut could provide an entry for the fireblight organism. After any hailstorm, check your pears for possible signs of fireblight injury. Hail usually precedes an outbreak of this leading killer of pears.

Most pears require cross-pollination, but one type called

Duchess does not. If you have room only for one pear tree, plant this variety. Some pears are pollen incompatible. Examples are Seckel and Bartlett. If you plant these two types of pears, a third variety will be needed to ensure fruit set. If you have any doubts about pollen compatibility, ask your nursery.

When space is at a premium, different cultivars of pear are sometimes grafted to the same tree. This type of tree will not need another variety grown nearby for cross-pollination. It will set its own pollen from the different types of pear growing on it.

PRUNING

Do not prune pear trees unless you absolutely must. Excessive pruning will delay bearing, stimulate succulent growth, and make the tree more susceptible to fireblight. Prune only to keep a tree balanced.

Pears should be trained to the modified leader system. This is not complicated. Basically, you want to develop a sturdy frame for the tree. You want wide crotch angles and a strong central stem. Usually with pears, the central leader does not develop properly. Choose the next highest branch and train it to be the leader. This is what is meant by *modified leader*.

The branch that you choose for your new leader cannot be just any branch. It has to be the highest branch on the tree. Train it so that it grows upward. Prune any branches that might interfere with its growth. With the other branches, select those with wide crotch angles. These are the ones you will train to build the framework of the tree. Branches with narrow crotch angles are to be avoided because they might not hold up under heavy loads of pears. Branches with wide crotch angles will build a sturdier tree.

Prune during dormancy (usually in the spring). The only exception is that you *must* prune immediately after any sign of fireblight. Otherwise the disease will spread throughout the entire tree and kill it. All diseased prunings must be picked up and removed. They should be either burned or placed in a plastic bag in the trash. Do not leave them lying around where the cat can drag them back into your yard or the neighbor's dog will play with them. These are diseased wood and their disease can spread back to your healthy pears if they are not properly disposed of.

When cutting diseased branches, sterilize your pruning shears before each cut is made. This will help prevent the spread of the disease by using your tools as a carrier. Always cut at least 6 inches below the diseased area to be sure to trap any disease organism that might have traveled downward into the noninfected parts.

After pruning is over and you have properly disposed of the diseased cuttings, each wound that was made by pruning should be properly taken care of. Otherwise they will be openings for the diseases to enter. A tree paint or wound dressing should do the job. Do not use ordinary house paint or try to "make-do" with some home remedy or you could seriously injure your pear tree.

Tree paint is sold under many brand names at nursery houses. Sometimes it can be obtained from your local garden or hardware store. Ask them about it. If it is not available locally, you will be able to order it through the mail. Do not buy a product unless the label on that product says it can be used for the desired purpose. Many store clerks are unfamiliar with the products they sell. Some of them will know less than you do so take their words with a grain of salt. Read the label before you buy anything.

Do not prune until you can do it right. If you have fireblight, do not wait. Go ahead and prune until you've gotten rid of the diseased wood. With other cuts, however, do not prune while waiting for your tree paint to arrive in the mail. That could take two to three weeks or longer. Open wounds will invite disease entry. Wait until the tree paint arrives.

It is best to prune in the early spring before the tree breaks dormancy. The only exception is pruning to control fireblight or some other disease. It will not kill your trees to prune them in the summer, during their periods of active growth, but it will set them back. If pruned too late in the season, it will leave the tree too tender for winter and injury will be apparent the following spring.

FIREBLIGHT

When talking about the diseases of the pear, this is the most important. Fireblight is the leading killer of pear trees. In the past, it limited the areas where pears can be grown to the dry regions of the Far West. Even today, the large commercial growers are located in the Western states.

Fireblight favors moist conditions and warm temperatures. Dampness is the crucial requirement. Fireblight is a bacterial disease that spreads mostly by insects and rain. The most likely carriers are flies, ants, aphids, and leafhoppers. Usually after a hailstorm you can expect to see wide outbreaks of this disease. The fresh wounds caused by the hail permit easy entry of the infection.

Initial infection usually begins in the terminal branches and on smaller twigs. Infected leaves or blossoms wilt and turn black. The tree takes on a scorched appearance, as if singed by fire, that gives this disease its name. The dead leaves will remain on all summer and a milky ooze will appear. This turns brown in a few days. Branches darken in infected areas and cankers (obtrusive sores) will appear. If the infected branch is cut open, it will be reddish-brown and soggy inside. Pruning and removal of infected branches is the recommended control for fireblight. There are no completely effective chemical controls for this disease. If fireblight is known to be a problem in your area, try planting the most resistant varieties you can obtain. And be prepared for battle.

INSECT PESTS

The most serious pests of pears are the codling moth, certain species of scale insects, pear psylla, and the pear thirp. Pests are not universal so do not automatically assume that you have them. See Chapter 12, under insect pests, for control of codling moth.

Scale. These are tiny insects with a waxy outer covering. The young are crawlers that appear in mid-May. They move to new feeding sites, molt, and lose their legs. They then attach themselves to the tree.

Scales cause damage by sucking the plant's juices. This weakens the tree and leaves small wounds that expose the tree to infection. Scale damage can be detected by discoloration. Red spots sometimes appear on leaves, stems, and fruit.

Scales are difficult to remove once they have attached themselves to the bark of the tree. Scrape them from the bark with a blunt instrument such as a butterknife. Be careful not to injure the tree. A dormant oil spray in the spring is recommended. Ladybugs and trichogramma wasps are also effective in controlling scale.

Pear Psylla. The adult is reddish-brown with translucent wings. They reach ⅛ of an inch long. The young insects are pale yellow, slightly flat, and become greenish or brown as they grow. The insect is covered with honeydew. The pear psylla scars the skin of the fruit with a sooty mold that grows on the honeydew.

Control with a dormant oil spray. During the fall, scrape rough bark off the trunk and larger branches of the tree. This helps remove potential hibernating places and will make for a more thorough job when you apply your dormant oil spray in the spring.

Pear Thirps. The adult is black with feathery wings and is about 1/16 of an inch long. The nymph is white and resembles the adult. It overwinters 5 to 7 inches below the soil inside a small cell. Pear thirps attack buds in early spring. The buds shrivel and become brown. The adult female lays her eggs in the pear blossom and causes the fruit to drop prematurely.

Control pear thirps by cultivating the soil beneath your pear trees to a depth of 6 inches. This cultivation should kill the last-stage nymphs. Use of a dormant oil spray is recommended.

Pear Midge. The adult is a very small fly that in many ways resembles a mosquito. The larvae are a pale orange maggot. The damage occurs when the adult female lays her eggs in the swelling buds. The maggot feeds inside the developing fruit. This causes malformed fruit that will drop prematurely. The infested fruits will be apparent by their deformed size and shape.

Control pear midge by collecting the bad fruit. Remove them and destroy them. Collection will be most effective if done before the middle of May. At that time, the larvae emerge. During June and July, cultivate under the pear tree to destroy larvae and pupae before they emerge as adults and attack the fruits.

Pear Slug. The adult is a black sawfly nearly ½ inch long. The larvae are green to black and resemble a snail or slug. The damage occurs when the larvae feed upon the upper surface of the leaves. This retards plant growth and fruit development. It also weakens the tree. Control the pear slug by hand removal of the insects from the leaves and drop them in a bucket of kerosene. Most people prefer to wear gloves when doing this chore. Do not under any circumstances get any kerosene on your tree or you could seriously injure it.

Pear Rust Mites. Similar to the apple rust mite, pear rust mites will very often attack apple and pear trees. These mites cause blisters to appear on the apple peel and leaves. They can also cause fruit buds to turn brown and flare open in the winter. The mites overwinter in the bud scales. Control with a dormant oil spray.

Syneta Leaf Beetle. The adult beetle is yellowish brown and about ¼ of an inch long. The larvae are small, fat, curved-bodied grubs. The adults scar and destroy the fruit. Sometimes fruits fall off because of the beetles feeding on the fruit stems. The grub burrows underground and feeds on the pear roots.

Control the beetles by placing large sheets of plastic under the tree. Then shake the tree a few times. Give quick jerking shakes. This will cause the beetles to fall to the ground where they can be collected and disposed of. The best time to do this is in cool weather (such as early mornings). In warm weather, the beetles fly away quickly when disturbed. In cool weather they are more sluggish. Destroy the pupae by cultivation in early spring.

HARVEST

The pear must be picked while it is still in the green stage. Do not allow pears to ripen on the tree. When they look ripe on the tree, they will be rotted inside. Ripening is best at temperatures of 65 to 75 degrees Fahrenheit, over a prolonged period of days in a well-ventilated area. For best quality, a pear should be ripened slowly. If held too long in cold storage, varieties such as Comice will never ripen. Pears can be ripened in special containers for fruit ripening or on sunny window sills. They will ripen if placed outdoors in a ventilated box on a sunny autumn day. If you are ripening fruit out-of-doors, use aluminum screening or some other measure to protect the fruit from insects. After a pear is ripe, place it in the refrigerator a couple of hours for best eating quality. This post-ripening chilling will restore fruit sugars and provide the best flavor.

Do not wait for pears to get soft before picking. They will be ready to be picked when they can be separated from the fruit spur without much resistance. When picking, gently twist the pear. Do not pull the fruit away from the spur. If it offers too much resistance, it is not ready yet for picking.

Fig. 13-1. The Stark Jumbo pear (courtesy Stark Bro's Nurseries & Orchards Co.).

Fig. 13-2. The Starking Delicious pear (courtesy Stark Bro's Nurseries & Orchards Co.).

Pears (Figs. 13-1 and 13-2) are a softer fruit than apples and they will not have as long of a storage life. They survive longest in their fresh state if they are kept under refrigeration. They will absorb odors from other foods. If stored in a refrigerator, place them in a sealed plastic bag. Some pears, such as Bartlett, can be stored for up to three months in such a manner.

Chapter 14

Quinces

Except for in parts of New England, quinces are not grown commercially in this country. It is terribly underrated as a home garden fruit as well. Quinces are popular in South America and they are enjoyed in Europe. They are especially at home in England where stewed fruits, fruit puddings, and fruitcakes are a tradition.

In the United States, any fruit that has to be cooked is apt to be considered a nuisance. This is partly because people do not want to spend their time cooking and partly because they do not know how to use this fruit. Here there is no demand for quinces except for jam or jelly.

The quince is a culinary fruit. It really has to be cooked to be enjoyed. If you do not like fruits that you have to cook, you probably will not care for quinces. Unless you've tried it, however, you are missing out on a rare taste treat.

The fruit is best made into jelly or preserves that will liven up toast, pancakes, or waffles. Another way to serve this fruit is as a dessert. First, cut it in half and remove the inner seeds and pulp. Bake it and let it cool. When it is cool, fill it with whipped cream or fruit cocktail and serve. One quince serves two people. If you plan on growing quinces, check your public library or bookstore for a good recipe book that offers recipes for cooking quince. It will be worthwhile.

JAPANESE FLOWERING QUINCE

The Japanese flowering quince (*Chaenomeles lagenaria*) is not a true quince. Here the name quince is a popular misnomer. Japanese flowering quinces are small bushes grown for their ornamental beauty. They have large saucer-cup shaped blossoms that range from orange to fire-engine red. The blossoms open up each spring for a spectacular display.

These plants do bear an "edible" fruit. Edible means that you can eat it without dropping dead in your tracks. It does not mean that you will want to eat it or like it. Fresh, the fruit is similar to rosehips. It is small, hard, seedy, and dry. Most people do not realize that these fruits are any good at all. Nevertheless, you can make jelly out of them.

It is not worth the effort to grow these bushes for their fruit. Much depends on how crazy you are about jelly. The primary reason to grow Japanese flowering quinces should be for the spring beauty that they will add to your garden. If you already have some growing in your yard, you might want to make use of the "fruit" they bear.

CLIMATE

Climate will be a limiting factor in determining where quinces can be grown successfully. Quinces do not grow well in the Deep South. Winters there are not sufficiently cold enough to satisfy the necessary chill requirement of the fruit. Conversely, severe cold will kill most quince trees. This makes them impractical to grow in very cold locations.

Before planting quince trees, contact your nursery or county agent to see if quinces can be successfully grown in your area. If the answer is no, you probably should not try to plant quince. Select a fruit more suitable to your region.

Quince trees are about as hardy as pear trees. Some quince trees are used as a dwarfing rootstock for pear trees. Chances are that if pears grow in your area so will quinces.

SITE

Air drainage is quite necessary for success with quinces. The flowers open up relatively early each spring and they are subject to frost injury. Trees planted on a hill or slope will sometimes escape late spring frosts that can kill blossoms. Low valleys where frost settle and windswept hilltops should be avoided.

Quinces require full sunlight to do their best. The trees should not be planted in the shade of a building or large tree. Quince trees are semidwarf in stature. They reach 15 to 20 feet high when mature. Space should not present a problem for growing this fruit.

146

The quince is a beautiful tree that becomes a showpiece when it is in full bloom. Large, white flowers will add beauty to your yard each spring. Plant your tree where it can receive admiring looks and comments from your neighbors. Do not hide it in your backyard or in some cryptic niche where it will not receive the attention it deserves.

Quince trees prefer a clay loam soil. They will not thrive in sandy soils. The soil should be well drained, but with a high water-holding capacity. Quinces are very sensitive to drought and water stress problems created by inadequate watering. If your soil does not hold water well, you must improve it before you set out your quince trees.

Quince trees will tolerate a wide range of soil acidity. If the soil becomes too acidic, however, it will be beneficial to add lime. If you feel that your soil is not heavy enough to support quince trees, visit a friend who has clay soil and borrow some to mix in your soil around the planting site. The important thing is to increase the water-holding capacity of your soil.

PLANTING

Planting of quince in the Eastern half of the United States should be completed as early in the spring as possible, Plant as soon as the land is ready to work in early spring. In the South, fall planting is acceptable. In other parts of the country, spring planting is recommended. Fall planting is risky in the North, because it could result in winter injury to the trees.

During planting, the roots should be kept moist and above freezing. They must also not be exposed to winds or hot, drying sunlight. It is usually best to let the roots of your tree soak a couple of hours in a tub while you are digging the planting holes for them. If the planting site is not ready, dig a temporary hole in the garden and heel in the roots in moist soil. A shady spot is preferable. As soon as possible, the tree should be planted to its permanent location.

Quince trees should be planted while they are still dormant or at the latest before much leaf growth occurs. Otherwise, the setback from transplanting will be too great and the tree might even die.

Dig a hole that will be large enough to contain the roots of your tree without bending them. The roots should be evenly extended when the tree is set in the hole. Do not allow the roots to all go in one direction or you will get poor anchorage. The depth of the hole is important and it must be adjusted according to the needs of the tree.

Do not put fresh manure into the planting hole. A well-rotted compost can be mixed with topsoil to increase its fertility (but it must be well rotted). Fresh manure can burn the roots and kill your tree. The addition of timed-release fertilizer pellets might be useful if the label on the packet says it is safe to add them. No other commercial fertilizer should be used because they are too strong and can kill the newly set tree.

Put the topsoil in the bottom of the hole. Fill up the hole halfway and then gently tamp down the topsoil. Do not use grass sod to fill the hole. If necessary, bring in good soil from another part of the garden. Fill in the hole completely, but leave a shallow saucer-like depression on top with about a 2-inch depth. This will help collect rainwater.

Water thoroughly and let it sink into the ground. Fill in any gaps made by adding the water, tamp down the soil and water again. The soil must be packed firmly around the tree roots. If air pockets are left, they could injure the tree and even kill it. Be careful when tamping down the soil that you do not injure the trees roots.

Remove any labels that are attached to the tree at planting time. If they are left on, the wire or string might girdle the tree after growth begins.

CULTURE

Quince trees are selfpollinating; only one tree is needed to bear fruit. If you want, you can plant two varieties. It will not be necessary to do this for cross-pollination purposes.

Do not bother to fertilize your tree until it starts to bear fruit. It is all right to use a timed-release fertilizer pellet at the time of planting if you prefer. It is not necessary to fertilize the tree much before it starts to bear. If the tree looks like it needs it you can fertilize. If you use a commercial fertilizer, use a well-balanced formula such as 10-10-10. A water-soluble fertilizer that can be absorbed by leaves works nicely. Be wary of overfertilizing your fruit tree or you can weaken or even kill it. This is worth repeating. One of the biggest mistakes made by beginners is to overfertilize their young fruit plants.

Weeds should be controlled. They will grow faster than the quince tree and rob the tree of nutrients and water if they are not kept down. You will want to remove weeds as a sanitary practice to keep out pests that like to harbor in weedy areas and tall grasses. Control weeds by hand hoeing. Be careful not to injure the tree while removing weeds. Keep weeds away from the base of the plant.

A mulch will aid in weed control as well as help to conserve moisture. Grass must also be kept mowed and not allowed to compete with the young trees. If you are growing your quince trees in sod culture, add extra water to see that your quince tree's needs are being met.

PRUNING

Quince trees grow erect and shapely. They require very little pruning. Prior to bearing, pruning should be minimal. Unpruned trees tend to bear younger than pruned trees. A good rule of thumb is to not prune too much. This is especially important during the early years. The tree will require some pruning to train it's growth so that it develops the proper shape.

The goal is to achieve a balance of growth. Any branches that become too long or grow faster than the other branches will need to be tapered back. Select branches with wide crotch angles. Those with narrow crotch angles will not hold up under heavy loads of fruit. If they split, they will split down the side of the tree causing serious injury and possibly shortening the life of the tree. Branches with wide crotch angles are better. If they split off, usually it will not affect the trunk. Whatever breaks that occur will usually be at points along the branch. These are easier to heal than the side of the tree. All areas of open wounds should be protected. If a branch breaks off, prune it so that there is no ragged edge and cover it with tree paint.

Prune in late winter or early spring. Summer pruning is not recommended. A quince tree should be pruned only when it is dormant (unless there is a special reason to do otherwise). Dormant trees suffer less setback than those in their active stages of growth. All diseased wood should be cut off and burned. Do not leave diseased wood lying around or it will help spread the disease. Burn cuttings or dispose of them by placing them in plastic garbage bags and set them out with the rest of the trash. If you merely move them to a different part of your yard, bugs will bring the diseases right back. Do not be afraid to prune an injured branch. You are doing the tree a favor.

During the first two years, select branches spaced at intervals along the trunk. Cut off the weak-looking branches and any that are lower than 2 feet from the ground (assuming your tree is larger than that size). Quince trees should be trained to the central leader system of pruning. A 5-year-old tree should have five to seven branches that are well-spaced around the trunk. If the leader gets too high, you can shorten it by pruning. Be forewarned, however, that cutting the leader will stimulate the growth of side branches.

HARVEST

Quinces have a long growing season and they should be ripe about the same time as are McIntosh apples. In most areas, this will be late September to October. Unlike most fruits, the quality of quinces will not be hurt by fall frosts. The fruit is at its peak when it is allowed to ripen on the tree. Even dead ripe, the fruit is not sweet. Unless you like sour fruits, do not try eating it fresh.

PESTS

The pests that bother pears and apples are the same culprits that will be after your quinces. Quinces, however, are likely to be less affected by insects because the bugs apparently prefer the other fruits. See Chapters 12 and 13 for some common possible pests.

Chapter 15

Cherries

One sure way life can be a "bowl of cherries" is if you grow your own. Your main requirements will be a sturdy tree (type depending upon your taste and climate), a pointed shovel, and probably some form of humus. There are three types of cherries commonly grown in the home garden: sweet cherries (*Prunus avium*), sour cherries (*Prunus cerasus*), and sweet and sour hybrids called Dukes. Duke cherries resemble both types. Sweet cherries are classified into two groups according to the firmness and shape of their fruit. Gean or heart varieties compose the soft-fleshed group. Biggareau is the name given the firm-fleshed group. See Figs. 15-1 through 15-3.

CLIMATE

Climate is the predominant factor in determining where cherries will grow successfully. Ordinarily, the tree does not flourish in areas with long, hot summers or where winter temperatures get high for brief periods. For this reason, cherry trees are not recommended for the South. They will, however, perform well at higher elevations, and if you live in a southern mountain range, you might do quite well growing cherries.

Sour cherry trees are more winter hardy than sweet cherry varieties. The ability of sweet cherries to withstand cold is comparable to peaches. If you live in an area where peaches grow, chances are that you will be able to grow cherries. Winter injury to the trunks of sweet cherry trees is a severe problem in many parts of

Fig. 15-1. The Northstar Cherry tree is the hardiest of the sour cherries. This tree makes a natural dwarf. This 4-year-old tree is of bearing age.

Fig. 15-2. The Stark Gold cherry. The yellow-colored sweet cherries are hardier than the reds (courtesy of Stark Bro's Nurseries & Orchards Co.).

Fig. 15-3. A young Montmorency cherry tree. Montmorency is the standard sour cherry by which all other sours are judged.

the country. Sour cherries will often thrive in these same areas. For most of the country, they are more dependable. Sour cherries are especially adapted to the central and southern Great Plains where other, less hardy fruits often fail.

SITE

Spring temperatures will be an important factor to consider when you are growing cherries. Cherry blossoms come out early and they are very susceptible to spring frosts. The sweet varieties form blossoms even earlier than the sour varieties. Hence they are even more likely to be injured by frost damage. Sites that are subject to heavy spring frosts are unacceptable for cherry growing. Avoid frost pockets by not planting in low-lying areas in your yard where cold air settles. The higher sites in your yard are more likely to have better air drainage and less chance of frost.

Cherries require a well-drained soil; a sandy loam is best. They are more sensitive than other fruits to the ill effects of poor drainage. If your soil has a heavy clay content, you will have drainage problems. Adding humus to your soil should help. See Chapter 3 for soil information. Bury a few shovelfuls of gravel below your planting to aid in drainage.

Lighter soils are essential for sweet cherries. They are more particular about soil than the sour varieties. Soils with low water-holding capacities, such as beach sand, are to be avoided. They are apt to dry out during hot periods and leave the tree subject to moisture stress. All soils are improved by the addition of organic matter, but with clay or sandy soils it is essential. Clay holds too much water; sand does not hold enough. Humus tends to act as a normalizer in both types.

PLANTING

Spring planting is recommended in areas where winters are

Fig. 15-4. Bing Cherries. Bing is the standard sweet cherry by which all other sweet cherries are judged (courtesy USDA).

harsh. In those areas where winters are mild, it is possible to plant in the fall. Plant cherry trees early in the spring as soon as the ground can be worked. It is necessary that trees be dormant at the time of planting. Trees that have broken dormancy will be severely setback by the transplanting operation. Cherry trees start growth early. If the tree has broken dormancy (started to leaf out) before it has had a chance to become established in its new location, it might die.

The only tool you will need to plant your cherry tree is a pointed shovel. The long-handled kind will be most comfortable to work with. Dig a hole large enough to hold the roots of your tree without cramming. While you are digging the hole, let your cherry tree roots soak in a tub of water. Do not let the roots dry out. When you are ready to plant, protect the tree roots from drying winds and sunlight. Place the tree into the hole. Be sure that the roots fit in without crowding. If the hole is too deep, remove the tree and partially fill it in with soil. The tree should set in a tub of water while you are fixing the hole. Add topsoil to make the hole less deep. When it looks about right, bring the tree back and plant it.

If you did not dig the hole deep enough, do so now. Do not try to force the tree in too small of a hole. Take the time to plant it right. It will be worth the extra effort and might mean the difference between success and failure. After planting, water the area thoroughly and weekly thereafter.

CULTURE

It will be important to get your cherry tree off to a good start. One way is to control weeds. Aside from being unsightly, weeds harbor pests and compete for plant nutrients and water. Control weeds by shallow cultivation around the base of the tree. A mulch will help check weed growth and conserve soil moisture at the same time.

Cherry trees will not require fertilizer, prior to bearing, unless your soil is lacking in basic fertility. In the third or fourth year of their growth, the tree will come into bearing. Then the addition of manure in a circle around the base of the tree is helpful in the spring. If you use fresh manure, a few shovelfuls of dirt should be tossed over the manure to keep gnats from breeding in it.

During extra-dry periods, water more often to avoid drought stress. If your tree has to endure stress for want of adequate water, it will delay its fruiting time, stunt its growth, and make it weaker and more susceptible to winter injuries as well as insect and disease pests.

Sweet and sour cherry trees have different growth habits. Sweet cherry trees tend to grow upright and they will grow into a much larger tree. Sour cherries spread out.

PRUNING

If your sour cherry tree was prepruned in the nursery, do not trim it down any further. If not, prune it back immediately after planting to achieve balanced growth. Sour cherry trees should be trained to the open center system. This is their natural growth habit. The tree will be roughly shaped like a vase. The goal of this method of training is to shape a tree so that as much sunlight as possible can enter into the insides of the tree. If you do not do this, the tree will tend to bear fruit only on the outer rim where the most sunshine strikes. This is the easiest of training methods.

Sweet cherry trees will naturally grow to the central leader system. This is the way they should be trained to grow. After the first season's growth, select branches with wide crotch angles. Prune off branches with narrow crotch angles.

When you have developed the basic framework of your tree, prune branches so that they all balance with each other and so that some are not longer than the others. It will be necessary to prune each year to maintain the balance. If the leader becomes injured, develop the tree to a modified leader system (see Chapter 4). This is necessary to maintain the upright growth of the tree. Do not prune sweet cherries very heavily before they come into fruiting or they will delay bearing. Remove dead or broken limbs.

Caution: Prune only with a specific purpose in mind. If you do not know what you are doing, it is better to not prune at all. Judicious pruning can be beneficial to the development of your fruit tree and help produce high-quality fruit. Irresponsible pruning can delay fruiting and, in severe cases, cause injury to the tree.

INSECT PESTS

The healthier your cherry tree the more capable it will be of defending itself against insects and diseases. The most common insect pests of the cherry include: the plum curculio, cherry fruitfly, aphids, pear slugs, and scales. Most of the "wormy" cherries in the United States are caused by the plum curculio or the cherry fruitfly.

Cherry Fruitfly. The adults are black with yellow bands

around their bodies. They are about one-half the size of houseflies. The maggots are white, ¼ of an inch long, and damage fruit by making it unappetizing and unfit for consumption. The adult female makes small slits in the fruit in which to lay her eggs. The larvae start feeding near the pit (which separates from the pulp fairly easily). The cherry will shrivel on one side and the pulp will looked decayed. There are likely to be small holes in the skin. When larvae development is completed within the cherries, the larvae will fall to the ground and change into pupae in the soil. Late fruiting varieties are less likely to contain larvae.

Control cherry fruitflies by destroying infested fruit and cultivating under the trees to destroy pupae. Pick and destroy all cherries that look damaged on the tree. Keep dropped cherries picked up and removed from the base of the tree.

Black Cherry Aphids. These are tiny little creatures that cluster on the stems and underside of leaves. Their sucking of plant juices causes the leaves to curl, turn yellow, and die. Most aphids overwinter in the egg stage. These eggs are laid on the twigs and bark of trees.

Control aphids with a dormant oil spray. If aphids become numerous during the growing season, introduce a natural predator insect such as ladybugs.

Rose Chafer. This is a gray or tan beetle with a reddish-brown head. It is slender, long-legged and about ½ of an inch long. Rose chafers feed on foliage, buds, flowers, and fruit.

Control rose chafer by cultivating areas underneath the tree where eggs are likely to have been deposited. For greatest effectiveness, cultivate in May or early June while the rose chafer is still in the pupal stage. Adults can be handpicked from the tree and dropped into a bucket of kerosene.

Cherry Fruitworm. The adult is a small charcoal-gray moth with a wingspan of ¼ inch. The larvae are a pale pink worm with a black head about ⅜ of an inch long. The larvae bores into the fruit and feeds on the pulp. It causes rough brown areas in the pulp and on the skin. The cherry fruitworm overwinters as a full-grown larva in a silken cocoon, that has been tunneled inside of a dead twig, under bark, or in debris left on the ground. It pupates in May and the adult emerges one month later.

Control fruitworms by pruning out dead branches and twigs. Remove the prunings and burn them to kill any overwintering larvae. Keep the debris and bark cleaned up from around the tree. This is especially important during the winter months. This will help to reduce the spring populations. Keep the area under the tree free of dropped fruits. Destroys cocoons whenever they appear.

Mineola Moth. The Mineola moth overwinters as larvae up in the tree. It becomes active in early spring. The larvae feed on the opening fruit buds. The insect then pupates and emerges as a moth in June. The female lays eggs. When the eggs hatch, the larvae from them attack the ripening cherries. Control moths with a dormant oil spray.

DISEASES

Healthy plants are the best insurance against disease. Set out only quality, disease-free trees. Keep them weeded, watered, and supplied with ample nutrients. Clean up windfallen fruits and maintain the garden in a sanitary state. This way disease problems can be minimized.

Ring Spot. Ring spot is a viral disease that attacks the sweet and sour varieties. On sour cherry trees, the symptoms of the virus will be visible for only one or two years after the initial infection. From then on, infected trees will show no sign of having the virus, other than decreased production and varying degrees of stunted growth. During the early stages of infection on the sour cherry, the trees will have stunted leaf growth and somewhat sparse foliage. Some leaves will have rings of dead growth and other leaves will be shotholed and shattered.

On sweet cherry trees, ring spot causes rings and shotholed patterns on the leaves. There will also be some discoloration of the foliage and some of the leaves will become tattered. The symptoms will be most severe in the early stages. Symptoms will occur on an annual basis. It will be most noticable on the early leaves formed in the spring. Control ring spot by planting only virus-free stock. Keep your trees isolated from any wild cherry trees.

Yellows. This is a viral disease that is on the increase. Yellows is especially a problem on sour cherry trees. About one-third of the sour cherry trees in old orchards are likely to be infected with yellows. The first indication of the disease can be identified by a green and yellow mottling of the leaves. This occurs on the older leaves. This will be followed by periodic waves of partial defoliation. The tree will start to lose leaves during the growing season for no apparent reason. This usually occurs from about three weeks to one month after petals have fallen.

When trees have been inflicted with yellows for a number of years, they develop large leaves and very few fruiting spurs. The spurs will bear small crops of large-size fruit. Eventually, the trees lose vigor and become very poor producers. The symptoms will be most noticable in the best producing areas with cool climates (such as those bordering the Great Lakes). In warmer areas of the country, symptoms might not even show up except as a loss in yield.

Control by planting virus-free stock. Avoid planting new cherry trees near old cherry trees.

X-Disease. The X-disease virus infects the sweet and sour cherry varieties. It harbors in wild cherry trees and especially in Choke cherries. Control this disease by planting only virus-free stock and by not planting new cherries near old or wild cherries.

Leaf Spot. This fungus overwinters on old leaves. In spring, the fungus spores are released from these leaves and carried by winds to new leaves. They germinate on the new leaves causing infection. Small brown spots changing to purple will develop on the leaves. These developing fungi will produce more spores in abundant quantity. They will spread to nearby leaves and infect your other fruit trees. If left uncontrolled, leaf spot can cause partial to complete defoliation of infected trees. Sometimes only a few leaves will be spotted. If the weather becomes favorable to leaf spot—that is damp or rainy—the disease will spread rapidly. On occasion, the tree can lose all of its leaves before the fruit is even harvested.

Control leaf spot by clean up of old leaves. In extreme cases, the use of a copper sulfate fungicide, such as bourdeaux mixture, will be desirable.

Black Knot. This fungus disease is easy to spot (see Fig. 31-1). Black knots appear in infected areas along the branches Control by pruning out the black knots, removing them from the planting area, and burning them.

Brown Rot. Brown rot fungus invades the fruit and causes it to turn brown and rot. This can be a problem, such as after a hailstorm, when the fruits have been injured. The fungus will also attack the flower blossoms. Control brown rot by pruning off infected flowers covered with gray spores.

Other Diseases. Cherry trees are sometimes attacked by other diseases that are not as common as the ones previously mentioned. Powdery mildew, leaf rust, and scab can occur. Control these diseases the same way you control any fungus disease. Remove the overwintering sites and remove infected areas before they spread.

Chapter 16

Apricots

Can you imagine a more lovely sight on a morning in July when your very own apricot tree is laden with golden fruits glistening in the sunlight? The apricot (*Prunus armenica*) blooms early in the spring. The blossoms of these trees are likely to be killed off each spring by frosts in all but the choicest locations. Climate will be the limiting factor as to where apricots can be grown. It is fruitless to grow apricots in areas not suited to them. If you live in an area where winter hardiness could be a problem, plant only the hardiest varieties of apricots. See Figs. 16-1 through 16-3.

SITE

Many apricots need to be cross-pollinated, but some do not. Always check with your nursery catalog to find out which varieties require cross-pollination and which do not. If they do not provide that information, play it safe and buy two apricot trees (one each of a different variety). It is better to assume a plant needs to be cross-pollinated.

If you need two trees, be sure and choose a location where they will have ample room to grow without crowding each other. When growing dwarfs, you need a minimum of 6 to 7 feet between them. Standard trees should be separated by 12 to 14 feet. Remember to visualize the mature tree when you are setting them out. That will give you some impression as to the size it will grow. Standard trees grow from 15 to 20 feet. Dwarf apricot trees grow from 8 to 12 feet.

Fig. 16-1. Stark's EarliOrange apricot (courtesy Stark Bro's Nurseries & Orchards Co.).

If you only have room for one tree, select one that is capable of self-pollination. Do not plant apricots that are too tender for your region. There have recently been introductions, from such places as the University of Minnesota, of hardy cultivars. These are the selections that northern growers will want to plant.

A sunny site is essential for growing quality apricots. Never plant apricots in the shade. Full sunlight is required for best growth and fruit production. The apricot unfurls its attractive flowers early

Fig. 16-2. A dormant, young apricot tree. A sunny site is essential for growing quality apricots.

Fig. 16-3. The Wilson Delicious Apricot (courtesy Stark Bro's Nurseries & Orchards Co.).

in the spring so it should be given frost protection. Avoid planting apricots in low or frosty areas. Remember cold air is heavier than warm air; a moderately elevated spot is preferable to one where cold air will collect.

Avoid planting apricots in the permanent sod parts of your lawn. Plant them in borders or along the edge. That way the trees do not have to compete with the grass for water and nutrients. If you plant them in the middle of your lawn, keep a circle under the base of the tree free of grass. There are metal or plastic products that you can buy to prevent the grass from spreading. Those items will save you the constant chore of removing the grass by hand.

A fertile loam soil is best. Poorly drained soils are not suitable for apricot production. Many soils will benefit if organic matter is added to the planting site. This encourages good root growth and improves the soil texture. With sandy or clay soils, it is necessary to add humus to the soil.

No matter what type of soil you have, your topsoil will usually be better than your subsoil. For this reason, it is a good practice to keep it separate from the subsoil so that when you fill in the planting hole you can do so using your best soil. It might be worthwhile to dig up some topsoil from other areas of your garden. You can purchase topsoil, but it is too expensive for outdoor plants. It is better to buy peat moss and composted manure to mix with dirt to improve your soil.

PLANTING

Apricots should be planted while they are still dormant. Never transplant trees in the middle of summer. In most parts of the country the planting of apricots should cease after June 1. Fall planting is acceptable in the South. It is not recommended to plant apricots in the fall in Northern states because winter cold injury can occur. Newly set trees are quite delicate and they need a good season's growth to get them off to a good start.

If conditions are not right for immediate planting, store the tree in an unheated cellar or basement. Keep the plants in a cool location so that they do not start to break dormancy. Never store dormant plants near a furnace. Keep roots moist, but not drenched. Do not let your trees freeze. Plan on planting as soon as conditions are right. If trees are kept dormant for too long they might never revive.

Soak the roots at least two hours before planting. Avoid exposing roots to the wind and sunlight while planting. Do not plant when roots might be exposed to freezing.

Plant the apricot tree 1 to 2 inches deeper than it grew at the nursery. You will be able to tell by looking at the crown area of the tree (that part near the soil line). If your apricot is a dwarf, be careful not to bury the grafted area beneath the soil. Otherwise the top part of the tree will start to form roots when it comes into contact with the soil. If this happens, you will not have a dwarf tree because it will revert to standard size. The grafted area—and you can tell where the tree has been grafted by close examination of the lower trunk—should be about 1 to 2 inches above the soil line.

Be sure to dig the hole big enough to accommodate the roots of your apricot without cramming or crowding. Some people dig holes that are too small and wonder why they have troubles. Dig a decent size hole. If that seems like too much work, do it in steps and take breaks when necessary.

When the roots are set into the planting hole, spread them evenly so that there is a balance and they do not all aim in one direction. This will help the tree to be better anchored. Fill the area around the roots with topsoil. If you add organic matter, be sure there are no air pockets left. Do this by gently tamping down on the soil after it has been filled halfway. Finish filling in the hole. Tamp the soil down and water it. Let the water soak in. When all of the water has vanished, add soil to any areas that need it and give another dose of water. The area around the base should form a shallow depression about 1 or 2 inches lower than the surface soil. This will enable rainwater to collect and it will help promote the tree's growth.

CULTURE

In dry areas, it will be necessary to provide extra water for your apricot trees. It is a good practice to water trees on a weekly basis. Set up a regular schedule and it will quickly become a habit. Make it something to be enjoyed and not considered a chore. Watering is very important. A temporary drought or prolonged dry period, especially during the month prior to harvest, will severely reduce fruit size and quality—even in areas where the annual rainfall is adequate. Trees planted in sod or newly set trees that have shallow roots will display symptoms of water stress, such as yellowing of leaves, before the damage occurs to the fruits.

Avoid frequent light sprinkling of plants. Soak the soil each time you water. Watering once a week is usually enough. Too heavy or frequent waterings can damage roots. With newly set trees and those grown on sandy soils, it is a good idea to water them more frequently. Heavy soils, such as those with considerable clay content, will require fewer frequent waterings than light sandy soils. Heavy soils are also subject to slower loss of nutrients to the subsoil.

A problem when growing apricots, that can not be over-stressed, is that of frost injury. It is necessary to protect apricots from frost damage to the blossoms and fruit. Some protection is offered by selecting sheltered locations. You can cover trees with burlap on nights when frost is predicted.

It is not an easy task to cover a large tree. Therefore, it is usually just the dwarfs that are covered for protection from frosts. There must be care taken so that the trees are not injured. A certain amount of damage will occur to blossoms or fruits from the act of covering the plant. The damage should be limited to a few broken twigs. This is minor when compared to the damage that frosts can cause. The cover must be left on until the air temperatures are safely above freezing. It has to be removed before temperatures get too warm and damaging heat builds up.

Another method that some growers find easier than covering their trees to protect them from frosts is the use of low-volume sprinkling. Protection depends upon a continuous film of unfrozen water covering the branches. This will release heat that protects the buds. Sprinkling must be continued until the temperature is safely above freezing or the night's effort will be lost.

Apricots will not need to be fertilized until they reach bearing age. Fertilize them in the spring with manure placed in a circle around the base of the tree. If you use fresh manure, toss a few shovelfuls of soil over the manure to keep the gnats from breeding in it.

PRUNING

Pruning should be minimal until the apricots begin to bear fruit. Fruit production usually begins in the third or fourth year after planting. Unpruned trees tend to bear younger than pruned ones. Some prefruiting pruning will be necessary. Branches that cross each other or impede sunlight to the center of the tree should be removed.

Train apricots to the open center system of pruning. An open center "vase-shaped" top will give the apricot fruit the needed exposure to sunlight to develop quality fruits.

To develop the largest fruits, it is a good practice to thin out the number of developing fruits. There will be a natural thinning out called the *June drop*. After June drop, you might not need to thin out any fruits. Some pruning can be done, but hand thinning is more effective with less chance of injury to the tree. Do not just thin at random. Remove the apricots that are the weakest or damaged. Leave a space of 7 inches between each apricot to achieve maximum-size fruits.

Resist the temptation to not thin out the fruits. If trees are allowed to overbear, they will put a great deal of their resources into fruit production and be drained so that they are left more susceptible to winter injury and disease or insect attack. On the other hand, do not thin out half of the apricots. There is a maximum size apricots will attain even under the best of conditions. You are not going to have apricots as big as watermelons so do not aim for that goal.

Size is only one factor of quality. Flavor is perhaps most important. To obtain the best flavor for your apricots, your trees will need full sunlight. If a low-hanging branch from a neighboring shade tree is in the way of your apricot tree, trim the branch. Of course, if that branch belongs to your neighbor's tree you should ask permission first. Usually you will be able to work out some aimiable agreement that will probably end in your giving your neighbor some free apricots when the time comes for harvest.

INSECT PESTS

The insect pests common to apricots are often the same as those that bother peaches and Japanese plums. These include the oriental fruit moth, plum curculio, and borer species. See Chapter 17.

Grasshoppers. Grasshoppers come in many sizes; some range up to 2 inches long. All have strong hind legs. They feed on all kinds of plants. They make large, ragged holes in leaves and comma-shaped bite-marks on leaf edges. Although they can appear anywhere in the continental United States, they are especially troublesome in the Great Plains. Ordinarily, grasshoppers do not bother fruit trees. They will, however, migrate to fruit trees after eating most of the green growth in fields or during periods of drought. Grasshoppers can strip the foliage off trees and leave them completely bare of leaves. This usually happens in August or July after a long dry spell.

Control grasshoppers by using a combination of tactics. A disease that affects grasshoppers is commercially available. It is called grasshopper spore. It does not immediately kill the pests, but it makes them sick and they slowly die. It is easy to use and quite effective at reducing large populations. Grasshopper spore comes in a box with two packets inside. One contains the spore and the larger packet contains a bran mixture. You will mix the spore and bran together and then sprinkle the combination over those areas with the largest concentration of grasshoppers. After a few days, you will notice a reduction in the number of grasshoppers. This treatment will last for several years, but the grasshoppers will reproduce faster than the disease organism. This is not a foolproof method of control.

Grasshoppers lay their eggs along the dense growth at the edges of roadsides, fields, and fences. Cultivate these areas in the late fall to help reduce next year's grasshopper population. Replace broadleafed weeds with perennial grasses. Crested wheat grass works nicely. It grows quickly and discourages egg laying more than native grasses. To destroy newly hatched grasshoppers, flood the area with water. Be careful not to injure your fruit trees.

Stink Bugs. These bugs are like their name implies, phew! They give off a foul odor. It is their odor that will give these unwelcome guests away. The adults vary in color and they are up to ⅝ of an inch long and ⅜ of an inch wide. The nymphs resemble the adults, but they are smaller. Stink bugs suck the sap from a tree and weaken it. The buds and fruit will not develop normally. Sometimes the fruit will become blemished with what is called "catfacing." The fruit will drop prematurely. Most stink bugs overwinter in weedy areas.

Control the bugs by eliminating overwintering nests. Keep grass mowed and weeds removed from around the base of the tree. Destroy damaged fruit and prune injured twigs.

Japanese Beetle. The Japanese beetle is shiny green with reddish-brown outer wings, oval shape and it is about ½ of an inch long and ¼ of an inch wide. The adult beetles will attack the foliage. The larvae feed upon roots, grasses, and other plants. Along with apricots, Japanese beetles are known to attack apples, cherries, nectarines, peaches, plums, cherries, crabapples, and quinces.

Control by biological means. A disease called Milky spore is commercially available. It is quite expensive. If you have a neighbor who has fruits or roses, you might want to buy some of this together and share it accordingly. The directions for its use will be on the package. There are a number of traps for Japanese beetles that use sex attractants to lure the beetles into the trap. These are quite effective and come with disposable bags. When the first bag is filled, it can be thrown away and a new bag can be attached.

DISEASES

Apricots are a stone fruit. They share the common diseases of other stone fruits such as plums. If plantings are maintained properly, disease will be less of a problem than insects.

Brown Rot. Brown rot attacks the fruit and causes it to turn brown and rot. This fungus will attack the flower blossoms as well. Control brown rot by pruning infected flowers that will be covered with gray spores.

Chapter 17

Plums

While plum trees are grown for their delectable fruits, the trees are also beautiful ornamentals. In spring, they are covered with large white blossoms, in summer they fruit, in autumn their leaves change color and fall, and in winter they cast a striking silhouette against the snow on cold, moonlit nights.

There are two species of plums that are most often grown. These are the European plum *(Prunus domestica)* and the Japanese plum *(Prunus salicina)*. Some species native to the United States are dealt with in Chapter 25.

EUROPEAN PLUMS

The European plum is sometimes called a blue plum because they usually bear blue fruits with amber-colored pulp. They are also known as "prunes." This label is not totally accurate because not all European plums are suitable for prune production. Nor are they all blue-fruited. For example, Green Gage is a European plum with green fruits. In most cases, however, it is safe to call them blue plums or prunes.

Most European plums have a high sugar content and they make excellent prunes when dried. These fruits are fine for fresh eating as well. European plums are often canned or made into preserves.

Climate

The climate that you live in will determine what kind of plums you can grow. Individual cultivars (varieties) must be considered also because there are differences in hardiness within the same plant species. The hardiest plums are the wild plums or hybrids with wild stock in them. The European are the next hardiest. These can be grown in many areas of the country, but they are not recommended for the humid Southeast.

European plums are slightly less hardy then apples and they will grow in most places apples can be grown. In the Deep South, European plums will have a difficult time receiving the chilling requirements they need.

Site

European plums open up their flowers late and often escape frosts. They should be planted in an area where they will have full sunshine. Do not plant them in the shade or they will be not as productive and they will yield lower-quality fruits. They need sunlight to help "sugar-up" the fruits.

Plums should be planted in an area with good air circulation. Avoid windy sites where strong winds are likely to knock fruits off the tree. A site with good air circulation means that plums are not to be planted in a corner with walls on two sides or a similar situation.

Remember to only select those cultivars that are suited to your climate to be assured of regular crops. With sheltered locations, you can sometimes create "miniclimates," but these conditions are not stable and it is better to grow the hardiest types of plums you can in order to avoid disappointment.

Any reasonably fertile, well-drained soil will grow plums (Figs. 17-1 through 17-4). Soils that are heavy or poorly drained will not be suitable for plum production. The best soils are those with a fertile loam. You will be able to increase the fertility of your soil by adding organic matter to it prior to the time of planting.

Soils with a poor water-holding capacity are to be avoided. If you must plant in such soil, be sure to toss in a few shovelfuls of gravel in the bottom of the planting hole to aid in drainage. On sandy soil, you will need to water more frequently than on other soils.

Planting

Spring is the best time to plant in most areas. Fall planting is acceptable in the South. Set your plum tree out early in the spring (as soon as the ground can be worked). Most European plums are capable of self-pollination. You need only plant one tree.

Fig. 17-1. The Earliblue Plum. Most European plums have a high sugar content (courtesy Stark Bro's Nurseries & Orchards Co.).

Fig. 17-2. Stark Blue Ribbon plums (courtesy Stark Bro's Nurseries & Orchards Co.).

Fig. 17-3. The Redheart plum. (courtesy Stark Bro's Nurseries & Orchards Co.).

If your soil has many small stones in it, remove them from the planting site. Soil should be sifted to a metal screen to rid it of such stones. The earth that is used in the planting hole should be good topsoil and it must be firmly packed around the roots. The roots have to be in close contact with the soil in order for the tree to "take." Gaps or "air pockets" will harm or kill the tree.

Follow directions for planting your plum that arrive with your order from your nursery. Be sure to dig a large enough hole so that the plum can be set in without bending its roots. Pack the soil firmly down once the hole is filled and water it thoroughly. Water the planting area once a week thereafter.

JAPANESE PLUMS

Japanese plums are the red-skinned varieties. They usually have an amber or red flesh. These are fresh-eating dessert fruits. Few things make a better treat than tree-ripened Japanese plums.

Climate

Japanese plums are not as hardy as European plums. It is a mistake to try to grow them in areas that are too cold for their culture. Japanese plums are adapted to most of the same regions where nectarines can be grown. Low winter temperatures hamper the production of Japanese plums in northern states. Some fruit buds will usually be killed at temperatures of 0 degrees Fahrenheit or lower and reduced crops result. Temperatures much below that will damage or kill trees. In the Deep South, insufficient winter chill can be a problem. Japanese plums are not adapted to the humid climate of the Southeast where diseases that attack the fruits can cause problems.

If winter hardiness is a problem in your area, you can try growing any of the hybrids of Japanese plums and sand cherries (see Chapter 25.). Bush cherries are extra hardy fruits, but the quality is not quite up to par with the Japanese plum.

Fig. 17-4. A dormant Mount Royal plum tree. A hardy blue plum for the North.

Site

Japanese plums require another variety of Japanese plum growing nearby for cross-pollination. Do not plant a solitary tree. When selecting a site for your plum, pick an area where you will have enough space to grow two or more plum trees. Remember when planting to visualize the mature tree and the space it will need (about 12 feet).

Japanese plums bloom fairly early in the spring and they are subject to frost damage to their blossoms. For this reason they must never be planted in a frost pocket (low areas where frosts settle). Choose a slightly elevated site with good air drainage. A slope is preferrable to a hilltop that might have gusty winds. The developing fruits are more cold tolerant than are the flowers. If late spring freezes occur during the time the fruits are developing, there will likely be less loss than if they should occur during the flowering stage.

Standard plum trees are not very large, but some people might prefer dwarfs. This is especially true if they do not have much room. This situation is not as crucial with plums as it is with apples because the plum tree at maturity is still quite manageable and easy to take care of.

PRUNING

European plums are pruned to train their growth differently than are Japanese plums. The European plums should be trained to the central leader system of pruning (the same as for training apples). The leader should rise above the highest branches and all competing branches should be removed or cut back. The upper limbs should be shortened so that the sunlight can filter into the tree. The lower limbs should be longer than the upper branches. This is sometimes called "Christmas tree" fashion because the goal is to train a tree with a pyramidal form (although not as pronounced as are Christmas trees). Branches must be selected with wide crotch angles. These will build a good framework able to hold up under the load of heavy crops.

Japanese plums should be trained to the open center system of pruning. The form you are aiming for with Japanese plums is the vase shape. The canopy of the tree should be pruned to open up the center areas to as much sunlight as possible. The more sunlight the higher the yield and better the quality of the plums.

With all pruning methods, prune as little as necessary prior to the time your plum tree reaches bearing age. The more pruning you do and the heavier cuts you make, the longer it will take for your tree to start to produce fruit. For this reason go easy on pruning. Prune only to remove diseased branches or wood and to shape the tree to the form you want the mature tree to take.

CULTURE

A regular schedule of watering is a good practice. In arid regions or during dry periods, it is essential. A temporary drought, especially during the weeks before harvest, can interfere with fruit development. This is the period of the final swell. A great deal of water is needed so that the plums will enlarge properly. If they do not receive sufficient water, fruit size and quality will be greatly diminished.

Weed control is important around newly set plants to get them off to a good start. You will want to control tall grass and weeds around mature plants as well. Such conditions provide habitats and hiding places for pests of all sorts, from insects to rodents. Keep weeds controlled and grass mowed down around your plum trees. A mulch will help control weeds and conserve soil moisture.

Most of the nutrients needed by plums will be present in practically all soils. The tree's growth and production can tell you which elements are deficient. For a fee, your county agent can run tests and a leaf analysis to determine the nutritional needs of your plum tree.

Nitrogen is the element that usually will be needed in greatest supply. Trees deficient in nitrogen will produce light green to yellow leaves and reduced shoot growth. Excess nitrogen causes rank growth, poor fruit development, color and flavor, and will subject the tree to winter injury by delaying the hardening-off process. When trees are planted in sod, extra fertilizer should be used to meet the needs of the grass and satisfy your tree's needs as well.

Keep competition for water and nutrients at a minimum by cultivating a bare area under the tree. Adding a mulch will help keep weeds down. Trees will not need fertilizer until the year that they begin bearing of fruit. Timed-release planting pellets are recommended to get trees off to a good start. Well-nourished trees will bear the best crops.

Once the tree comes into bearing, a regular fertilizing program each spring before growth starts is recommended. Animal manures make an excellent fertilizer. Spread manure evenly in a circle under the branch areas. Avoid touching the trunk of the tree with fresh manure. If you use a commercial fertilizer, a balanced formula such as 10-10-10 is best. A formula that contains only nitrogen will create deficiencies in phosphorous and potash uptake in the tree. An alternative to spring feeding is the application of water-soluble fertilizers on a two-week basis up to July 15. Foliar feeding is one of the most efficient methods of feeding your tree.

It will be more important to thin out excess fruits when you are growing Japanese plums than when you are growing European plums. Wait until after June drop before thinning out fruits. That way you will be able to calculate how many, if any, fruits need to be thinned out. Remove only those fruits that are weak or bruised.

DISEASES

Brown rot destroys more plums than any other disease pest. This is especially true in areas where it rains during and just before harvest. Removal of rotting fruit and "mummies" (fruits that have shriveled) from the tree will help to control the spread of the brown rot fungus.

INSECT PESTS

The same insects that bother the European plum also bother the Japanese plum. The worst offenders are the plum curculio, Oystershell scale, and borer species. The plum curculio is the insect primarily responsible for wormy plums. Also a menace to all temperate fruits, this is an extremely difficult pest to control.

Plum Curculio. The adult is a small, grayish-brown snout beetle with black and white markings. They have four prominent humps on their backs. The larvae are white with brown heads, ⅜ of an inch long, legless, and slightly curved. The damage the adult beetle does is unsurpassed by other insect pests of temperate fruits. This pest will bother all of your other tree fruits if you do not watch out for it.

The adult feeds on the fruit (usually) in the spring while they are developing. The female will make a crescent-shaped scar in the fruit, in which she lays her eggs. These scars look like a half-moon, are very easy to recognize, and always indicate the presence of the plum curculio. The larvae develop inside the fruit while eating out tunnels. Fruit that is infested with plum curculio usually falls off the tree before it has matured.

Control the problem by picking up and destroying all dropped fruits. Cultivate the soil around plum trees during the late spring and early summer to destroy the larvae and pupae in the soil. The adult curculio hibernates in old leaves or debris left on the ground during winter. Remove trash where beetles can find shelter and apply your winter mulch late in the season.

Plum curculios prefer shade. Prune trees properly to open them to sunlight. Keep trees strong and healthy by giving them ample nourishment and water. Weak, sickly trees are always more susceptible to insect attacks. Attract songbirds to your garden; they are a natural predator of the plum curculio. Provide netting to protect fruits such as cherries that the birds might eat.

American Plum Borer. There are many borer species. Some of the adult forms are moths and others are beetles. The larvae also come in different forms and colors. Most larvae range from 1 inch to 1½ inches in length. They feed upon the growing tissues of the trunks, limbs, and roots. When present, they will usually leave a *frass* (looks like sawdust) or gum near the entry hole. Borers can severely weaken trees. Sometimes they will kill trees if damage is bad enough.

Control borers by removing all broken, diseased, or dead branches. Keep all wounds treated as soon as possible. Try to maintain healthy trees. Control egg-laying by coating trunks with whitewash (made from diluting lime in water). The lime should be barnyard or garden lime—*not* the citrus-fruit type. Tree wraps such as aluminum foil will usually discourage borers. Be sure the insect does not get underneath the wrap. Change wraps each spring.

Oystershell Scale. These are tiny insects with a waxlike coat. They are crawling insects. Oystershell scale look like tiny oysters. They suck plant juices and cause discoloration of the leaves, stems and fruits. Scales secrete a waxy substance around their bodies after they have attached themselves to the bark of your tree. This makes them difficult to remove.

Control the problem with a dormant oil spray. They can be scraped off with a dull knife, but be very careful in so doing. A predator insect, such as the ladybug, is helpful.

Spider Mites. These are tiny creatures that feed upon the underside of leaves. You will need a magnifying glass to see them, but the damage they do will be apparent. They cause little yellow specks to appear on leaves and they weave very fine webs around them. Their feeding stunts the growth of the plant and fruit development.

Control mites with dormant oil spray. During the growing season, you can control spider mites by introducing a natural predator such as the ladybug.

Chapter 18

Peaches

The peach (*Prunus persica*) is often called the queen of fruits. Canned peaches or those bought in stores cannot compete with those you grow yourself. Commercial varieties are chosen for their capability to withstand shipping and they are usually picked while still a bit green. At home, you will be able to pick your peaches at the peak of their ripeness. Tree-ripened peaches have a better flavor. You will be able to choose any variety that you want to grow, including those types that are too soft for shipping—but oh so good!

Peaches are not usually practical for people in the northern states. Some cultivars, such as Reliance, are supported to be hardy to minus 30 degrees Fahrenheit. Nevertheless, they still might not survive the rugged winters of places such as central or northern Wisconsin.

Sometimes trees can be sheltered somewhat by use of burlap to protect them from drying winds and subzero temperatures. That also can be a problem. If the timing of application or removal is not exact, it can cause failure. For example, if peaches are covered too early in the fall they will not harden off properly. They will be more susceptible to winter injury. If they are uncovered too early in the spring, frosts and fluctuating temperatures can kill them. If they are uncovered too late, heat damage can occur. For these reasons, raising peaches is not recommended for northern states.

If you insist on trying to grow peaches in the North, select miniature trees that can be raised in containers that are portable and can be taken indoors during inclement weather. Container growing will solve a nematode problem unless you use dirt from your yard to use as media. The container must be well drained. Overwatering and underwatering are the two main causes of plant death when plants are grown in containers. Be careful not to go to extremes. Use the finger test. If the top soil is damp, do not water. If it feels dry, water. Do not allow trees to stand in water or to dry out. Use common sense.

Over three-fourths of all peaches grown in the world come from the United States. Due to the warming effect of the Great Lakes, peaches are grown in parts of Michigan and up into some of the Canadian provinces. For the most part, however, peaches are a crop for the Middle South and South Atlantic states. You can grow almost anything in California.

Peach yields will vary, but a full-grown tree can produce up to three or more bushels of peaches. With dwarfs, yields will be somewhat smaller—but good nonetheless.

There are two kinds of peaches the *clingstone* and the *freestone*. The freestone is the most often grown in the home garden and for fresh eating. The clingstone is grown for canning. Peaches come in white and yellow. The yellow type are favored. See Figs. 18-1, 18-2 and 18-3.

Be extremely careful when cultivating around your peach trees. More than 90 percent of the roots of peaches lay in the first 1½ feet of soil. It is a very shallow-rooted tree. Water your peach trees well, especially during dry periods, because they will suffer from drought quickly due to their shallow roots.

CLIMATE

Climate is the limiting factor in determining where peaches will successfully grow. Low winter temperatures hamper the growing of peaches in northern states. Some fruit buds of peaches are usually killed at temperatures below 0 degrees Fahrenheit and a reduced crop follows. Lower temperatures can cause damage or even death to the peach tree. Along the southern borders of the country, winter temperatures might be too high. Only those cultivars with a low chill requirement will thrive in these areas. For those who do not live in places where extremes in weather prevail, the peach is an excellent fruit to grow. It is well-suited for its wide adaptability, long ripening period, and ease of growing. Peaches are among the fastest growing of fruits.

178

Fig. 18-1. The Stark Encore peach. The peach is often called the queen of fruits (courtesy Stark Bro's Nurseries & Orchards Co.).

SITE

Peaches should not be planted in low or frosty areas where frost damage to developing fruits can occur. A moderately elevated ground that provides good drainage is best. Temperatures below 30 degrees Fahrenheit in the spring will kill most young fruits.

Peaches grow extremely fast and often bear a year or two after planting. If you will be growing a standard-size tree, select a site with more open space than is needed when growing a dwarf. Peaches can be kept small by pruning and maintained in a 10- to 12-foot space (if necessary).

Nearly all peaches set fruit with their own pollen. Therefore, you need plant only one tree. Avoid selfsterile varieties because they will require extra attention. It is easier to grow those types that set fruit without cross-pollination from another variety nearby.

The soil should be a fertile loam. Poorly drained soils are not suitable for growing peaches. Peach trees are very heavy feeders and they will require supplemental fertilizers for best growth.

Plant peaches in full sunlight. Shade will lower production and

Fig. 18-2. The July Elberta peach (courtesy Stark Bro's Nurseries & Orchards Co.).

Fig. 18-3. The Stark Early White Giant peach (courtesy Stark Bro's Nurseries & Orchards Co.).

the quality of the fruits. Add plenty of organic matter to soils when you are preparing them for planting. Areas that have been cultivated for several years will have fewer weeds and a lower insect population. If nematodes are a problem in your area, it is advisable to sterilize the soil you will be planting in, and perhaps for several feet around the planting site. Steam treatment is safer for the beginner to use than chemicals; it is also easier and less expensive. All nematodes might not be killed by the treatment and they multiply very rapidly. If you can give your tree at least a year's leeway in combating these pests, it will get them off to a good start. Established trees are stronger and better able to fend for themselves than are newly set trees.

PLANTING

Plant peach trees in the spring except in those areas where fall planting is acceptable. Soak roots in a tub of water for two or three hours prior to planting. This will help them begin to grow.

Plant the tree as soon as possible after it arrives from the nursery. It is best to plant as early in the spring as you can, but when most dangers of frost are behind you. If you set out a tree and discover that frost is predicted for that evening, protect the base of the tree with a light mulch of straw. Cover the top of the tree with burlap. This cloth should be left on until the outside temperatures have suitably warmed. Do not remove it too early or you will have lost your efforts. Do not leave it on all day or high temperatures can build up and injure the tree.

The planting hole must be big enough to hold the roots of the tree without cramming. Spread the roots out evenly when setting the trees. If you are growing a dwarf, remember to keep the grafted area (near the crown) at least 2 inches above the soil line. Otherwise the tree will revert to standard size. The grafted area is easy to recognize on the lower trunk. There will be a change of color where the trees have been grafted, and possibly some scar tissue.

Do not plant peach trees near oaks or where oak trees previously grew. A fungus disease called mushroom root rot will attack your peach trees.

CULTURE

Because peaches grow so fast, they will require a good deal of attention. Water them on a weekly basis and more often on sandy soils. Fertilize them with a timed-release fertilizer at planting time or with a soluble foliar spray every two or three weeks until August

1. Even prior to bearing. This will help to achieve rapid growth. A heavy dose of manure in the spring is also a good practice.

Weed control is important when you are growing peaches. Although peaches are among the fastest growing of fruits, weeds can be even faster growing—especially given ideal conditions. Keep weeds under control on a routine basis and weeding will not be a major chore. If weeds are left to grow, they will compete with your peaches and be a real burden to deal with.

When watering your peach tree, avoid frequent and light applications. Soak them thoroughly. Too heavy or too frequent waterings can damage peach trees. People who have heavier clay soils will not have to water as often as those growing peaches on light, sandy soils. Do not wait until your peach leaves turn yellow from drought stress before watering them. Water them on a regular basis. Once you get the feel for it, you will automatically know when to water your plants.

If in doubt, try a moisture test. Take a stick and shove it into the ground under your peach tree. Be careful not to injure roots. Pull out the stick. If the stick is soaking wet, you probably have drainage problems. If it is dry, your tree needs water. The stick will indicate moisture levels in the soil. Only about half of all moisture in the soil will be available to your tree. The rest of the water in the soil will be tied up with organic and nonorganic molecules and processes.

There are commercial devices to tell you when to water. If you like to spend money and it makes you feel good to have this gadget or that, then one of these devices is for you. A smart grower never depends too much upon mechanical devices. Develop your own skills and you will not be at a loss for what to do.

PRUNING

Pruning is more important for peach trees than practically any other fruit tree. Prune to achieve three purposes: to shape the tree, thin it out, and stimulate fruit production.

Prune to train the growth habit to the open center system. This is the natural growth tendency. The goal is to open up the canopy (leaf area) of the tree to a maximum amount of sunlight. The higher the levels of sunlight available to your tree, the better the production and quality of fruits. The open center system will produce a vase-shaped tree.

Do as little pruning as necessary to shape the tree, prior to bearing. Overpruning tends to delay bearing and reduce yields. See Chapter 4.

During the dormant season, prune to remove excess twiggy growth. Be careful not to overprune as these short spurs and twigs are where the peaches will be borne. Additional thinning will be necessary after fruit set and the young fruits start developing. You will be able to do this without any tools. Usually it is best to wait until after June drop. This is the time in June when the tree drops excess fruits. These dropped fruits should be cleared from under the tree to discourage insect pests.

Because peaches are such heavy bearers, additional thinning out of fruits will be desirable. Remember that there are two separate processes involved in thinning. These are the process of thinning out pruning wood and the process of thinning out the fruits. Trees that are overloaded with fruit must have the crop thinned out to produce fruit of adequate size and quality, and to prevent limb breakage. Heavy crops cause weight problems on limbs. It will be tempting to leave all of the fruit on the peach tree, but by thinning out the fruits those left on will develop better size and superior quality. A good rule of thumb is to figure on a distance of 6 to 8 inches between each peach. Earlier-ripening varieties need the greater spacing and they should be thinned early to produce large-size peaches. Later-ripening varieties can be thinned at the pit-hardening stage without much loss in final size.

Peaches bear fruit on the previous season's growth. This is known as one-year-old wood. Prune to maintain the maximum amount of fruiting wood. The heaviest loads will always be on the outer third of the tree. Prune to keep the tree producing new wood. In some areas, you will be able to prune in the summer immediately after harvest from those branches that bore fruit. This will stimulate the growth of new fruiting wood. In areas where winter cold injury can be a problem, it is best to do all pruning during the dormant stages of the peach in the early spring.

DISEASES

Peach trees are short-lived and subject to attack by many viruses. Usually peach trees live longer when grown in the northern areas (unless they are damaged by winter cold). The only major disease to worry about is brown rot. It attacks the fruit. For information on this disease, see Chapter 15.

INSECT PESTS

The insect pests that bother peaches the most are the oriental fruit moth, the plum curculio, and borer species. Identify any pest before taking control measures. That way your measures can be most effective.

Oriental Fruit Moth. The adult is a gray moth with a ½-inch wingspan. The larva is a pink worm with a brown head. Larvae bore into the stem end of the fruit and feed on the pulp. Sometimes the damage to the fruit will not be readily apparent. These creatures, through their destructive feeding habits, can increase the tree's susceptibility to disease. In the areas where early ripening varieties can be grown, the peaches can be picked before this insect has had the chance to attack the fruit.

Control by a dormant oil spray. Also cultivate the soil in the spring before the blossoms open to a depth of 4 inches. This will destroy many of the overwintering larvae.

Green June Beetle. The adult is a somewhat flattened green beetle about 1 inch long. The larva is a white grub that crawls on its back. Larvae feed on the roots of grasses. The adult beetle feeds on the leaves and fruits of the peach.

Control beetles by cultivating the soil under the tree. Adult beetles can be handpicked and dropped into a bucket of kerosene.

Periodical Cicada. The adults are black with red eyes. The wing has an orange vein except for the black near the lower edge. The nymphs are a pale beige. They look something like crayfish. The adult females injure the stems and limbs of the peach by their egg laying. The damaged area is rough and limbs break easily. Nymphs feed on the roots and weaken the tree. Control this problem by attracting songbirds to your garden.

Tarnished Plant Bug. The adults vary in color. They are ⅝ of an inch long and ⅜ of an inch wide. The nymphs resemble the adults. These pests feed upon twigs, preventing new growth. They are most prevalent in the South. The tarnished plant bug will overwinter in weedy areas.

Control by eliminating weeds and possible nesting sites. Destroy any infested fruit, and prune damaged twigs.

Nematodes. This is a major menace to peach trees and other fruit trees, especially in the South. Nematodes are small, thin, colorless roundworms. While only a few species are plant parasites, the damage they cause is immense. Most of these plant parasites are so small that they are not visible except under a microscope. Northern growers are fortunate because these areas with rugged winters do not favor a buildup of nematodes. Nematodes are a soil-borne insect.

Most nematodes live around roots and feed upon them. Some

types actually live within the root tissue. There are some nematode species called *foliar nematodes*. These pests move up onto the stems and leaves of plants where they feed. Peach trees suffering from nematode damage often look like they are suffering from water stress (with yellowing leaves). The trees will decline and might even die if the populations get built up too high.

Control is difficult. Temperature and moisture levels in the soil have an affect upon nematode populations. They become inactive during cold periods and heat can also injure them. In the Imperial Valley of California, farmers plow their fields to expose them to the dessication of the hot sun and drying winds. In most parts of the country, cultivation is not an effective control.

Partial control can be achieved by sterilizing the soil, either by steam or a soil fumigant, prior to planting. This method will only last for a few months as the soil eventually becomes reinfested. For the newly set peach tree, those few months can mean the difference between success or failure. Consult your county agent if serious problems arise.

The time to worry about nematodes is before you plant. If you find nematodes are a problem in your area, you can plant resistant varieties. Some peaches are more resistant to nematode damage than others or grafted onto rootstock that is resistant. Your nursery can supply you with resistant varieties.

Chapter 19

Nectarines

Nectarine (*Prunus persica* var. *nucifera*) are becoming more and more popular with home growers. Along with their attractive, smooth, and highly colored skins, they have a flavor that is hard to resist. See Figs. 19-1, 19-2, and 19-3. Often people who do not like peaches are crazy about nectarines. Some commercial nectarine growers in California expect that the nectarine will soon pass the peach in popularity.

For the home grower who lives in the eastern half of the United States, it is more practical to grow peaches. Yet with special care and attention, you might be able to successfully raise nectarines.

CLIMATE

Nectarines are best suited for the western half of the United States and other areas with a dry climate. In the eastern half of the country, conditions can get quite humid. This is not a good thing for nectarines as it helps favor fungus diseases and fruit-rot organisms. In the East, especially the humid Southeast, nectarines will have too many problems with fruit rot. The smooth-skinned nectarine cannot protect itself from fruit rot as well as the fuzzy-skinned peach.

Climate and humidity are the principal limiting factors for the home production of nectarines. The fruit is only about as hardy as peaches and cannot be grown in areas where winterkill occurs. It has a chill requirement so it is not suited for the Deep South. There are a few varieties that are adapted to low chill conditions. Consult

Fig. 19-1. The Stark Early Bird nectarine (courtesy Stark Bro's Nurseries & Orchards Co.).

your nursery if that is a problem in your area.

In the North, winter hardiness is always a problem. If you live in an area where you can grow peaches, you will be able to grow nectarines unless your climate is too humid. A rainy period before harvest can result in fruits rotting on the tree. If your area is too cold, do not attempt to grow nectarines unless you are growing miniature varieties in portable containers. These fruits go inside during inclement weather and winter. You must remember to take them inside. If you do not, the plant might die.

Too many times people try to grow a fruit that is not sufficiently hardy enough for the growing conditions of the region. To do so will be fruitless. It is a waste of time, labor, money, and it creates frustrated hopes. You must live within the reality of the climate of your area. To do otherwise is to invite defeat and frustration.

SITE

Nectarines require a full day's sunlight to do their best. Sunlight is needed for rapid growth. The nectarine is among the fastest growing fruits. Sunlight is also needed to develop fruit quality and yield. Do not plant nectarines in an area where they will be shaded by tall buildings or trees.

Nectarines are somewhat tender and should not be planted in areas that might be subject to frosts or cold spells in the spring. Avoid low spots in the yard. Also avoid windswept hilltops. Temperatures during winter will be several degrees colder with the wind blowing. In the summer, the winds increase the transpiration rate of the trees and contribute to drought stress. Do not plant nectarines in windy locations. Another reason to avoid windy sites is that strong winds can knock ripening fruits off the tree and spoil them before you get a chance to pick them. Nobody wants to pick up fruits off the ground. Insects and rot organisms will quickly enter them, lowering the fruit quality.

Fig. 19-2. A nectarine tree. Notice the long, graceful leaves.

Fig. 19-3. The Stark Earliblaze nectarine. (courtesy Stark Bro's Nurseries & Orchards Co.).

An ideal site is a slightly elevated slope that will provide the necessary air drainage to help keep frost damage at a minimal level.

Nearly all nectarines are capable of setting their own fruit through self-pollination. You need plant only one tree to get fruit. There are exceptions. Always be sure to read your nursery brochure thoroughly. Check for any pollination requirements.

SOIL

Good water drainage is more important than fertility in determining a good nectarine soil. Nectarines do not like "wet feet." They need a soil where water does not linger on the surface. Heavy, water-logged soils must be modified to correct drainage problems before nectarines can be successfully grown.

An ideal nectarine soil is one that is slightly acidic and rich in organic matter. You can increase the natural fertility of your soil by adding composts to it prior to planting. A well-rotted compost is best. Many soils, especially in the South, are troubled with heavy nematode populations. These root-feeding pests can do as much damage to the nectarines as they do to the peach. Check your soil for nematodes before planting. If you have a high nematode population, steam treatment of the planting area is advisable. Chemical treatments are best for beginners to avoid because they are hazardous and require greater expertise to administer. Don't be particularily worried about potential problems. You will have enough real things to worry about.

PLANTING

Nectarine trees do not become very large when mature. Most varieties are capable of self-pollination. The tree should not be crowded between something or stuck up against a wall. Plant them in an area where they will have plenty of open air and sunshine surrounding them.

Dig a large enough hole to accommodate the tree's roots without squeezing them. A long-handled shovel is the best tool to use for this operation. When setting the tree in the planting hole, be sure to evenly spread out the roots so that they do not all bend in one direction. Roots that all bend one way will make for a poorly anchored tree.

Handle the dormant tree with care. Your nectarine tree is dormant, but not dead. If you are too rough with it, you can cause it injury and lessen your chance for a successful transplanting. Soak roots prior to planting. This will enable them to take up more water during a few hours than they will all week in the ground. Do not soak trees overnight or for several days or the roots will become water-logged and the tree might die.

Use only good topsoil for filling in the hole and pack it firmly around your tree's roots. The subsoil that is low in humus and fertility should be replaced with good soil even if you have to dig it out of another corner of your yard.

Leave a shallow depression around the base of your tree. A few inches will do. This will help collect rainwater and keep the tree from drying out too fast. Water all newly set plants on a regular basis. This will be about once a week, but more often on sandy soils. This is crucial to help establish the young tree.

When watering, always give the area around the tree a good soaking. Light, frequent waterings can encourage trees to become shallow-rooted because roots develop toward the source of water. Such trees are more subject to drought stress and are less able to resist winter cold injury.

CULTURE

The nectarine is a genetic mutant of the peach. Technically, it is a "fuzzless" peach. It lacks only the gene that accounts for the fuzz on the peach. Consequently, nectarines are smooth skinned. Occasionally, you will find nectarines growing in your peach tree or peaches growing on your nectarine tree.

The same single gene that separates these two fruits is also responsible for the differences in plant culture. For example, the nectarine—because of its smooth skin—is more susceptible to disease and insect attacks than the peach. Apparently, the fuzz on the peach, which many people peel off, is one of nature's defenses. In the Eastern half of the United States, there is more rainfall and a higher level of humidity than in the Western half. These humid conditions tend to favor the development of fruit rot organisms. For this reason, the nectarine is predominantly grown in the Western and drier areas of the country. In California, irrigation is used to meet its water needs. If you live in the Eastern half of the country, you might want to plant peaches instead. If you plant nectarines, be prepared to protect them and to suffer a higher percentage of fruit loss to disease and insects than you would if you were growing peaches.

The nectarine is a very rapid grower. It will not take too many seasons before it begins to bear. Usually by the second or third season after planting you will have a crop of nectarines. Trees set heavily with fruit and they will need to be thinned out to maintain the size and quality of the nectarines.

Fruit Thinning

Thinning out the number of developing fruits will help to increase the size of your nectarines. This should be done shortly after June drop. Some of the fruits will naturally be thinned out in the June drop process. Wait until after then to determine how much more thinning, if any, you will need to do.

If you thin out fruits before June drop, you might lose more nectarines than you bargained for. The tree will naturally lose some of the fruit at this time. Usually, the tree loses the weakest and smallest fruits. These are the ones that you want to get rid of because they will not develop into prime nectarines.

Plan on spacing fruits about 6 to 8 inches apart for best size. Thin fruits by gently twisting off the blemished fruits. If they do not want to come off easily, leave them on. Any fruit that will not come off without a struggle should be allowed to mature and ripen. The fruits that come off with a simple twist are those that would fall off later in strong winds or produce inferior fruits anyway.

It will be tempting to leave all of the nectarines on the tree. Nevertheless, by pruning out the fruits those remaining will become much larger. Although you can prune for thinning, it is better to thin out the fruits than to cut out the fruiting wood. If you do prune, do so in the early spring while the tree is dormant. Be very careful not to prune too many branches or you will not have any fruit.

Fertilizing the Prebearing Tree

Nectarines are rapid growers and quite heavy feeders. They should be fertilized prior to fruit bearing. Fertilize each spring with an application of manure. Composted manure is best, but you can use the fresh manure provided you do not get too close to the tree so that the manure touches the trunk. Apply the manure in a circle under the branch spread. Do not apply manure after the first of August or the tree will not be able to harden off properly.

Fresh manure is an excellent breeding ground for gnats. These tiny flies get into the eyes and bite the face, hands, and other exposed areas of the body. To prevent gnats from breeding in the manure, always cover it with a few shovelfuls of dirt. You do not have to use your best soil to cover it, but cover it so that none of the fresh manure is exposed.

Nectarines require adequate water to keep up with their rapid growth. Trees should be mulched to help control weeds and conserve water. Extra nitrogen should be added to mulched plantings to help decompose the mulch in the early years of the tree's setting. The quantity of the fertilizer should be in relation to the tree's age and vigor. Be extremely careful not to get carried away and overfertilize young trees. Too much fertilizer will cause plants to become sick and die. When using a commercial fertilizer such as 10-10-10, one cup for every ¼ inch of the trunk's diameter will suffice for the growing season.

PRUNING

Pruning is very important to your nectarine tree. When growing nectarines, as with peaches, you prune for one of three reasons: to shape the tree, thin it out, and to stimulate fruit production.

Trees are shaped to the open center system of training. Most often they naturally grow this way so it will not involve much effort on your part to grow the tree in this manner. Pruning should be light the first year or two and only done where necessary.

Prior to the time your nectarine reaches bearing age the only pruning you should do is for training the tree or removing diseased wood. All other pruning will be counterproductive and tend to delay the bearing of fruit.

If the tree grows too upright or gets too tall, it is sometimes advisable to prune the top. This will encourage the side branches to produce. Once a tree has reached bearing age, annual pruning will be desirable to stimulate fruit production.

Fruit is always borne on 1-year-old wood. The continual production of 1-year-old fruiting wood is possible by the annual pruning of the tree. Prune those branches that bore fruit after the harvest. Next year they will produce new growth and the following year fruit again. This is the best pattern to follow.

When pruning, always use the proper tools and make clean cuts. Trees can be injured if you just whack away at them. They are living things and require the same tender loving care that all living things respond to. If you do not know what you are doing, do not do it. Never prune your nectarine tree unless you have a specific reason to do so.

HARVEST

Nectarines will not all ripen all at once. They are at their best quality when picked fully ripe. Nectarines differ from peaches in skin texture, flavor and aroma. Just as with the peach, they are a soft fruit and they bruise easily. Handle nectarines gently.

Store nectarines under refrigeration for best care. They must be kept away from excessively moist conditions that encourage the development of rot. The fresh fruits can be stored for two to three weeks without excessive loss of quality. Longer storage usually results in the internal breakdown of the nectarine. Stored fruit should be checked regularly for rotting or internal breakdown. Use the fruit as close to its prime quality as possible. For longer storage, can or freeze the fruits.

Chapter 20

Mulberries

Mulberry plants are very difficult to get started. They do not seem to be fully hardy in the North. Check with your nursery company to see if mulberries will grow in your area before you order any plants. The fruit resembles the blackberry in size, shape, form, and flavor. It is borne in abundance and makes scrumptious pies, jams, or preserves. Best of all, you can pick the ripe fruit and pop it into your mouth—by the handful.

No yard is too small for a mulberry planting. This fruit can be trained to grow in many forms: as bushes, hedges, or trees. The tree form is the most popular and productive of fruits.

CLIMATE

There is a mulberry species for almost everybody. Mulberries grow under a wide range of climatic conditions. In regions where winter hardiness is the first consideration in selection of fruits, growers should plant only a hardy variety such as the Russian mulberry (*Morus alba* var. *tartarica*). This is the hardiest species of mulberry and it will thrive in severe climates. The Russian mulberry is often used for windbreaks on the Great Plains.

For the South, the native red mulberry (*Morus rubrum*) is appropriate. It is found growing wild throughout many areas of the Southeastern United States. The red mulberry grows the tallest tree. It reaches heights of over 30 feet.

If you live in California or similar areas, you will be able to grow the black mulberry (*Morus nigra*). This is the least hardy of the species, but it bears the largest fruits.

SITE

Mulberries prefer a damp location. The mulberry blossom is not very showy or ornamental, but it is very hardy. Mulberry blossoms are called *catkins*. There are two kinds of catkins: male and female. The male catkin is long and slender. The female catkin is short and thick. They give off a greenish-yellow pollen that is carried by the wind. These trees are wind-pollinated.

The mulberry is *dioecious*. The male (staminate) flowers and the female (pistillate) flowers are borne on separate plants. Only the females bear fruit. It is important, when ordering mulberries, to get the fruiting kind. Nonfruiting mulberries are sold for ornamental purposes.

It is also important to recognize this fact when it comes time to select a site. You will need enough room for at least two plants—one of each sex.

Frosts will not usually affect your mulberry flowers (catkins). This is a good plant to set out in those areas of your yard where less hardy fruits usually suffer from frost damage. Because the mulberry is wind-pollinated, a cold spell in the spring that might lower bee activity could reduce the fruit set of your apples, but it will not affect your mulberries.

Mulberry plants prefer a fertile loam, but they will grow almost anywhere if they have access to ample moisture. The soil must have a high water-holding capacity. Add plenty of peat moss if the soil is low in fertility and add lime to neutralize the acidity of the peat.

PLANTING

Follow the directions for planting your mulberry trees or bushes that come along with your order. It is always a good practice to read the instructions before planting.

The only tool you will need will be a pointed, long-handled shovel. Dig the holes. Remember that when you are planting mulberries you will have to plant more than one, dig a separate hole for each tree you set out. The holes should be spaced no closer than 15 feet between them. This will give the tree ample space to spread out.

A pitchfork will be handy in moving large clumps of leaves. If you do not have a pitchfork, you can lift leaves with your hands. On sandy or clay soils, leaves or other forms of humus should be added to improve the planting site. For sandy soil, it will help to better retain moisture. On clay soil it will loosen them up.

The hole you dig for each tree must be big enough to place the roots of the tree in without bending. If the hole is too small, remove the tree and enlarge it. If the hole is too large, partially fill it in before you return to planting. While you are working on the planting hole, you should have the mulberry plants soaking their roots in a tub of water. Be sure to keep roots out of direct sunlight and drying winds during the planting operation.

If you have extremely poor soils, you will want to dig a larger hole and add alternate layers of dirt and leaves. Well-rotted manure and peat moss can be used as a substitute or in combination with leaves.

Some nurseries will recommend that you stake young trees to bamboo or some other kind of support poles. They might even include such supports with your nursery trees. Even if they do not, you might want to use one of your own. This will be a necessity in areas that are extremely windy. Strong winds can severely injure newly set trees.

The stakes you use can be of any form provided they are long and sturdy. Any stake shorter than 4 feet probably will not provide you with the protection you need. The stake will not easily go into the ground so it should be hammered into position. Tap the top of it gently. Be sure that the stake is secure before you tie the tree to it. The tree must be planted before the stake is put into the ground. Tie the two with soft string; never use wire. Each year you will want to check the string to see that the tree is not being girdled.

When the tree is set out, its roots must come in close contact with the soil. Never should leaves be in direct contact with roots. Soil must be firmly packed around the roots to prevent air pockets from forming. These gaps will cause root injury and can kill the tree.

Spring planting is recommended except for those areas of the South where you can plant in the fall. The early morning or in the evening before sunset are the best times to plant rather than under the hot, afternoon sun.

If you will be planting mulberries as a hedge, set them fairly close together (no farther than 3 feet apart). A 2-foot space between each plant will provide a dense hedge, but few berries. Use only small plants for hedges, seedlings, or hedge grade. Do not plant young trees and cut them down to hedge size or you might kill them.

They have already been trained as trees so they must be allowed to grow in that form.

When setting out mulberry plants to raise as trees, they will need a greater space between them than they do when growing them for hedges or shrubs. Always visualize the trees as a mature plant. That will help you to avoid planting them too close together.

CULTURE

Mulberries, once started, grow with little need for attention. It usually takes about a couple of years for the trees to become established. Once established, they are hardly a bother at all. Newly set trees, however, will require extra attention to get them off to a good start.

A yearly application of manure in the early spring will aid growth. It will not be necessary until the trees begin to bear fruits.

The major problem with growing mulberries is that they can become quite messy. They are likely to litter your yard with windfallen fruits. If you like an emaculate yard, you will not want to grow mulberries. This litter can present a sanitation problem. You will want to rake up windfallen fruits to keep them from attracting insects. This is quite a chore. If your mulberries are growing in sod, tall grasses must be kept down.

Mulberry plants should be given plenty of water during the growing season. This is especially important during fruit development. During periods of drought, additional watering is recommended.

Hoeing under the newly set trees is a good practice. This will help rid the area of weeds. Be careful not to hoe too deeply or you will injure your tree. If weeds are allowed to run rampant, they will likely take over and rob your mulberry tree of nutrients and water. Weeds that grow tall can shade young trees from receiving the sunlight they need, prevent air circulation, and encourage mildew and other diseases.

With mature plants, weeding is also a good idea. Usually, shallow cultivation with a hoe works best. A good way to keep the weed population down is with a mulch. Mulches help smother weeds and prevent their growth. They also have the added benefit of conserving soil moisture. In the case of organic mulches, they add vital nutrients to the soil as they decay. A winter mulch will help protect the root system of your mulberry from cold and fluctuating temperatures. It is essential to use a winter mulch in areas where winters are severe.

PRUNING HEDGES

Mulberries need to be pruned differently when grown in hedge culture than when grown as trees. Train the bushes the same as for any hedge. Hedge pruning shears should be used to keep all growth in line the way you want it to be. Heavy pruning will not be necessary the first season. After that, it will be best to prune moderately heavy. This will help keep down the size and encourage the production of branches. Use only small plants for hedges. They are less expensive to buy and will be easier to train.

You will be able to train your hedges to many patterns. Much depends upon how formal you want your hedge to be and how much fruit you want to produce. Naturally, the more you prune the less fruiting wood you will have. Some people prefer to grow mulberries with a round head. This will produce the most fruits, more so than any other hedge shape, and it is fairly easy to maintain—once established. The plant can also be trained to square or exotic shapes if you prefer.

Birds like to eat mulberries. So plan on sharing some with them. You can put netting over your bushes if there is a problem with birds.

PRUNING TREES

If you have room, you will probably want to grow mulberries in their tree form. This is the most productive way to grow them (providing larger yields). It is also the easiest way because it requires less maintenance labor. Prune trees to train their growth patterns so that you will not have to do a great deal of corrective pruning later on when the trees have matured.

It is necessary with newly set trees to train them to tree form. Even those that are "tree grade" from the nursery will require some pruning to keep their shape. If left unattended, lower branches will develop and the tree will take on a bush form.

Train mulberries to the central leader system. This is the same method used for apples. The highest branch should arise above all other branches. No branch should be allowed to compete with this top branch. The side branches should be tapered so that the lower limbs are shorter than the upper. This will allow the sunlight to filter through.

The central leader system of pruning is sometimes called "Christmas tree" fashion because it tends to form trees slightly pyramidal in form.

When the mulberry begins to bear, which is usually in its fourth year after planting, it will not be necessary to do much pruning. Thinning mulberries will not increase their size.

Prior to bearing age, a minimum amount of pruning works best. If young trees are overpruned, it can set them back and they will delay bearing fruits. All pruning has a dwarfing effect upon plants. Keep this in mind.

INSECT PESTS

The major insect pest of any consequence to the mulberry plant is the silkworm. This is not too common in this country except in those areas where silk is produced commercially. Other insects can become a problem, but surprisingly the mulberry does not have a great deal of insect pests. Most can be controlled through sanitary garden practices (such as keeping windfalls picked up). If insects become too numerous or are reducing the yield, contact your county agent for assistance.

DISEASES

There are three common diseases that infect mulberries: canker, popcorn disease, and mildew.

Canker. Canker disease produces cankers (sores) on the branches of the mulberry tree. Control the problem by pruning the infected areas. Cut at least 12 inches below the canker, preferably while the tree is dormant. Sterilize your pruning shears with each cut so that you do not spread the disease. Rubbing alcohol or a solution of 1 part bleach to 3 parts water can be used for this purpose.

Popcorn Disease. This disease occurs mostly in the South. It is not serious. Fruit that gets infected does not ripen properly. It looks more like popcorn; hence the name. Popcorn disease will usually go away by itself after awhile.

Mildew. Various kinds of mildew can present problems on the leaves of trees located in areas of heavy shade or with poor air circulation. Usually when this happens only a few leaves will be killed. Control mildew by pruning to increase air circulation and planting trees in full sunlight.

HARVEST

Mulberries are very tender and they crush easily in the hand. The fruits are sweet when ripe and they leave a telltale purple stain on hands and clothing. Wear rubber gloves to avoid this discoloration. Pick the fruit, placing them gently into small containers, or pop them into your mouth. The fresh fruit will keep several days in the refrigerator.

Mulberries are a home garden fruit. They are too tender to withstand shipping and do not ripen all at once. These two qualities keep them out of the commercial market. It is an advantage for the fruit to ripen over a period of weeks instead of all at once.

Mulberries are best when they are tree ripened. As the fruits ripen, they can be served fresh for desserts or frozen or canned for later use. Home-baked mulberry pie, made from your own mulberries, will be a delicious treat on cold winter nights.

Part 4
Native Fruits and Melons

Chapter 21

Juneberries: The Birds' Favorite Fruit

Everybody loves these shiny black berries—especially the birds. Just as soon as the berries start to ripen, birds will flock around. One day you will have a tree loaded with berries, the next day no fruit will be left. You absolutely must protect your Juneberry tree from birds or you will not have any fruits.

The Juneberry *(Amelanchier alnifolia)* is a native fruit found throughout the United States and Canada. The Juneberry grows into a large shrub that can be trained as a small tree. It is an excellent fruit for the home grower. It is fairly easy to grow and provides ornamental beauty in the spring when its lacy-white blossoms cover the tree.

The Juneberry is not a true berry. It is technically a *pome* (like the apple). Because of its small size and resemblance to blueberries, it is called a berry by most people. If you examine the fruit closely, you will see that its structure more resembles the apple. Juneberries differ from blueberries in several ways. The Juneberry has a large, hard pit. Blueberries have several soft seeds that are barely noticable when eaten.

The Juneberry is known by different common names around the country. In New England, it is called the *Shadblow* or *Serviceberry*. In Alaska, it is called the *Saskatoon Blueberry*.

Juneberries are a fruit that you will enjoy no matter what name you call them. They can be eaten fresh, baked into pies, or used in many other ways. Some people think that Juneberries make a better-tasting pie than blueberries.

CLIMATE

The Juneberry is among the hardiest of fruits. This is an ideal fruit for people who live in rugged climates where nothing else seems to grow. Juneberries can be grown in Alaska and the Yukon. They are that hardy.

The fruit does better in the Far North than in the Deep South. In areas of the South, there might be problems with insufficient winter chill. Juneberries do not grow well in central and southern Florida because winters there are not sufficiently cold enough to meet the Juneberry's chill requirements.

SITE

The Juneberry opens its blossoms early in the spring. The tree in bloom makes a spectacular display. Its abundant flowers resemble lacy-white clouds. The flowers are extremely hardy. Frosts do not seem to injure the blossoms.

The Juneberry is capable of self-pollination. It does not need another variety nearby for cross-pollinating. It is also a compact plant. Its natural growth habit will be to form a shrub, but it is best trained to form a small tree.

Unlike most fruits, Juneberries seem to be content growing under shady conditions. They are often found growing wild at the edge of the forest where some sunlight filters through. Plant the Juneberry anywhere in your yard, but it is best to avoid heavy shade.

Although Juneberries somewhat resemble blueberries, they have opposite needs. Juneberries do not like an acidic soil. Juneberries are one of the few fruits that grow better in a "basic" or slightly alkaline soil. The addition of lime prior to planting will help "sweeten" the soil for Juneberry culture.

Never plant Juneberries next to blueberries. If you plant the two fruits close together, you might accidentally lime your blueberries—killing them. Soils can leach nutrients as well. Keep blueberry plantings separate.

Juneberries are somewhat tolerant of drought. They require a well-drained soil. A sandy loam is best.

PLANTING

In the milder parts of the United States, the trees can be

planted any time the ground is not frozen during the late fall, winter, or spring. In the colder regions, spring planting is recommended. winter injury could result from plants set out in the fall. Never set out trees in frozen ground.

The roots are more tender to cold than are other portions. If the trees are being handled in the winter or early spring, use great care to prevent cold injury to the roots. In general the later in the spring the trees are set out the poorer the growth response will be because of the poor establishment of the new root system when the top growth begins.

Plant by first digging a hole big enough to hold the entire root system without cramming. Trees should be set out at about the same depth as they grew in the nursery. You will be able to tell from looking at the lower trunk where that was.

Stand the tree upright in the hole with one hand while you fill the hole in with topsoil using your other hand. If the hole is too deep, remove the tree and add soil to the hole to make it less deep—then resume planting. If the hole is not deep enough, remove the tree and deepen the hole so that it will fit the roots of the tree without crowding. Never try to force a tree into a hole that is too small for it.

It is necessary that the tree be planted so that it will grow as upright as possible. You will not want a tree that leans. It will not be as sturdy or as attractive. To keep the tree upright while you are planting, hold one hand on the trunk while you add soil with the other. Tamp the soil down every now and then with your foot, and adjust the tree so that it remains in as straight a position as possible. If you are fortunate to have a helper, have them hold the tree while you fill in the hole.

Place topsoil nearest tree roots. If you are using a loose organic material such as leaves, place a shovelful of dirt over them so they do not come in direct contact with the roots. Pack soil firmly around your roots. If air pockets are left, they can seriously injure or even kill your tree. Leave a shallow basin about 2 inches deep around the base of the tree. This will be most helpful in collecting rainwater. Water the tree on a weekly basis or whenever the crust of the topsoil becomes dry. On sandy soils, you will have to water your Juneberry plant more often. On clay and heavy soils, it will not be necessary to water it as frequently. Everytime you water, soak the area thoroughly (do not just sprinkle). This will help the roots to spread out and become better established.

Wrap your tree immediately after planting to protect the trunk from rodents and sunscald. If you do not have a commercial tree wrap, aluminum foil works nicely. Wrap it tightly and use adhesive tape around the edges to keep the foil from being blown off in gusty winds.

CULTURE

Juneberries will not require much work and they are very hardy. Because they are tolerant of drought, they will survive longer than other fruits if neglected. Do not neglect newly set trees or you could delay their fruiting.

Juneberries are easier to grow than blueberries and they are hardier too. This is a nice fruit for people who do not have a great deal of time to spend in their garden. It also fits nicely into small urban lots and takes the pollution abuse that torments many of America's cities.

It does not need fertilizer before it reaches bearing age. Upon bearing, an annual spring application of manure will suffice. Juneberry trees are not terribly productive. You might have to plant several to have as many fruits as you prefer.

A mulch to control weeds and conserve moisture is recommended.

PRUNING

Juneberries require training to grow into the tree form. The early shaping of the tree should be accomplished with as little pruning as practical. Severe pruning of young trees will delay their time of bearing fruits. Trees that receive only a small amount of pruning from the time of planting to the time of bearing are almost invariably larger in stature and fruit earlier than heavier pruned trees of the same age.

Prune your Juneberry to train its growth habit. Juneberries should be trained to the central leader system. Mostly it will be just a matter of keeping the branches well balanced for even growth. If tree training is left to chance, corrective pruning will become necessary at later dates. Nevertheless, the Juneberry is not that demanding when it comes to training. Prune to maintain the tree's shape. If one branch grows longer than another, it should be cut to balance the tree.

Prune to remove suckers from the base of the tree. Suckers are shoots that will come up at the base of your tree. If you let the suckers grow, they will form a shrub and sap your tree of its strength. If the suckers are carefully detached from your tree at the root, they can be used to form new plants. If you want to start a new plant from a sucker, it is best to remove the sucker in early spring while the tree is still dormant. A portion of rootstem should be attached to the sucker to achieve the greatest success. The "new" plant should then be treated as any other newly set tree.

The best time for pruning is early in the spring while the tree is still dormant. Winter pruning is ill-advised because it will injure trees even as hardy as the Juneberry. The fruiting wood is very brittle in the winter. Summer pruning can be done, but is best avoided because it has a tendency to setback the tree's growth.

PESTS

Birds are the major pests of Juneberries. To protect the ripening fruit, cover the trees with netting or cheesecloth. Be sure to wrap it tight around the tree so there are no open spaces under the canopy (treetop) where the birds can get in. Tie the netting securely to the branches so that it does not blow off in the gusts of wind.

Use soft string when tying the netting. Never tie with wire that can scrape or girdle the tree. Remove the netting after harvest season is over and put it in safe storage for next season's use.

Never plant Juneberries near junipers. Junipers sometimes harbor disease that attack Juneberry trees.

Chapter 22

Cranberries

Although usually thought of strictly as a commercial crop, the cranberry (*Vaccinium macrocarpon*) can be enjoyed in the home garden as well. See Fig. 22-1. This fruit requires preparation of its own special bed. It is labor intensive in its cultural requirements. If you do not have a good deal of time to spend taking care of things, you will not want to plant cranberries. On the other hand, growing your own cranberries can be a rewarding experience and you might set a trend within your garden circle. Cranberries are an unusual fruit and hardy enough to grow in Alaska when given adequate winter protection.

The cranberry, was first introduced to the New England Pilgrims by the native Americans. Cranberries are native to the acidic soil and peat bogs of the northern United States and Canada. These wetlands were called *cranberry meadows* in the early days. Originally, cranberries were an American Indian crop. They traded cranberries to white settlers, especially merchants, for merchandise.

Commercial production of cranberries did not begin until the nineteenth century. In 1820, the cranberry industry started in Cape Cod, Massachusetts. Before that time, cranberries were purchased from Indian tribes who harvested them from the wind. Cranberries grew as far south as Missouri and were quite abundant in the marshlands of Wisconsin.

The earliest mention of Wisconsin cranberries is in an account,

Fig. 22-1. Although usually thought of as strictly a commercial crop, cranberries can be enjoyed in the home garden as well.

Fort on the Mississippi, written by Pierre LeSueur in 1700. LeSueur, a French explorer, established a trading post on Madeline Island in 1693. Located in the Chequamegon Bay region of Lake Superior, Madeline Island was home for a band of Chippewa Indians. Today, Wisconsin leads the world in the production of cranberries.

Before commercial production began in Wisconsin, in the early 1850s, it was common for thousands of people to turn out on the public lands for the cranberry harvest. There are numerous accounts in the Milwaukee *Sentinel* of such happenings. It was a colorful sort of time, when whole families got together for the fall harvest. These gatherings often took on a festive mood.

The cranberry is relatively new among cultivated fruits. There are several reasons why it got off to such a late start. Cranberries are native to boglands and marshy areas which Europeans generally avoided for fear of contracting the dreaded diseases of that era. Also, the fruit is extremely tart. Europeans were used to sweet fruits, such as apples or cherries, and did not find the cranberry as appealing as other native fruits.

It was the Indians who taught Europeans how to use the cranberry. It was eaten at special occasions and remains today a standard fare for Thanksgiving and Christmas.

The cranberry has many uses and most Americans are familiar with cranberry sauce. The largest use for cranberries is now juice. Cranberry juice accounts for almost half of all production. This drink is usually sweetened with sugar to make it more appealing to the tastebuds. This use of cranberries was introduced to the commercial market in the early 1950s and has been a major boon to the cranberry industry.

CLIMATE

Climate is not as limiting as culture in the growing of cranberries. The southern limits seem to be around Missouri. In the North, they can be grown anywhere, given winter protection and adequate care. One reason the cranberry can survive in rugged climates is because it grows so low to the ground. It never becomes a bush, but rather sprawls along the ground. Usually winter snows form a protective "mulch" over the plants.

If you live in a dry region, you will not want to attempt to grow cranberry plants. Cranberries require a great deal of water for growing and for protecting them from frosts and insect pests. Do not try to grow cranberries unless you have access to plenty of water.

SITE

Cranberries grow best in an acidic bog. Unless you live in a swamp, you will probably have to prepare a special bed for them. The bed should be flat. It should not be on a slope. Hilltops are not recommended because the soil will drain too well.

Usually when cranberries are grown commercially, they are planted in areas where they receive maximum sunlight. For the home grower, they probably will do OK in your backyard under semishady conditions. Heavy shade is not recommended.

The size of the bed you put in will be dependent upon your needs and specifications. Cranberries spread by underground runners. You might want to confine your bed with rock walls that go at least 1 foot under the soil surface. This will keep the cranberries from spreading and make it easier to take care of them.

Select a site where children won't be playing or people won't be walking in your cranberry bed. Cranberries can be attractive as a bed attached to the house or in a location where they are not going to be trampled.

The cranberry plant likes an acidic peat bog. You can create this type of environment for them by adding plenty of peat moss to the planting mix when setting them out. The requirements of cranberries for an acidic soil is similar to that of blueberries (except that cranberries like it more moist).

Most garden soil is poor cranberry soil. Plan on digging out the original soil from where you put your cranberry bed. Dig at least 1 foot deep. Replace the soil with a mixture of 3 parts divided equally; one-third peat moss, one-third composted manure, and one-third sand. Use only composted manure because fresh manure will injure plants. Depending upon the size of the bed, toss in a cup or two of aluminum sulfate to help acidify the soil. Mix it in thoroughly. Read the directions on the package for exact usage.

The soils of most gardens will need to be replaced entirely by new soil. Use a mix you prepare yourself or purchase a commercial premixed planting "medium" (soil) for acid-loving plants.

PLANTING

Cranberries are propagated by cuttings. The nursery will send you cuttings to plant. Set the cuttings in the bed in rows. Have 4-foot rows with 6 inches between the cuttings within each row. The rows should be about 1 foot apart, depending upon the size of your bed. If you are growing a large bed, and expect to get into it, you will need open space to walk. For most, home growers however, this will not be the case.

Lay the cuttings in their planting site and cover them lightly with the planting mix. Do not stick them in so they are standing up. Lay them in along their side. Do not put more than 1 inch of dirt on them. It will be OK if part of the cutting is left exposed.

Water your plants well and keep the bed watered throughout the entire growing season. The soil should not be allowed to dry out.

It should be kept moist, but not drenched, at all times. Although they can be grown on dry land, the moisture needs of cranberries must be met.

Cuttings send out trailing stems along the ground. From these stems come the shoots that bear fruit. It takes a couple of years for cranberries to become established. They should be fruiting by the fourth year.

CULTURE

Cranberries are very shallow rooted and they need an ample supply of moisture. Drought can be a major concern because moisture stress can seriously set back your plants.

Cranberries require a long growth season. Blossoming in May, the fruit will not be ready to harvest until October. Because fall frosts can be a problem for the ripening fruits, there must be some consideration for protecting the plants. Cranberries can be safeguarded against both spring and fall frosts by irrigation. Two types are used:

☐ Flooding the bed.
☐ Sprinkler irrigation.

For the home gardener, sprinkler irrigation is the easiest to use.

The sprinklers must be kept on to provide a constant mist of water over the bed throughout the period of frost. The sprinklers should not be stopped until the temperatures have sufficiently warmed so that the plants will be in no danger.

Flooding of the beds is another way to protect cranberries from frosts. The beds can stand in water for some time, but they should not be constantly under water or problems will occur. Drain the beds when the danger of frost is past.

Weeds will be the biggest pest in your cranberry bed. Because cranberries are shallow-rooted, cultivation, if any, should be made very shallowly. It is best to just yank out weeds by hand. You will have to take pains so that you do not yank out the cranberry plants along with your weeds. Use both hands when weeding. Cover one hand over the cranberry plants to push them back while the other hand yanks out the weeds.

Cranberries can be mulched with peat moss or sawdust to help control weeds and conserve moisture. Do not use leaves or other mulch materials that will compact and smother plants. If you use sawdust, you will want to add composted manure to the mulch so that as it decomposes it does not rob nitrogen from the cranberry plants. It will be necessary to control weeds or they will take over the bed.

Cranberry plants are evergreen, woody, and trailing in their growth habits. They have a shallow fibrous root system. That is very similar to blueberries. They have no root hairs.

Leaves tend to be arranged in a spiral fashion. In the auxiliary (leaf stem end) of each leaf, there are auxiliary buds that grow into upright branches. These are the fruiting branches. You can stimulate the growth of these upright branches by cutting off the tips of the shoots.

PESTS

Most of the insects and other pests that bother the cranberry are the same pests as those that bother the blueberry. See Chapter 23 for more information on pests.

The cranberry fruitworm will attack the cranberry. The larval form is a wormlike creature that bores into the developing fruits, feeding upon them. Damaged fruits are not of any use. Nobody wants cranberries with little worms inside.

Leafhoppers can also become a nuisance if the bed gets too dry. Occasional flooding of beds will control all insect pests. For this reason, the cranberry can be grown practically free of insects.

HARVEST

The berries turn red when they are ripe. The shade of red depends upon the cultivar. Some will be fire-engine red and others will be more of a deep, almost black, red. Cranberries are a firm fruit. To tell if the berries are good, try the bounce test. Good berries have a slight bounce to them. Do not go about trying to dribble your berries. They are not that bouncy and you do not want to bruise the fruit.

Cranberries are tart when ripe and they never get sweet. They are best for culinary use. If you put them in the juicer, you will want to add sugar and water to have a palatable drink.

Harvest cranberries during the Indian summer days of October. You do not have to pick each little berry off each vine by hand. That would be a tiresome and time-consuming task. To harvest, simply flood the bed so that the water is standing. Take an ordinary garden rake and gently rake the berries off the vines. Do not apply too much pressure or you will rake up the plants. Ripe berries will come loose without much resistance. The good berries will float.

Once you think you have raked most of them, all you will have to do is to scoop them up. Skim the berries off the top of the water-filled bed.

HIGHBUSH CRANBERRIES

The highbush cranberry (*Viburnum trilobum*) is not really a cranberry, but is called this because it bears red, tart fruits with a vague resemblance to the cranberry when made into jelly. These plants are sold by many nurseries mostly for ornamental purposes. The fruit is edible when used for jelly or similar purposes.

The fresh fruit are not at all alike. Highbush cranberries are soft and mushy while regular cranberries are firm when ripe.

It is easier to grow highbush cranberries than the real kind. No special bed is needed. You can plant this shrub in your lawn. It is not fussy about climate.

Planting

Always select a site where your shrub can receive full sunlight. Because the flowers are so pretty, you can place this plant in a prominent area of your yard. The highbush cranberry likes a fertile loam with ample moisture available. It is capable of self-pollination.

Dig a hole big enough to hold the roots of the plant without bending them. Set the roots in while you fill the hole with your best topsoil. Water it thoroughly and weekly thereafter. Control weeds and tall grass with a mulch.

Pruning

Highbush cranberries require fairly heavy pruning to maintain the size of the plant and stimulate fruiting wood. The plants will tend to become "leggy" if they are not pruned. Discourage this development by heavy pruning. This will encourage dense branches to develop.

The plant is easier to grow than real cranberries. It will need to be pruned each year for best growth and highest yield. If you are crazy about jelly, you might like this plant. Otherwise, its major purpose is as an ornamental.

Its main pest is mildew. This can be controlled by pruning to maintain good air circulation.

Chapter 23

Blueberries

Growing your own blueberries (Fig. 23-1) can be more work than you might imagine—depending upon where you live. In the North, blueberries are not entirely winter hardy and each year cane dieback will occur.

Blueberries require their own bed (growing area) and special care. Because of these factors, blueberries are not recommended for beginners.

Winter temperatures and the length of the growing season determine where blueberries will grow. Blueberries can tolerate temperatures down to minus 20 degrees Fahrenheit before serious injury is done to the fruiting buds. Sometimes buds will survive slightly lower temperature. You will not get a full crop of fruit if it drops much below minus 20 degrees Fahrenheit. A heavy snow cover will usually protect the wild varieties, but snow will not protect the common garden variety (because of its height). This is a major reason not to grow blueberries in areas with severe winters.

Another factor that is important to blueberry culture is the length of the growing season. Blueberries need at least 40 days after fruiting before the first killing frost to allow the plant to mature. The earliest-bearing varieties require about 100 frost-free days to survive and produce fruit. Some varieties will survive in an area with a shorter growing season, but they will not be very productive.

To protect the bushes from spring frosts, use overhead sprinklers. A constant fine mist of water will keep the bushes

Fig. 23-1. Blueberries (courtesy Stark Bro's Nurseries & Orchards Co.).

warmer than the surrounding area. An alternative method to protect plants from frosts is to use burlap to wrap them up with on nights when frosts are predicted. You will find, however, that sprinklers are an easier method. All you have to do is turn on the knob. Whatever system you use, it should remain in effect until the outside temperatures have sufficiently warmed.

TYPES

The garden blueberry is the highbush blueberry (*Vaccinium corybosum*). This is the blueberry most people will grow. If you live in the South, the rabbiteye blueberry (*Vaccinium ashei*) is the species that you should grow. There are a number of wild species, but the lowbush blueberry (*Vaccinium augustifolium*) is the most significant. This is the blueberry grown in Maine. These plants are not selections from the wild. They are actually wild blueberries being "supervised" for maximum yield.

SITE

Most garden soil is not good blueberry soil. Plan on replacing the soil in the area where you grow your blueberries. Blueberries require an acidic soil. This is the most crucial requirement of blueberries. Iron is more readily available in acidic soils than in alkaline soils. An adequate supply of iron is vital to blueberries. If the soil is deficient, your plants will develop a condition called *iron chlorosis*. This is indicated by yellowing leaves in the middle of the growing season. Do not jump the gun if you see yellow leaves because they can also indicate drought stress or the autumn season.

Before planting blueberries, you must have a pH test made of your soil to determine its acidity. Your local county agent will take such a test for a fee or you can test your own soil with any of a number of commercially available soil pH testing kits.

Dig out an area for your blueberry bed. A sunny location is preferred. Dig a trench about 1 foot deep. When planting blueberries, it is easiest to plan on entirely replacing your original soil. You can buy a prepared commercial soil mix for acid-loving plants or you can make your own mix.

Prepare your own mix by using 3 parts equally: 1 part sand, 1 part peat moss, and 1 part composted manure. Sprinkle in aluminum sulfate to help acidify it, and mix thoroughly. Read the directions on the label of your box of aluminum sulfate to determine how much you will need to add. A substitute for aluminum sulfate is *chelated iron*, but that is more expensive.

Avoid planting blueberries in low-lying areas where spring frosts settle. Choose a somewhat sheltered location that has plenty of sunlight.

PLANTING

Plant blueberries in late April or early May. Space the bushes about 3 feet apart. The planting hole must be big enough to fit the roots without crowding. If you use the trench method, you will want to hold one hand on the bush while filling in the area around your plant with the other hand. Once all of the bushes are firmly set into the ground so that they are capable of standing up by themselves, you will be able to come back with your shovel and fill in any gaps in between plantings. Be sure to tamp the soil down after planting to prevent any air pockets from forming. Water the area thoroughly, immediately after planting, and each week thereafter.

Because blueberries are shallow-rooted, they should be

mulched to help conserve moisture and check weed growth. Do not apply fresh manure to the planting site.

CULTURE

Blueberry soil should be kept damp to the touch. The shallow roots will not be able to go too deep for water. If the soil dries out, your plants will suffer. It will be necessary to monitor the acidity of your soil from time to time. Be sure that it does not change. *Never* lime blueberry soil. If your leaves are turning yellow or if some of your leaves are yellowing during the regular growing season, it could be indicative of iron deficiency. Correct the situation at once! Iron chlorosis can lead to the death of your blueberry plant. The fastest remedy is to apply chelated iron (which is commercially available). A soluble form such as a fertilizer (foliage spray kind) for acid-loving plants will be fast and effective. Later on you will be able to add aluminum sulfate or other acidifiers to the soil.

Sometimes leaves turn yellow because of drought stress. In that case, the problem they have is not iron chlorosis, but simply a lack of water. Of course your leaves will turn yellow in the fall. The leaves change color before they fall.

Fertilize your blueberries each spring with an application of manure; composted manure is preferable to fresh manure. If you use fresh manure, be certain that you do not get it too close to the plant. If you use a commercial fertilizer, a water-soluble foliar spray is best. Add iron chelate or acidifier to soils each spring to keep the acid levels in balance.

PRUNING

Blueberries will not produce very much (if any) fruit the first few years after planting, As they age and come into full bearing, it will be necessary to prune them to keep them from overbearing. If the plants produce too much fruit, the berries will be small and the next year's crop is likely to be sparse. To avoid setback, always prune in the spring while the plant is still dormant. The only exception to this rule is when you must prune to control disease or insects.

During the first two or three years, prune out only the dead or broken branches or branches that grew too high (over 3 feet) and are likely to be subject to winterkill. Each year after the third, remove some of the small, bushy branches and spindly shoots. Always leave the most productive shoots. These are easy to recognize. They are thick, hard, and over 3 inches long. Heavier pruning will result in larger berries, but it will be a smaller crop. Moderate pruning is advised.

After the fifth year, prune the weakest and oldest canes at the base of the plant. Some plants will produce very tall canes. Cut these back to the average height of the plant. Annual pruning will encourage more productive growth.

To prevent disease infection after pruning, remove clippings far away from the plant. Burn them or shred them up for your compost pile. Treat all cuts with a tree paint or wound dressing.

PEST CONTROL

Birds, especially young robins, will eat the ripe fruit. It will be necessary to protect your crop from birds. The best way is to place netting or cheesecloth over the bushes about the time the fruit is starting to ripen. Tie the netting to wooden stakes and secure it so that there will be no loose areas where the birds can enter. Be sure that you use a netting that will allow plenty of sunshine to enter. It takes from three to five weeks for blueberries to fully ripen, depending upon the variety. You will have to remove the netting once or twice a week for picking.

Weeds are easily controlled by mulch and hand weeding. Do not, however, go away and leave your blueberries for the summer or you will have a patch of weeds when you return. It will be easier to pull out weeds, a few at a time when you first spot them, than to wait for the place to be overrun with them.

Insects will not be a major concern with blueberries. Usually the ones that attack the blueberry plant are the same pests that attack your other fruits. They include rose chafer, picnic beetle, apple maggot, curculio, tent caterpillar, scales, the cranberry fruit-worm, and others. The control methods for these pests are the same as with other home fruits. If you are using a netting to keep out birds, it will also discourage some insects.

Ordinary meadow mice can kill the bushes by chewing off bark. Rabbits sometimes chew the twigs during winter months. Traps or poisoning can be effective against mice and fencing will discourage rabbits. See Chapter 2.

VARIETAL SELECTION

For the most part the varieties (cultivars) you select will belong to the highbush variety.

Highbush Blueberries. These are the common blueberry grown in home gardens. It is also the blueberry of commerce in Michigan, North Carolina, and New Jersey. They were produced by controlled hybridization of selected superior wild plants. Highbush varieties can grow up to 6 feet.

Half-High Blueberries. These were developed by crossing the highbush selections with lowbush types. The goal was to achieve a plant with the quality of the highbush, but lower in stature and with a shorter growing season. The plants grow only about 4 feet.

Rabbiteye Blueberries. Rabbiteye blueberries are primarily grown in the southern states and California. They require the same general culture as other blueberries, but they are more tolerant of heat and drought. The quality of the fruit is inferior to the highbush fruit.

There are many selections of blueberries available. Contact your favorite nursery for those that are best suited for your area. Always plant at least two cultivars of the same category (highbush, half-high, or rabbiteye) for cross-pollination and larger crops. The following are some general recommendations. Your local nursery will be able to offer you a wider selection:

☐ For the South and Southern California, Tiftblue and Woodard (Rabbiteye types).

☐ For the Northcentral states, Northland and Bluehave (half-high types).

☐ For the rest of the country, Bluecrop, Rubel, Earliblue, Berkely, Pemberton, ronococas (highbush types).

Chapter 24

Huckleberries

The garden huckleberry (*Solanum melanocerasum*) is sometimes used as a substitute for blueberries—but it is not even related. It is not a huckleberry either. The common name of huckleberry attributed to it is a misnomer. This fruit is one of the many products of Luther Burbank's work. Burbank was a famous horticulturist. It is called the *wonderberry* in some garden catalogs.

This fruit should not be confused with the real huckleberry. See the last section in this chapter. The garden huckleberry belongs to the same family as the tomato, potato, and eggplant. The cultural requirements for its growth are the same as for the tomato. It is an annual grown from seed (although it sometimes reseeds itself).

The garden huckleberry is a culinary fruit. It is often baked into pies some people claim rivals the taste of blueberry pies. In all fairness that is an exaggeration. Perhaps those people have dull taste buds or they are not familiar with the taste of blueberries. It is true that the berries are black when ripe and about the same size as blueberries. They are even slightly tart, but that is where the resemblance ends.

Blueberries can be eaten and enjoyed fresh off the bush. The garden huckleberry must be cooked first. What garden huckleberries really taste like are unripe tomatoes. Of course, there are some people who like to eat their tomatoes while still green. To confuse them with blueberries is stretching the imagination.

Under no circumstances and in no way does the garden

huckleberry compete with blueberries. They are inferior. Nevertheless, they are fairly easy to grow and pies and sauce can be made from them. Incidentally, for the best-tasting pie it will help to add a little lemon juice.

The garden huckleberry has some vitamin C, but it is not important nutritionally.

SITE

Garden huckleberries can be grown on many kinds of soil. They perform best on a fertile, but sandy loam. The soil should be well-drained, but not dry out too quickly. Supply plenty of organic matter. Avoid heavy clay or muck soils.

Do not grow garden huckleberries in the same spot year after year or in areas where other members of the solanaceae plant family are grown (peppers, tomatoes, and potatoes).

In the North, it is most practical to start plants indoors. Garden huckleberries can be directly seeded in the South and areas with a long growing season. An eight-week-old plant is the best size for transplanting into the garden.

The plants will be very sensitive to frosts. Do not set them out too early. Wait until all danger of frost is past and soil and air temperatures are favorable.

If a late spring frost threatens your plants after they have been set out, you can protect them with paper plant protectors, baskets, or small cardboard cartons. You can make cartons out of old milk containers—assuming you have a lot of them—or can obtain them from your neighbors.

PLANTING

You can sow seed directly into your vegetable garden in a row. To get a head start, however, it is advisable to grow plants indoors early in the spring. Take them outside on warm, sunny days to acclimate the plants, for planting outdoors, later in the season. If you do not precondition plants to life outdoors with the sun and wind, they will be too tender and die after being set out. Setting them out for short periods of time will condition the plants to life outdoors. They will adjust without too much setback.

Set the plants in an area that has not been planted previously with tomatoes, eggplants, peppers, or potatoes. All of these plants are related. If any disease or insect pest has built up in the soil, it will likely attack your garden huckleberries.

Plants are always grown in rows as more than one. This is the easiest and most productive way to grow them. It makes for an easy harvest.

When setting out plants, leave 6-inch spaces between them within the row. Water the plants well and on a regular basis. This is especially important during dry spells. Be sure to soak the ground thoroughly when watering; do not merely sprinkle the area. It is best to not turn the hose on the plant. Let the water run along the sides.

CULTURE

Water plants and weed them regularly. A mulch can be used to conserve soil moisture and check weed growth. Because plants are grown as an annual, a water-soluble foliar spray fertilizer is effective. An alternative is to sidedress (place along the rows, without touching the plants) the plants with manure in the spring. If you use fresh manure, cover it with dirt to keep the gnats from breeding in it. Composted manure can be added at anytime, but it might be too expensive to use very heavily.

DISEASES

There are a number of diseases that will attack your garden huckleberries. Most of these are the same as will attack similar plants such as tomatoes.

Blossom-end Rot. The first symptom is a water-soaked spot near the blossom end of the fruit. This spot will enlarge and turn brown, gradually covering most of the fruit. The tissue of the area will shrink and become leathery. Blossom-end rot is caused by a variety of factors, including a calcium deficiency. To avoid this problem, maintain a uniform supply of moisture by mulching plants and watering them regularly. If you suspect that you have a calcium deficiency, apply garden lime to your soil.

Anthracnose. This disease can cause small, sunken spots to appear on the ripening fruit. Good air circulation and a sunny location help to prevent this problem.

Fusarium and Verticillium Wilt. Both are soil-borne diseases that cause the plant to turn yellow and die. To avoid these wilt diseases, rotate crops and never plant in soil where tomatoes, potatoes, and other solanaceous crops have been growing.

INSECT PESTS

The same insects that bother your other vegetables will probably take a whack at your garden huckleberries.

Cutworms. Cutworms can damage or destroy young, newly set plants. Use cardboard collars around the base of each plant to stop cutworms.

Hornworms and Fruitworms. Hornworms and fruitworms can cause damage. An effective control is to handpick them and destroy them. Wear gloves because this chore will get messy.

TRUE HUCKLEBERRIES

The true huckleberry (*Gaylussacia baccata*) is grown in the wild. It is rarely grown in home gardens. You will probably have to select plants from the wild or go to a nursery that specializes in native plants to obtain specimens.

Huckleberries are sometimes mistaken for blueberries. They do resemble and taste something like blueberries. They even grow best under the same culture as blueberries. Nevertheless, the fruit of the huckleberry is quite distinguished. It has 10 large and hard seeds in each fruit. In blueberries, the seeds are soft and not noticable.

Plant breeders have not yet taken a serious interest in huckleberries because they are similar to blueberries and blueberries are a superior fruit. The 10 hard seeds in the huckleberry are perhaps its biggest drawback. These seeds are not appreciated by those eating the fruit fresh or in pies.

When growing huckleberries, prepare the bed as if the blueberry culture. Give them a sunny location with some shade. They like moist conditions. Use blueberry culture techniques for growing huckleberries. See Chapter 23.

You will have to protect the ripening fruits from birds. To do this, cover the bushes with netting or cheesecloth. Tie it securely so that it does not hang loosely. This will allow sunlight and air to filter through, but it will keep the birds out.

Chapter 25

Bush Cherries

Imagine going into your garden and picking cherries without expending a lot of effort in yard work! Bush cherries can give you precisely such an experience. Bush cherries, or perhaps more accurately, cherry-plums (Fig. 25-1) are a hardy fruit for those areas where plant hardiness is a must. Cherry-plum cultivars are the result of crossing the hardy native sand cherry with several oriental plum cultivars. These fruits are productive and they can be trained to grow as a bush or small tree. The fruits are usually red in color. They can be eaten fresh, used in pies or preserves, or for canning.

CLIMATE

Bush cherries are extremely hardy. They will grow in rugged areas where neither cherries nor most plums will grow. This is a fruit to grow if you live in such an area. Bush cherries will withstand the toughest of winters. The only real trouble will be the problem field mice and rodents cause by eating the bark of these fruit plants.

There are different varieties of bush cherries, and naturally, some grow best in different regions. For example, the beach plum is an excellent fruit for people who live along the coastal areas of the Northeast and Northwest. It is tolerant of the highly alkaline soils and salt spray that comes from ocean breezes that can ruin many plants.

People who live in the drier areas of the Great Plains will find

Fig. 25-1. Bush cherries are actually wild plums.

sand cherries an easy fruit to grow. They are rugged enough to survive severe winters and they are drought resistant.

SITE

Select a location that receives plenty of sunlight. Bush cherries will not be as productive in the shade. Some are capable of self-pollination, but others are not and they will need another variety nearby in order to bear fruit. Be sure to read what the pollination requirements are in your nursery catalog. If there's any doubt, buy two bush cherries and plant them near each other.

Bush cherry plants tend to grow in bush form. Nevertheless, they can be trained to grow as small trees. Determine the landscape advantages of how you want your plant to grow and provide adequate space.

Plant bush cherries in a well-drained soil. The best soils are sandy or gravelly loams. Do not plant bush cherries in areas with poor drainage.

It is a good idea to increase the fertility of the soil by adding peat moss and composted manure. This will help plants to get off to a good start. At planting, you may wish to use a time-release fertilizer tablet for each bush you set out. Bush cherries will bear on bleak soils, but as with other fruits they respond to good growing conditions and fertilization.

PLANTING

Spring planting is recommended for the northern half of the country. Bush cherries start growth soon after they are planted. It is a good practice to set out these plants as early in the spring as the soil can be worked.

Plant each bush in a separate hole. The hole must be large enough to accommodate all of the roots without bending. Set the bush in the hole and pack the soil firmly around the roots. Use only good topsoil. When the hole is filled, thoroughly water the area around it. Water plants on a weekly basis. Water them more often on sandy soils and less often on clay soils.

During dry spells, additional waterings will be necessary. Even though bush cherries are drought tolerant, they will perform much better given good growing conditions and ample supplies of water. Plants can live through droughts, but they are not likely to bear heavy crops (if any) under such circumstances.

If you will be setting out more than one bush, a space of 3 to 4 feet between each plant will give them plenty of room to grow. You can grow plants closer for hedgerows, but it will reduce fruit yield. If you are training plants for the tree form, the bushes should be set farther apart (such as 6 feet).

PRUNING

The pruning of bush cherries will depend upon what you are aiming for: hedge, tree, or bush. Some plants such as the sand cherry never get very large and trying to train them to the tree form is not practical. They are best grown as a hedge or bush. The bush form is most productive. Other types, especially the cherry-plum hybrids, will develop into lovely and ornamental trees if so trained.

Select the larger-grade nursery stock when growing plants in the tree form and choose the smaller grades for hedges. When planting for growing as a bush, any grade stock will do. The larger and more expensive plants will probably bear quicker.

VARIETAL SELECTION

The best varieties are the hybrids. Most of these are the result of crosses of the native sand cherry and various species of Japanese plums. Your nursery catalog will list the types that they offer. Choose plants that will be best suited for your region. Among the newer cultivars (varieties) are Compass, Red Diamond, and Oka. There are many more. Most hybrids will require cross-pollination from another cherry-plum growing nearby.

Sand Cherries. The sand cherry (*Prunus besseyi*) is a cherry like plum that grows wild throughout the midwestern United States. It is often used by commercial nurseries as a dwarfing rootstock for plums, cherries, and peaches. Plums grafted on to the sand cherry (rootstock) will produce a dwarf tree.

Sand cherries are easy to grow and they are quite rugged. Although native to the Great Plains, they can be cultivated in gardens as far north as Alaska. They are small in stature (rarely exceeding 3 feet in height). This probably helps them to survive northern winters because the snow serves as a natural "mulch."

Any sunny site will do for your sand cherries, provided it has good air circulation and the soil is well-drained. The blossoms are quite hardy and rarely injured by frosts.

Sand cherries are capable of self-pollination. You need only plant one bush if you have limited room. Nevertheless, it will be worthwhile to plant several because the fruit is of good quality, albeit inferior to that of regular cherries and plums.

Sand cherries prefer a sandy soil. They will hold up to drought far longer than most other fruits, but they will perform better when given adequate water. The plant might survive a drought, but it probably will not bear fruit under such circumstances.

Nanking Bush Cherry. The Nanking bush cherry (*Prunus tomentosa*) is one of the most popular bush cherries. It bears fairly large fruits of good quality. It serves a dual role as a fruit provider and as ornamentation. Nanking bush cherries are especially becoming in spring when their delicate white blossoms virtually cover the plant. The bush grows to about 6 feet and is best trained as a bush or hedge. These are extremely hardy plants and they are often used to fence in yards.

The bright red fruits are slightly tart. That will not keep people from eating them right off the bush.

Beach Plums. The beach plum (*Prunus maritima*) is an excellent plum for growing along the coast. It is quite tolerant of salt conditions and it should be considered by urban dwellers in northern cities who experience salt injury to their plants from run-offs near roads and sidewalks.

The fruit is tart and best for jam. It bears a large, dark-blue plum smaller than most plums, but larger than cherries. It is hardy and it will grow in a wide range of areas and locations. Drainage is not usually much of a problem for the beach plum because it is able to tolerate high soil-moisture conditions. Nevertheless, do not deliberately set these plants out in areas with poor drainage conditions.

The only pruning necessary for growing bush cherries is to shape the plant to the form you prefer or to remove diseased and dead wood.

Chapter 26

Unusual Fruits

There are fruits for every taste. The three fruits described in this chapter are not related but each has certain characteristics that put them in a class by themselves. Although they can be quite delightful, each can also be somewhat of a nuisance. The fruits are chokecherries, persimmons, and pawpaw.

Chokecherry fruit is very astringent when ripe. The bitter taste of the berries will make you immediately start to choke or gag. This plant can become a hiding place for insects that will attack your other fruit plants and ornamentals.

Ripe persimmons are somewhat puckery to the taste and filled with what seems like a limitless number of little seeds. These seeds tend to get caught in crevices between your teeth. The plant requires a great deal of labor to maintain it. Persimmons will send up shoots from its roots called suckers. These suckers have to be cut out every year.

Pawpaws taste like bananas—with seeds. The fruits are very messy to eat and they are likely to leave traces on your face as the pulp squirts out at you. Children usually like to eat the ripe fruit fresh from the tree. They also will use the fruit as bombs. The squishy pawpaw makes a nice splash on an unsuspecting target. The windfallen fruits will litter the yard and attract flies as they decay.

CHOKECHERRIES

The chokecherry (*Padus virginiana*) grows wild throughout

much of the country east of the Rocky Mountains. You can tell when you are in chokecherry country from the heady perfume even before you notice the tiny white blossoms hanging profusely in grapelike clusters. Most years, they are one of the earliest-blooming shrubs.

When the chokecherry is loaded with fruit it is quite pretty, but don't let looks deceive you. The berries are not something that you will want to grab and eat by the handful. People who are unacquainted with chokecherries often make that mistake. They regret it soon after. Once the berries are in their mouths they will start to gag you.

The fruit of the chokecherry resembles the wild black cherry (*Padus serotina*). You will be able to quickly tell the difference by the taste. Wild black cherries are edible when ripe; chokecherries you will not want to eat raw. Chokecherries have to be cooked and have lots of sugar added to them before you can enjoy them.

Chokecherries are small fruits with a large pit. They are near black when ripe. Chokecherries make an excellent jelly or jam. They have a beautiful deep red color when used in jelly. They can also be cooked into a sauce for topping ice cream or cake. Naturally, the pits should be strained.

Danger. Like other wild cherries, the leaves and pits of chokecherries are poisonous. They contain a substance that breaks down into hydrocyanic acid. If ingested, they can cause cyanide poisoning that can result in death. Do not try to make a "tea" out of the leaves of this plant; it will be poisonous.

Climate

Winter injury is not a problem for growing chokecherries. They are hardy enough to withstand the winters in most parts of the country. The chokecherry seems to thrive almost anywhere. It is quite drought tolerant and it will survive dry spells that would kill other fruit plants.

Chokecherries grow wild in many areas of the country east of the Rockies. They can be found growing in their natural habitat at the edge of woodlands. Sometimes they will grow alongside wild black cherries or pin cherries (*Padus pennsylvanica*).

Chokecherries will grow in areas that other more tender fruits cannot. This is a fruit for those who live in hostile climates.

Site

Give chokecherries plenty of room to grow and lots of sunshine for best results. Although chokecherries will grow in shady places, they do not fruit as well as when they are given the benefit of full sunlight.

Chokecherries will open their flowers early. This will usually be one of the first fruits to bloom in the spring. The beauty of the blossoms will be a pleasure you will long remember.

Chokecherry flowers seem to be quite hardy. Apparently spring frosts do not affect them or they cause only limited damage. Chokecherries will still bear fruit even after late spring freezes have killed the blossoms on your other fruits.

Chokecherries spread from root suckers. This will cause any planting to become a thicket if it is not controlled. Usually it is best to grow chokecherries as a shrub rather than in tree form. To train the chokecherry to tree form is not practical because of the heavy suckering habit and natural tendency to form a shrub. Chokecherries form a fairly large shrub that grows up to 12 feet high and almost as wide. When selecting a site for your chokecherry, be sure that it will have plenty of room to grow.

Although ornamental, the chokecherry is better used in a corner of your garden rather than any central location. This is because it is such a vigorous grower that it will take over the entire garden if not kept under control. It also grows quite tall and will produce shade for other plants.

Planting

Chokecherries will grow on most any type of soil, provided that it is well-drained. A sandy loam seems to work best. The plants seem to like to grow in oak-leaf areas. This suggests that they prefer a slightly acid soil.

Although you can transplant chokecherries from those growing in the wild, it is not recommended because they might have a disease. The plants obtained from nurseries might not be totally free of disease, but they usually have been isolated. There are no cultivars of chokecherry or chokecherry breeding programs presently underway. There simply is not enough interest in this fruit. All chokecherry plants that you buy from a nursery will be selections from the wild.

When planting, keep the roots moist. Soak them in a bucket of water for a few hours. Dig a hole wide enough and deep enough to hold the roots without crowding. Add leafmold (decayed leaves) to the planting hole and cover the leaves with soil before setting in the tree. Generous use of peat moss will help get the plant off to a good start. Once the hole is filled, tamp the soil down and water it thoroughly and weekly thereafter.

Culture

The chokecherry is pretty much of a carefree plant. Once it is planted, you only need to take care of it the first couple of years to allow it to become established. After that, only minimal care will be required for pruning dead branches and for insect control.

Chokecherries are not heavy feeders. They seem to bear fruit under starvation conditions. Use of manure in the spring will undoubtedly help growth. If you have limited fertilizer available, use it on your other plants and don't worry about your chokecherry unless it displays signs of deficiency such as yellowing leaves and stunted growth.

Once established, chokecherries do not even require watering. They seem to thrive even during droughts, but supplemental watering is recommended during such times. The quality of the fruit will suffer after prolonged dry periods. This will not be terribly important because the fruit has to be cooked anyway. The shriveled fruits will be just as flavorful as the other. If there is a water shortage, do not waste it on your chokecherries.

Newly set plants are a different story. They will require some care to get them off to a good start. They should be weeded regularly and watered once a week. They should be planted in good soil or a well-composted manure should be added to help growth.

Pruning

Chokecherries are rarely pruned as a training technique. That would take too much work and the fruit is not worth that much bother. Pruning should be confined to removing branches that are broken or diseased.

The biggest chore will be pruning out the shoots that sucker up around the roots. These can be removed any time of the year. The sooner you remove them the smaller they will be and the easier they will be to remove. Do not wait until the end of the summer or until the plant goes dormant to cut out the suckers. Prune them down to ground level at first sight. If you want chokecherries for other locations, in the spring you can dig up a few of the suckers. Be sure that you get some of the root with the plants for good growth. You will not be able to use all the suckers produced.

Disease

Chokecherries are subject to the same diseases as are wild cherry and plum trees. They can also harbor diseases that will attack your regular cherry or plum trees. Do not plant them too close to your other tree fruits.

Black Knot. Black knot is a fungus disease that is a major problem with chokecherries. This disease appears as black, knot-like swellings on branches. Control by pruning off these swellings and burning them.

Other Pests. The tent caterpillar is the major insect pest. This is more so because of the potential harm it can do to your other fruits than due to its effect on the chokecherry. Control tent caterpillars by removing their nests and burning them. Other insects will on occasion bother your trees, but for the most part insects do not like the fruit and the leaves are poisonous to them.

Harvest

Chokecherry harvest will be a delight. The fruits are best picked while wearing rubber gloves. Otherwise, your hands will get a purple stain from handling the little berries that will crush easily in your fingers. The whole family can participate in the harvest as the shrubs are very abundant bearers.

The best way to pick chokecherries is by a process known as *creaming.* Here you just run your fingers down the clusters and let the fruits drop off into your bucket. Use a container that is dry and cool. If you use a metal bucket, clean it out first. Hot buckets will quicken decay and molds. Chokecherries are readily perishable and they do not keep for any prolonged period of time. They can be refrigerated, but not for very long. They are not anything you want to eat fresh so it is best to prepare them for turning into jelly, juice, or wine.

PERSIMMONS

There are two species of persimmons cultivated in this country. They are the American persimmon (*Diospyros virginiana*) and the Japanese persimmon (*Diospyros kaki*). The American persimmon is the hardiest variety, but the Japanese persimmon has sweeter and better-quality fruit.

Persimmons are rarely grown in the United States except in the home garden. Most people apparently do not care for them. It is one of those fruits best suited to culinary use and many people probably do not know how to use them. Persimmon makes a flavorful, but seedy jam. It can also be cooked into a sauce and used to fill cookies—something akin to fig bars. If you want other ideas or recipes for their use, consult your public library or local bookstore. English and Japanese cookbooks are the ones to check.

The fruit is not generally desirable for fresh eating. Nevertheless, the Japanese varieties are superior to the American in this respect. The fruit is somewhat puckery and very seedy. All those little seeds tend to get caught in your teeth. Some of the Japanese varieties are less seedy and are sweet enough to be eaten fresh.

It is extremely difficult to obtain fresh persimmons from your local grocer in most parts of the country. If you want persimmons, you probably will have to grow your own.

Site

Persimmons should not be planted in areas with severe winters. The American persimmon is hardier than the Japanese plant and can be grown in marginal areas where the latter will not survive. If you can grow apricots in your area, you probably can grow persimmons.

Persimmons are a semihardy plant. They bloom late and normally escape spring frosts. When grown in marginal areas, such as northern Illinois, the tree should be set out in a sheltered location.

Persimmons like as much sunlight as possible. This is especially important for the ripening fruit. Sunlight encourages the production of fruit sugars. The more sunlight the better the flavor of the fruit.

Persimmons grow on a large tree up to 30 feet or more. Give them plenty of room when setting them out. This is not a tree for small yards. Some of the Japanese varieties will grow smaller and they are preferable to the American varieties for that reason as well as their superior fruit. The American persimmon is more hardy and, being native to the eastern half of the United States, it is easier to grow. Japanese persimmons are usually grown only in California or the South.

Planting

Plant persimmons in a permanent location. Once they are planted, do not try to move them. They develop a different type of rooting system than most fruits. The persimmon has what is called a *taproot*. This is a very long central root with root hairs on it instead of the usual fibrous branching roots. Taproots go down very deep and they are not easy to transplant. Only very small trees should be transplanted (and with care).

Dig a deep hole for your persimmon tree; use a long-handled shovel for best results. Be sure that the hole is deep enough so that the taproot can fit in without curling up. Hold the tree with one hand while filling in the hole with the other. Keep the tree held so that the root will not curl. Tamp the soil down gently and water the area thoroughly.

Culture

Persimmons are fairly vigorous growers despite their taproot system. An annual application of manure in the spring is recommended. Place the manure in a circle under the tree. Spread it heavily but evenly around the tree. Do not touch the tree with the manure. If you are using fresh manure, toss a few shovelfuls of dirt over it.

Use a mulch to keep weeds down and to maintain an even soil moisture level. If weeds get to be a problem, take a hoe and whack them out of the way. Water the tree at weekly intervals and provide extra water during prolonged dry spells.

Pruning

The trees develop suckers from around the roots. These will sap the tree's strength and cause bushy growth if left unattended. Prune all suckers out each year.

Persimmons are fairly upright in their growth and should be trained to the central leader system. Keep pruning cuts at a minimum during the early years so as not to delay fruit production. Prune mostly to remove suckers and injured branches. Cover all wounds (except for suckers) with a tree paint or wound dressing.

Harvest

Persimmons do not ripen until late in the fall. They are not injured by fall frosts as are most other fruits. Despite their apparent hardiness, persimmons are a soft fruit and they will easily bruise. They should be handled gently when picked and placed into the basket with care.

Persimmons will hang onto the tree over winter if they are left alone. Unlike most fruits, these fruits can stand the freezing and thawing and still be edible in the spring!

Some growers handle persimmons like pears. They pick them

while the fruit is still a bit green and firm, and ripen them slowly. There is no real advantage to such methods. It is easier to just pick the fruits when they ripen.

Persimmon trees are heavy bearers of fruit. They will provide you with more than enough fruits to satisfy the needs of your immediate family. Unless you are crazy about jam, there is likely to be a surplus of fruits for friends and relatives.

Pests

The persimmon does not have many pests. Usually the same bugs that bother apricots will annoy your persimmon plants. By keeping weeds and tall grasses mowed and windfalls picked up, you should not run into many problems. If a pest problem develops call your county agent for assistance.

PAWPAW

The pawpaw (*Asimina triloba*) is given several common names and sometimes even the same name will have a different spelling. For example, pawpaw is spelled paw paw, papaw, or papa. It is called the Great Plains banana, in some areas because of the bananalike flavor of its fruit. What can become confusing is if you are talking with someone from England. The British call papayas pawpaw and refer to pawpaw as custard apples. This is one fruit where it might help to know the botanical name.

Pawpaws are actually a member of a tropical plant family and only moderately hardy. When it ripens, the fruit changes from green to yellow to a coppery shade. At the last stage, it is fully ripe and ready to be picked. The flesh will be cream yellow. Because the pawpaw are grown as selections from the wild, the fruits will not be uniform in size, shape, or quality. There will be a great deal of variability as to the quality of fruits from different trees.

The fruit is quite soft. It resembles the consistency of custard. Some people like this fruit, but others do not.

Site

Because pawpaws are essentially a tropical species they are not recommended for the North. They can grow successfully in some northern states, such as Michigan, but only because the Great Lakes help to modify temperatures. At the same latitude in Minnesota or western Wisconsin, they will fail. Winter injury is a leading cause of death when pawpaws are grown in the North. The paw paw tends to favor the more humid climate of the eastern half of the country.

Pawpaws will grow to be large trees. It should be set out where it will have ample room to grow. This tree is probably better placed in a sunny corner of your yard than in a focal point. It will have unusual purple flowers in the spring. The attractiveness of the blossoms is a matter of opinion.

Do not plant pawpaw trees where they might shade your other fruits. Although they can grow in shade, full sunlight is preferred. There is no point in planting this tree in your best location because it is not worth any special favor.

Pawpaws prefer a fertile loam. The soil should be well drained, but with access to an ample supply of moisture. The pawpaw likes plenty of water.

Planting

The pawpaw grows to be a large tree (30 feet or more). It will not be practical to move it after it gets too big. Plant it in a permanent location. Dig a hole large enough so that the roots will not be crammed when the tree is set in. Soak roots two hours before planting.

Fill the planting hole with good topsoil after setting in the tree. Hold the tree with one hand so you can keep it straight. Tamp down the soil gently, but firmly to get rid of any possible air pockets. Water the area thoroughly.

Culture

The pawpaw plant does not need any special care. It is not a popular plant and you will not be able to be sure of the quality of the fruits. Do not waste too much time caring for this tree because it might turn out to be a considerable disappointment.

Naturally, all fruits do better when watered regularly and given fertilizer. An application of manure in the spring is probably all it will take. Control weeds by hand hoeing. A surface mulch will help to check weed growth and keep the soil moist.

Pruning

Prune the pawpaw plant to train it to the central leader system. See Chapter 4. Prune also to remove dead or diseased wood. Sometimes severely pruning helps to stimulate the fruiting on a mature tree. While trees are young, however, it is best to prune them as little as possible. The effect of overpruning might be to delay bearing age by several years.

Because this tree gets to be quite large, it will be necessary to cut off some of the branches to allow sunlight into the area. It is too much work to try to keep this tree small by pruning.

Harvest

The pawpaw is best picked when fully ripe. The outside of the ripe fruits will be a coppery-brown color and inside it will be a rich creamy yellow. The fruit will be soft and smell something like a banana.

The bearing habits of the trees differ. Most pawpaws do not seem to be heavy producers. Of course there are exceptions. Because there is not uniformity in fruit production from tree to tree, pawpaws are not recommended. If you like to try the exotic, however, this fruit fits that description.

Chapter 27

Jelly Fruits

If you are very busy and do not have the time or desire to put a great deal of effort into growing traditional fruits, you can still benefit from your landscape. Many plants bear edible fruits. Some are also ornamentals. The fact that a fruit is "edible," however, does not necessarily mean that it tastes good. But with some cookery your tart raw fruits can be turned into delightful snacks. There are a few easy-to-grow species that should be planted primarily for their ornamental value, but whose fruits can be used. These plants produce fruit that is best used to make jelly. Some of the fruits, such as crabapples, can also be made into pickles or apple jack (hard cider). All of the following fruits can be used to make jelly.

EUROPEAN MOUNTAIN ASH

The European Mountain Ash (*Sorbus aucuparia*) is grown primarily as an ornamental tree. The ripe fruit, which are clusters of orange to red berries, can be made into jelly. This is one of the few practical uses of the fruit. It is not something that you will want to snack on right off the tree. The berries are small, hard, and have a very astringent taste. They are quite popular with several species of birds.

Site

The mountain ash is adapted to a wide range of climates and it grows almost anywhere. It is popular as a deciduous (leaf-falling) ornamental because of its brilliant colored fruits and the attractive foliage and shape of the tree. These can be seen growing in public parks and especially in the eastern half of the country.

Plant mountain ash in full sunlight. There is no worry about frost injury with this tree because it is extremely hardy. Because the tree is so attractive, you will not want to hide it. Plant your tree where it can receive the admiring glances and comments that it deserves. The tree develops into a moderate-sized shade tree. It should be given plenty of room to grow.

Any good soil will do. Naturally, soils that are high in organic matter or have a good water-holding capacity will promote a faster growth of the tree assuming all other factors are equal.

Planting

Plant mountain ash early in the spring in northern areas. In the South, fall planting is acceptable. Sod culture is the most common method of growing these trees. Plant them right in the lawn.

Use a shovel to cut the grass sod with the blade. Go around in a circle and apply pressure with your foot. Lift out the clumps of grass carefully. You can use them to top the planting hole later on.

Dig out the hole. Be certain that you allow enough room in the hole to set the roots of your tree in without crowding them. Do not plant the tree until the hole is big enough to hold it.

Set the tree in the hole and fill it in with topsoil. A timed-release fertilizer pellet can be added if the label says it is safe to do so. Do not add any fertilizer to the planting hole. Water the tree thoroughly; then water it once a week. Soak the ground. Remember that the grass will use some of the water so supply enough to meet the needs of the grass and the tree.

Caring for Mountain Ash

These trees will be practically care free. Weeds will not be a problem when mountain ash is grown in grass sod. The grass around them should be kept mowed. A tree wrap is useful and especially for the early years of the tree's life. Use grass shears to cut grass underneath the tree. That will avoid accidental mechanical damage that could happen when lawnmowers get too close.

The fruit or berries are small and hard. Harvest them when they turn bright red or bright orange. They are dry-fleshed and puckery and do not make good eating in their raw state. Pick what you need for jelly. If there are any berries left on the tree, birds can feed on them overwinter.

ROSEHIPS

All roses are ornamentals, but the single-flowered varieties produce the best rosehips. In case you are not familiar with rosehips, they are the fruit of the rosebush. They are sometimes called *rose apples*. If you examine rosehips closely, you will notice that they do look something like an apple in miniature form, but the fruit is dry-fleshed. Rosehips are a rich source of vitamin C.

The fruiting rose (*Rosa rurifolia*) produces large, single, 5-petal rose-pink flowers in early summer. After it has finished flowering, the bush will start to form rosehips.

Climate is not a problem with this rosebush because it is hardier than the hybrid roses that are bred for their double flowers. On occasion, they will die during winter, but usually that does not happen. A winter mulch can protect plants in areas with severe winters.

Planting

Follow the directions that come from your nursery. Rose bushes do not require cross-pollination. If you prefer, they can be grown as a single-specimen planting.

The only tool you will need is a long-handled shovel with a pointed blade. Dig a hole large enough to hold the roots of your rosebush without squeezing them. If the hole is not large enough, enlargen it before you set out your rosebush. It might not seem important, but proper planting can mean the difference between success and failure for your plant.

Roses are heavy feeders. They should be planted in a rich fertile loam. In most cases, you can improve your soil by adding a mixture of peat moss and well-rotted manure. Do not use fresh manure in the planting hole. The peat moss will help retain moisture. An adequate supply of water is one of the secrets of growing roses.

When growing roses in poor soil, it is best to dig a deeper hole than necessary and fill it with alternate layers of leaves and dirt. This will greatly improve the soil. On soils that have poor drainage, you must dig a deeper hole and at the bottom toss a few shovelfuls of gravel. Be sure to spread the gravel around evenly so that it is level. This will greatly improve drainage.

The roots of your rosebush should not come into direct contact with leaves or other organic matter. Pack soil firmly around roots to prevent any air pockets from developing. Once the hole is filled with soil, tamp it down gently but firmly. Leave a slight depression around the base of the bush so that rainwater will have a place to flow. Soak the bush after planting and water it weekly.

Caring for Your Rosebushes

Roses are ornamental and they deserve special treatment. Place them in a sunny location where you can show them off to your neighbors and friends. If planted in the shade, roses will not fare as well.

Keep weeds down and cut tall grass around rose plants. Because they are such heavy feeders, it is best to cultivate an area around them where the grass does not grow rather than to allow the grass to grow right up to them. A mulch will help keep down weeds and conserve soil moisture.

Fertilize your roses every year in the spring with a heavy application of manure in a circle around the base of the bush. If available, wood ashes should also be incorporated (dug in) to the soil. Cover fresh manure with dirt so that it does not become a breeding ground for gnats.

Prune your roses to remove diseased and broken branches and to maintain size control over them. Depending upon how fastidious you are, this can mean heavy pruning or light pruning. The bushes can grow fairly high and become "leggy" so it is important to prune them to stimulate the production of side branches.

When selecting rose varieties with the rosehips in mind, consult your nursery company and be sure they offer what you want. The beautiful new hybrid roses will provide you with a wealth of blossoms, but no fruit.

RUSSIAN OLIVES

The showy silvery foliage of the Russian Olive (*Elaeagnus augustifolia*) is quite attractive. This is especially true when planted among evergreens. It forms a willowy-type tree with weeping branches.

The Russian Olive is an extremely hardy tree and very drought resistant. It grows well in poor soils and is often used to help prevent soil erosion. In the Great Plains, it is sometimes planted for windbreaks. Most of the time it is planted as an ornamental lawn tree.

The fruit are small and hard. They are not a desirable fruit to eat raw. They can be made into jelly or blended with bland fruits to add zest to jams or preserves. Here is a tree for rugged climates that will provide jelly for your toast.

Planting

Follow the directions that come from your nursery for planting your Russian Olive tree. Russian Olives can be grown in hedge and bush forms as well as the tree form. Be sure to order tree-size plants if you want them to grow in tree form. Never plant tree-size specimens with the idea of turning them into hedges. Use hedge-grade plants for making hedgerows.

Use a long-handled shovel with a pointed blade, do dig a hole big enough to contain the roots of the tree without cramming them in. If the hole is not large enough for the roots, make it larger before you proceed to plant. With sandy or poor soils, you will want to dig a fairly large hole so that you can add alternating layers of leaves and dirt to it. This will help improve the soil and make it better able to hold water. With clay soils, you will also want to dig a larger hole. At the bottom, you should add a few shovelfuls of gravel. Spread the gravel out evenly. Then add alternating layers of leaves and dirt before you set in your tree.

The roots of your tree must not come in contact with leaves or gravel because that might injure them. Pack good topsoil firmly around roots. Tamp down the soil gently, but firmly. When the hole is filled, there should be a slight depression around the base of the tree (not exceeding 2 inches). Soak the tree well and water it on a weekly basis. On sandy soils, if you are having a dry spell it might be necessary to water daily or semidaily the first week or two.

Caring for Your Russian Olive

Depending upon what form you choose to grow your Russian Olive, care will range from relatively easy to quite time-consuming. If you grow the plants as hedgerows or bushes, they will naturally require a great deal of pruning. If they are grown as trees, they will require practically no care at all. The only pruning required for trees will be occasionally to remove broken branches or for aesthetics.

CRAB APPLES

Crab apples in bloom will bring great beauty to your yard. Flowering crabs come in many sizes and colors. They range from deep red to white-flowered in dwarf shape, pyramid shape, or shade-tree sizes. There is a crab apple just right for your garden. There are some varieties that are double-flowered, but the single-flowered types are best for fruits.

Crab apples are as hardy as apples and sometimes they are a

little hardier. They grow well throughout the same regions where apples grow. For instructions on planting and culture, see Chapter 12. The only difference with crab apples is that they will be much easier to grow and you will not have to worry about pruning them except for broken branches.

Remember that the main reason to grow crabs will be for their sensational beauty. Do not hide these trees. The crab apple fruit is inferior to apples, but it still a fruit worthwhile to grow. This is especially true for those people who like apples, but do not have the time to care for them.

Check with your nursery company to see what crab apple varieties they offer. Some of the best to plant for fruit are Hyslop, Dolgo, Whitney, and Chestnut crab.

Chapter 28

Marvellous Melons

For many Americans the Fourth of July means fireworks, parades, picnics, and watermelons! It doesn't seem like summer without eating your fill of watermelon. Other melons, often called dessert melons—muskmelon, honeydew, cantaloupe, are all part of the treasures of summer. And when you grow them in your own garden, there is a special satisfaction at harvest time.

Melons are not the easiest of plants to grow. They require regular attention and some tender loving care to produce quality fruits. Melons also require warm weather, a long growing season, lots of water, and plenty of sunshine. Whether growing dessert melons or watermelons, it is best to provide irrigation.

FRUIT OR VEGETABLE?

The melon is a vegetable that is eaten as a fruit. Melons belong to the Curcurbitaceae botanical group that is also called the gourd family. This group includes cucumbers, squash, pumpkins, and gourds, as well as melons. Although there are many species of melons, those most commonly grown are the dessert melons (musk - melon, honeydew, and cantaloupes) and watermelon.

All melons are vegetables. It will be easier to grow them if they are located in the vegetable garden and not spread out among your fruit trees. Melons are an annual trailing vine grown from seed. In most areas of the United States, they must be started out from seed each spring.

DESSERT MELONS

Cantaloupes, muskmelons and honeydew melons are usually classified as dessert melons to distinguish them from watermelons. The watermelon (*Citrullus lanatus*) has slightly different cultural habits. It is dealt with separately later in this chapter.

Dessert melons can be classified according to their skin type: *netted* and *non-netted*. Muskmelons have netted skins. Honeydews and true cantaloupes have non-netted skins. Some people call all dessert melons "cantaloupes," but this is a popular misnomer. True cantaloupes (*Cucumis melo* var. *cantalupensis*) are rarely grown in the United States except in California or in areas where they are grown by such ethnic groups as Afghans, Armenians, and Iranians. Cantaloupe seed is rare to come by and not usually offered by many nursery houses in the United States. If you want to grow true cantaloupes, buy seed from someone who grows these melons.

The muskmelon (*Cucumis melo* var. *reticulatus*) is highly spiced and tends to have a stronger aroma than most cantaloupes. Also, muskmelons have a netted skin. Most nursery houses that sell vegetable seeds offer a wide selection of muskmelon seed from which you can choose the best for your area and preference. There are many new varieties and superior hybrids.

Honeydew and cassaba melons (*Cucumis melo* var. *inodorous*), also called winter melons, usually require a longer growing season than most muskmelons. They do not fare as well when grown in the North. There are some types of honeydew with a shorter growing period requirement that are available for Northern growers. If you have the patience and start plants early indoors, you should be able to grow any of the melon species.

Transplants

Melons require a long growing season and they are best started indoors in pots, especially in the North. Dessert melons are basically a subtropical plant from Iran. In most Northern areas, the summer season is not sufficiently long enough for the melons to reach maturity. This is especially true for honeydew types. Although there are some hybrids developed for earlier fruiting, it is advisable (or more common) to start plants indoors during March or April. Transplants can be set out in the garden—after all danger of frost is past—in late spring or early summer.

Use a hill system to grow melons. Melons need to cross-pollinate with another melon of the same type in order to set fruit. Usually four to five seeds are planted in each pot.

The melon seeds require a temperature of approximately 60 degrees Fahrenheit to germinate. If pots are on the window sill during the day, they should be removed to another area of the room as soon as the sun sets. Window sills have a tendency to turn quite chilly after the sun goes down. Melons are extremely sensitive to cold. Young plants can be stunted by the cold or even killed in extreme cases.

Be careful not to start the plants too early in the spring. Because melons are a trailing vine, their growth will become a nuisance if they are allowed to become too big before it is safe to plant them outdoors. Some people like to start their melon seed in a cold frame outdoors early in the spring and transplant them to the garden later when the soil has warmed. This is not recommended for the beginner because it involves greater work and higher risks of plant losses. Building a cold frame is not a simple task despite what some popular gardening magazines tell you. Unless the structure is properly built, problems will occur. It can let in cold drafts of air that can adversely affect plant growth or even kill tender young plants. If you forget to open the top during the middle of the day, temperatures can build up to extremely high levels, creating stress on the young plants. It is best for beginners to start plants indoors.

The ideal containers for starting melons are small peat pots that are available commercially as Jiffy Pots or a similar brand name. These pots can be transplanted—pot and all—into the garden when ready. When using these pots, you will need a tray under them to catch excess water.

Your melon pots must be filled with a growing medium. Soil from your garden is not recommended because it might contain diseases or insects. If you steam your soil, that can eliminate most pests. Commercially available potting soil that is free of disease or insect organisms is probably the easiest thing to use.

Some mixes have nutrients in them. The mixes can be purchased fairly inexpensively in large plastic bags. One bag will usually fill several pots. With this product, all you have to do is open the bag and fill the pots. Then you are ready to plant your seeds. Water seeds after planting. Do not soak the pots, but keep them moist to the touch and in a warm place. During the day, they can be set on the window sill, but before the sun sets they should be removed. Do not allow the pots to dry out completely.

When the young plants have germinated, their primary needs are for sunlight and water. Do *not* fertilize them. It is too easy to overfertilize and kill young plants. The young plants will be able to obtain whatever nutrients they need from the soil mix they are grown in (unless grown in sterile beach sand) that should suffice them until they are set out in their permanent location in the garden. The plants are ready to be transplanted only when all danger of frost is past. It does not matter how large or small the plants are. The outside temperatures must be warm enough for them to be safely transplanted or they will be injured or die.

Before plants are set out permanently, it is a good idea to gradually adjust them to outdoor life. Do this by setting out the pots on warm days (above 50 degrees Fahrenheit) and taking them in before the temperature drops in the early evening. This helps to expose the plants to the weather and other elements of outdoor life. It will make them tougher. Plants grown indoors experience shock when suddenly set outside without this prior "conditioning." They might even die.

Site

Melons like a warm, moist soil. They thrive in highly fertile, light sandy loam. Mix well-rotted manure and barnyard lime into the soil area where the transplants will be set out. Remember that melons are trailing vines that require a great deal of space. Prepare a bed for your melon patch. Have as much as 6 to 8 feet for each hill planted. Where limited space is a problem, so-called bush melons will produce a more compact growth. Generally the fruits are not as large as the regular melons and they might lack in other quality characteristics.

Sunshine—and plenty of it—is a must for your melon patch. If you plant your patch in a shady area, you might obtain growth, but never have any fruits. When grown in a sunny area, your melons will be their most productive.

Planting

Plant your melons on hills. Place one or two pots together to form a hill and space each hill at least 5 feet from each other in a row. You can plant double rows by planting two rows of hills with a 3- or 4-foot space between them.

Work a little well-rotted manure into the soil around each hill. Be sure the manure is well-rotted and *not* fresh or you will injure the young transplants.

If you live in an area where there is a fairly long growing season or if you prefer to directly sow your melon seeds (instead of using transplants), plant after all danger of frost is past. One packet of seed should be enough for at least a dozen hills. It is best to not try to fight nature. If you live in the North, plant only those varieties that are early ripening. They will provide you with the best chance for success.

Culture

The area around your melon hills should be kept free of weeds and grasses. A hoe will be an adequate tool for cultivating the area. Because of the trailing nature of the melon vines, it is not advisable to use a rototiller for controlling weeds or you could injure the vines. It is important to be very careful while cultivating. Hand weed areas closest to the base of the hills. That way you will not accidentally uproot plants.

Water and sunlight are the crucial factors for growing melons. Most garden soils are sufficiently fertile to meet the melons' needs. If a soil is lacking in nutrients, plants will show signs of abnormal development, yellowing leaves, or stunted growth. Such soils can be readily corrected by simply mixing in some well-rotted manure. Be sure it is well-rotted.

Melons need water. This point can not be overstressed. On light sandy soils, they can be watered every morning. Use a good dose of water for each hill (not a sprinkle). Water thoroughly around the base of each hill. On heavy soils, you might only have to water two or three times a week. A good melon soil is damp to the touch, but not drenched. Standing water can injure plants. It is crucial to water plants during periods of drought or extremely dry weather.

The best method of watering is to hose down the soil around the base of each hill. Use of a lawn sprinkler is not recommended. The constant sprinkling of water on the plants' leaves, without giving them a chance to dry off, will encourage the development of mildew and other leaf diseases. Although such diseases usually do not kill the plant, they can sap some of the vigor that otherwise would go into fruit production.

Harvest

Dessert melons should be allowed to ripen on the vine in order to achieve their highest quality. Some honeydew melons can be picked while still green and they will ripen off the vine as long as the melon was picked at a mature stage of development. Nevertheless, most muskmelons and cantaloupes will never ripen properly if they are picked prematurely. For top-quality melons, allow them to ripen on-the-vine.

Dessert melons are ripe when they slip off the vine easily. Ripe fruits have a distinctive aroma and take on a characteristic color. Honeydew and cassaba types turn white.

Varietal Selection

Most dessert melons can be grown in any part of the country, including the North, if they are started in pots indoors to extend the growing season. For best results, consult your garden catalog for those cultivars best suited to your area. Listed below are some general recommendations for some cultivars. Your nursery might offer a wider selection. Included is the name of the plant, approximate number of days to maturity, flesh color, and approximate weight of the ripe melons.

Cantaloupe

Persian Small: 110 days, deep orange flesh, 6 pounds.

Honeydew

Honeydew: 110 days, light green flesh, 6 pounds.
Earlidew: 85 days, green flesh, 6 pounds Best for Northern growers.
Honeyloupe: 88 days, light orange flesh, 3-5 pounds. Hybrid of muskmelon and honeydew.

Muskmelon

Saticoy: 90 days, orange flesh, 4-5 pounds.
Kangold: 88 days, salmon flesh, 4-5 pounds.
Mainerock: 75 days, orange-salmon flesh, 2-3 pounds.
Hales Jumbo: 88 days, salmon-orange flesh, 3 pounds.

WATERMELONS

Sunshine and plenty of water are the secrets of success in watermelon growing. Water is a more crucial factor than for any other fruit. If you do not have access to supplemental water sources or live in an area where rainfall is sparse, growing watermelons is not recommended. They must have adequate supplies of water to grow properly.

Transplants

The watermelon is an annual trailing vine grown from seed. It has a long growing season requirement and is best started out as transplants in the North. They can be seeded directly only after all danger of frost is past.

To grow watermelon, use the hill system the same as for dessert melons. Watermelons will take up a slightly larger space unless you are growing the compact, so-called bush types. These will produce smaller melons, but might be more convenient for people with small yards.

In the North, transplants are recommended. Plant four to five seeds in each pot. The seeds require a temperature of near 60 degrees Fahrenheit to germinate. See the instructions for transplants for dessert melons. Watermelons are basically a tropical plant from Africa. Wild specimens can still be found growing in the African interior. The use of transplants extends the growing season for Northern growers.

Site

Watermelons like a warm, moist soil. Unlike dessert melons, watermelons prefer a slightly acidic soil. Mix plenty of peat moss and well-rotted manure into the soil where your transplants will be set out. Do *not* lime your watermelon patch.

Because of their trailing growth habit, watermelons belong in your vegetable garden. That is the only place you will likely have enough space for them. They can be a nuisance anywhere else.

Direct seeding of watermelons is a common practice for those who do not like work with transplants. Plant seeds only after all danger of frost is past because watermelons are very sensitive to cold. Young plants can be killed or have their growth severely stunted by frost damage or sudden cold snaps. If plants are already in the garden and a frost warning is imminent, growers are advised to take precautions to protect their watermelon patch. Commercially available products can help prevent frost injury. An item called Hotcaps (little plastic cups) can be used on very small seedlings. If the vines have any growth on them, a mulch is preferable. Mulches are the least expensive way to protect young transplants. They must be heavy enough to keep the plants from getting cold. Remove them once all danger is past and temperatures have safely warmed to the upper 40s.

Organic mulches such as straw are best. Cover the entire plant with a heavy layer and do not remove it until the outside temperatures have reached at least 50 degrees Fahrenheit. If temperatures climb only into the 40s, there is still a risk that they will suddenly drop.

Planting

If you are directly sowing seed, do so *only* after all danger of frost is past. A typical packet of watermelon seed will plant only about a half-dozen hills. Plant at least 4 to 5 seeds per hill. Hills should be spaced in rows 3×6 feet.

Work plenty of organic matter into the soil when you are planting watermelon. Peat moss will help make the soil acidic (as watermelons prefer). Keep hills moist until seeds germinate. After germination, water hills once each morning (except on heavy soils). Gardens with clay or other heavy soils will need to be watered only two or three times a week.

Culture

Keep your watermelon patch free of weeds and grass. Such vegetation tends to choke out the young melon plants unless controlled. The most practical method is to weed with a garden hoe or by hand. Nearest the hills it is best to weed by hand because all cultivation must be shallow to avoid uprooting the melon plants.

Mulches are sometimes used for weed control and to conserve soil moisture. Because of the trailing-vine nature of watermelons, it might be difficult to keep a neat mulch. Some people merely use mulch to fill in all those areas in the patch where the watermelons are not growing. A layer of organic mulch around the base of each hill is most effective. It is in the hills that the plants are rooted and receive their moisture. These are also the key areas to be watered.

Watermelons, more than any other vegetable, need water. Watermelons consist of 92 percent water. Any drought stress will severely shrink the size of the melons and the quality of the fruits will suffer as well.

Caring for your watermelon plants is quite easy. It is mostly a matter of weeding, mulching, and watering on a regular basis. If the plants look deficient in nutrients, an addition of well-rotted manure should be piled around the base of each hill. The use of a liquid foliar fertilizer, such as Rapid-Gro, will go to work immediately in plants that are lacking, correcting any deficiency symptoms. Signs that something is wrong include stunted growth, yellowing leaves, or abnormal growth. If there is any question about what problem is affecting your plants, consult your county agent for assistance. For the most part, watermelons benefit from additional fertilizers.

Harvest

There are several types of watermelons. The large and red-fleshed types are the most popular. There are some yellow-fleshed varieties. These are colorful when made into melon balls or for variety and novelty at parties. Watermelons should be allowed to ripen on the vine for their best flavor. Ripe watermelons are not as aromatic as are ripe cantaloupe, honeydew, or muskmelon. Usually the melons, when ripe, will be full bodied in size and the area that touches the ground will be a deepening yellow. Use of the thumb or middle finger should make a hollow "thunk" sound when the melon is ripe. It is this sound that is the only real way to tell if the fruits are ripe—other than cutting them open.

Varietal Selection

For a full list of cultivars for your area, consult your favorite nursery catalog. Below are listed some popular selections and their characteristics. Included is the name of the plant, approximate number of days to maturity, flesh color, and approximate weight of ripe melons.

Compact "Bush-Types"

Kengarden: 80 days, pinkish-red flesh, 6-7 pounds.
Sugar bush: 80 days, red flesh, 6-8 pounds.

Small Melons

Sugar Baby: 80 days, light red flesh, 1-pound melons.
Yellow Doll: 65 days, yellow flesh, 6-8 pounds.
Northern Sweet: 75 days, dark red flesh, 8-10 pounds.
Seedless: 84 days, red flesh 10-15 pounds. Special Note: Seedless requires cross-pollination with regular varieties in order to set fruits.

Large Melons

Jubilee: 95 days, red flesh, 25-35 pounds.
Charleston Grey: 85 days, red flesh, 18-25 pounds.
Crimson Sweet: 90 days, red flesh, 25-40 pounds.
Black Diamond: 90 days, bright red flesh, 40-50 pounds.

Part 5
After Planting

Chapter 29

Preserving Produce

If you have followed instructions well, your garden should have produced so many fruits and berries that you will save some to put away. You will be able to store some fruits for fresh use. Others you might want to can, freeze, or dry. Some fruits can be made into jellies, jams, preserves, or fruit butters—such as apple butter. Crabapples can be pickled and watermelon rinds made into pickles. Some cooks like to add fruits to their relishes. The latest trend is to dry fruits into *fruit leathers*. Whichever way you preserve your produce, during chilly winter nights you will be able to enjoy the fruits of last summer along with the memories of your gardening experience.

CAUSES OF FOOD SPOILAGE

To understand food preservation, it is necessary to consider the reasons for food spoilage. The primary cause of food spoilage in the United States is microbiological. Living organisms such as yeasts, bacteria, and molds cause *microbial spoilage*.

Relatives to these organisms are the micro-biological food-borne diseases such as salmonella or staphylloccocci. The most dangerous of the foodborne diseases is botulism; it can result in death.

Another cause of food spoilage is vermin. Rodents or insects will eat food or contaminate it. These vermin ruin much of the human food supply each year.

There is a natural force in food spoilage called *senescence*. This is the aging process brought about chiefly by the continuing respiration of the fruits. This aging process causes a chemical breakdown of the fruits. They deteriorate and lose vitamins and quality.

Enzymes affect both the aging and chemical qualities of the fruits. All living things produce enzymes to ensure the metabolic reactions necessary for the organism to survive. These enzymes continue to operate even after the fruit is harvested. Preservation methods have been developed to control (slow down or destroy) the enzyme activity.

An important, but often overlooked, cause of food spoilage is poor handling. Bruising, crushing, cutting, and other physical damage encourages more rapid deterioration. It also makes it easier for insects to invade the fruit.

FRESH STORAGE

Most fruits can be stored in their fresh state for only a short period. Small fruits such as berries require refrigeration. Even under the best of conditions, berries will last only two weeks. Grapes will not last even that long before they break down physically. Other fruits, such as apples, can be kept for several months without any serious deterioration. Fruits that keep well in their fresh state for prolonged periods of time are apples, quinces, and persimmons.

Not all apples are created equal. Some varieties, such as Delicious, are more suitable for keeping over winter than are other varieties. Apples are divided into three general types: summer apples, fall apples, and winter apples. Winter apples are the best keepers. Fall apples keep the second longest, and summer apples do not keep well at all.

The best-keeping apples are also the hardest. Keeping them in storage can even improve their quality and make them easier to eat. Certain conditions are required to store fruits properly. Because respiration (hence aging) increases with temperature, fruits survive best when stored in a room that is between 36 to 40 degrees Fahrenheit. When storing fruit in a basement, be sure that it is not near a furnace or your fruit will rapidly deteriorate. Some old farmhouses have root cellars. These are ideal places to store fruits. They are warm enough to keep the fruit from freezing, but cool enough to maintain them at their top quality for fresh eating.

The humidity (amount of moisture in the air) is also an important factor to consider in the storage of your fruit. If the air is too moist, it will cause fruits to deteriorate rapidly or encourage the growth of molds. If the air is too dry, fruit will lose moisture and start to shrivel.

Various fruits have different keeping qualities. Persimmons and quinces are not as difficult to store as apples. These fruits can survive freezing temperatures with very little, if any, damage to their quality. Apples must not be allowed to freeze or they will rapidly break down and spoil.

Another consideration to storing fresh fruits is that of vermin. A certain amount of loss to insects and rodents can be expected. But a clean storage place will help prevent the fruits from becoming winter food for vermin. Do not allow your root cellar, basement, or fruit-storage room to become a rodent-infested pit. That is no place to store anything you want to eat. Before putting away any fruit for the winter, clean out the room you put it in. Remove empty cartons and any debris left from the previous winter. Clear and damp dust shelves before reloading them.

Sweep out the area. Rodent droppings on shelves or on the floor indicate the presence of mice. If you're using a regular room other than a root cellar, clean it and allow it to dry thoroughly before using it. Seal all outside mouse entrances before storing your fruit. Consider setting out traps or poisons. A note word of caution: mice have been known to carry poison meal around to other places, including infesting food. Wash all suspect fruits carefully before use and cut off any parts that look suspicious. You do not want to be ingesting little bits of rat poison with each bite of apple.

Bugs should not be a problem in a clean environment. Most bugs do not like the cold. Once a room is cleaned for the winter, only a few bugs will come back.

Fruit is alive. Your apples are living organisms and they must not be put into airtight containers in their fresh state. Expect some losses to pests, but use common sense to keep these losses to a minimal level.

Air Circulation. When storing fresh fruits, it is important to maintain good air circulation around the storage area. Do not set bushel baskets on top of each other. Use steel or wooden shelves to separate containers. You must use containers that have outlets for air because fruit "breathes." It will not keep without air circulation. If fruit is built up layer upon layer, it increases the respiration rate. If you use wooden or cardboard crate boxes to store fruit, do not pile them one on top of the other. Separate them one crate high per shelf.

This will keep your fruits in better quality and help them to last longer.

Fruits such as peaches, nectarines, apricots, and plums can be kept in a root cellar for a month to six weeks without depreciable loss of quality. Generally, the softer the fruit the shorter the lifespan for its use as a fresh-eating item.

CANNING

Canning is probably the most practical and economical method of preserving home fruits. For one thing, it is a way to save fruits that otherwise might be wasted. It is wisest to only can the amount to be used within one year. Fruit held longer will be safe to eat if it has a good seal and no signs of spoilage. Nevertheless, there is likely to be some nutrient loss. This is especially true if the canned goods are held at temperatures above 70 degrees Fahrenheit. Any canned fruit that you are not able to use can be given away or sold. A Christmas gift of home-canned peaches from your very own peach tree is one gift your friends will know came from the heart.

As a beginner, it is important that you know about the various microorganisms discussed previously and the factors that cause food spoilage. Bacteria are the most serious of the foes to deal with in canning because they are more difficult to kill by heat than are yeasts or molds.

A very important concept to acquaint yourself with is that of the acidity of foods. Acid in canned foods is expressed as *pH value*. Foods with a pH of 4.5 or lower are called *high-acid foods*. Those with a higher pH number are called *low-acid foods*. Because few bacteria can survive in an acid environment, high-acid fruits are easier to can than vegetables that are predominantly low in acid.

Botulism is a deadly poison that forms from the bacteria spores that bear the same name. These spores produce a deadly toxin in low-acid foods in the absence of oxygen. They will not grow in high-acid foods that can be safely processed in boiling water at 212 degrees Fahrenheit. Such temperatures will kill most yeasts and molds.

In canning, the fruit is preserved by applying heat to prepared fruit in containers so that those microorganisms that cause spoilage or food poisoning are destroyed and enzymes that cause undesirable changes are inactivated. It also depends upon sealing the fruit in airtight containers to keep out all possible contaminants.

Canning is not a difficult skill to master, but it must be done properly to be successful. Instructions must be followed to a T. Any shortcuts could lead to disaster or a health hazard.

Equipment

Buy glass jars that are specifically made for home canning. Experienced canners can sometimes substitute, but the beginner should never take chances. You won't be saving any money if you or your children have to have your stomachs pumped from eating contaminated fruits.

Glass canning jars come in many sizes. The pint and quart sizes are the most popular. The pint size is the most practical for small families or single people and the quart size works best for larger families. Once the seal has been broken by opening, the jar's contents should be kept under refrigeration.

Always check jars before using to be sure they are not cracked or nicked. Wash jars in hot, soapy water, and rinse well. Even if your jars are brand new, wash them in hot soapy water and rinse well. Do not dry jars with a towel; turn them upside down in a drying rack and let the jars air dry.

Jar enclosures—the lids and rings that fit the canning jars—usually have to be bought separately from the jars. Be sure to only buy those enclosures that fit the size of the jars you are using. Do not try to make do with others. These enclosures are designed to properly fit home canning jars correctly and they are made of materials that will provide a proper seal.

Wash lids and rings in HOT soapy water and rinse well. Do not towel dry these items; set them into the rack to air-dry.

There are two basic types of canners: *water-bath canners* and *steam-pressure canners*. These are available at most hardware stores or places where cookware is sold.

The Basics of Canning Fruit

Home canned fruits will be no better than the raw products you use to make them. Choose fruits of good quality with no bruises or soft spots. Use only fresh, firm, and ripe fruits. Once processed, the fruits will not get any riper. Avoid green or overripe fruits.

Sugar or sugar-water syrup is often used to process fruits. Fruits can be canned without sweetening in their own juice or in water. For cold-packed fruits, you will have to add water because the fruits' own juices are retained until the fruits are processed.

258

Preparing The Fruit

Wash all fruit thoroughly, but gently, to remove dirt and bacteria. Wash small quantities at a time so that you will be able to do a more thorough job. If you wash too many fruits at a time, it might be necessary to rinse them again later to clean off any dirt that resettled on them. Do not soak fruits or they will lose nutrients and flavor. Be sure to wash fresh fruits only in cold water. Do not use soap or hot water. Peel and cut or slice produce according to preference.

The preparation depends upon the fruit. Apples will be peeled and cored. Be sure to remove all the tiny bits of core because they are very annoying when caught in the throat. Usually apples are sliced.

Fruits such as peaches, apricots, and plums are almost invariably pitted before canning. To enhance the flavor, one pit can be left in each jar. Apricots need not be peeled. A common method of peeling peaches (or tomatoes) is to immerse the fruit briefly in a container of very hot water. This loosens the peel so that the thin outside layer comes off quite readily. Each fruit has specific times and procedures required to properly process that fruit. Check with your county extension home economist for instructions on how to can specific fruits.

Cold Packing

Cold packing is the recommended method of canning produce, using either a pressure cooker or a regular canner. Vegetables, other than pickles, *must* be canned by this method for safety. It is also much preferred for fruits (other than for jellies, jams, or preserves).

In addition to your canner, long-handled tongs (to pick lids and rings out of boiling water), a canning funnel (which resembles a bottomless metal cup), a large spoon, and a ladle will be handy items. Be sure you set out more than a sufficient supply of clean glass jars before you start. You will have to be sure they are sterile at the last minute.

Cold Packing Canner

A canner is a super-large kettle (often made of dark blue porcelain. It has its own cover and two gripping handles (similar to the handles cups have). It also has a wire rack that sets inside and contains spaces for several glass jars. After washing and rinsing the jars, as previously described, they can be sterilized for canning by setting them upside down on the rack and letting the boiling water steam them for several minutes. Handle them by the bottoms when you remove them. Use tongs to remove the lids and rings.

Fruit is ordinarily put raw in the jars. Use a canning funnel to cut down on waste and mess. Pack the fruit in fairly tightly because it cooks down (shrinks) during processing. Put enough syrup, juice, or water to cover the solid fruit in the jar. The fruit at the top of the container will darken if not covered with the liquid. Leave about 1½ inches of space between the lid and the contents of the jar because there will be some expansion of the food during processing.

Put the lid on the jar immediately after it has been filled. Screw the top on just slightly. Do not tighten the cover at this time. Wait until the jars have cooled and sealed. The lid should still have enough "give" to let some steam escape, but not be so loose that it pops off.

Set the jars carefully on the rack in an upright position. Do not completely fill your canner until the jars are on the rack. As you place the jars on the metal rack, the water level will rise. It should be at least 2 inches above the jar tops during the processing. Add more hot water, if needed, to obtain the preferred level. Place the canner on the medium to hot heat. Cover and leave it covered for the set time required to process the fruit.

Follow directions for specific fruits in timing the processing. See Table 29-1. To cold pack fruits, they must be processed in a boiling-water bath. Be careful to allow enough time for processing. Do not try to shorten the required time.

After processing, carefully set the jars out of the canner onto a rack (or table protected by a towel) to cool. Avoid unnecessary handling of the jars until the lids have sealed. When jar lids seal, they will have a slightly indented look. If you are in the same room, you will also hear a slight "popping" sound as each jar seals. To test the seal (after the jars have cooled and if you are in doubt), press down gently on the center of the lid. If it feels indented and does not spring back up, the jar is sealed. This method assumes you are using conventional metal lids.

When the jars are cool, firmly tighten the tops. The fruit is now canned and ready to be put in the pantry or on some other storage space. Remember that canned fruits keep longer if the temperatures stay under 70 degrees Fahrenheit and above freezing where they are stored. *Never* store canned fruits near a stove or furnace.

Table 29-1 Processing Fruit.

Fruit	Time Required	Container
Apricots, Nectarines, Peaches, and Plums	25 minutes 30 minutes	pints quarts
Apples, Pears	15 minutes 20 minutes	pints quarts
Berries	10 minutes 15 minutes	pints quarts

Check Jars for Seal

This point can not be overstressed. Be sure each jar is sealed before you put it away. If the jar has not sealed, it might be because you used insufficient water or, more frequently, because you did not allow the proper time for processing. Set aside any jars that did not seal. The contents will have to be reprocessed or eaten soon. Eat the fruit at the next meal or refrigerate it.

Re-can unsealed jars right away. Empty the contents and pack and process the fruit as if it were fresh. It is a lot of work to can fruits. If you do the job right the first time, it will save you much grief later on.

It is a good practice to label jars after they have cooled. The label should state what the jar contains and the date it was canned. This makes it easier to, for example, quickly distinguish peaches from apricots. It also lets you use the oldest fruit first.

Cold Packing Pressure Cooker

Using a pressure cooker reduces processing time. This method relies on steam under pressure. Follow the directions that come with your pressure cooker.

The pressure cooker uses the same general procedures as for the regular canner. With a canner, you must watch timing and be sure the water level is high enough. With pressure canning, it is necessary to watch the pressure gauge as well as to keep track of the time. Steam has a tremendous amount of force. If the pressure gets too high, you could have an explosion. Nevertheless, those who use steam cookers usually prefer not to use any other method. They are very efficient, save time, and (in regard to your health) are the safest method of canning.

Follow the instructions for cold-packing canning. Be sure to adjust the timing and watch the pressure.

Open Kettle

The open kettle method of canning is best reserved for jellies, jams, and preserves. Never use it for vegetables or low-acid food not being pickled or jellied.

Prepare the fruit as previously indicated. Using your largest kettle, season the fruit as preferred and cook. The fruit will have to reach a rolling boil and stay that way for a period of time. Stir frequently with a long-handled spoon. Do not leave the spoon in the kettle between stirs. It will become too hot to handle. Follow your recipe for exact timing. In general, larger quantities require more time than do smaller amounts. For example, a pint of apples can be processed in 15 minutes, but a quart takes 25 minutes.

While the fruit is boiling, sterilize your (already clean) jars, lids, and rings. Set a canning funnel on a sterilized jar. Pour the boiling hot fruit into it. Fill to about 1½ inches from the top. Remove the funnel. Wipe the top of jar with a clean, damp paper towel to remove any fruit. Place the lid and ring on the jar. Screw the ring tightly. Set each jar aside in a safe place until you are sure it has sealed. Refer to the section: Check Jars For Seal. Fill each jar the same way, but do not let the fruit cool. It must be at or near the boiling point to properly preserve your fruit and to seal.

FREEZING FRUIT

Of all of the methods of home preservation, freezing is the simplest and least time consuming. The color, fresh flavor, and nutritive value of most fruits are high in quality after freezing. They tend to appear and taste more "garden fresh" than with any other method of preservation. Freezing fruits successfully requires that they be carefully prepared, packaged, and properly frozen.

To freeze fruits, you must have a freezer. In some rural areas it is possible to rent a frozen foods locker, but this practice is diminishing. Storage temperatures must be 0 degrees Fahrenheit or below to help prevent unfavorable changes in the food's chemistry—including bacterial growth.

If you are using the freezer compartment of your refrigerator, you must adjust your temperature-control dial so the freezer will be at its lowest point. Freezers and most two-door, freezer-refrigerator combinations are best for long-term storage of frozen produce.

Most fruits require packing in sugar or syrup to prevent undesirable changes in the flavor of the frozen product. Sugar, plus the acidity of the fruit, helps to retard enzyme activity in fruit stored at 0 degrees Fahrenheit or below.

Packages

The material you select for packaging your frozen fruits must meet certain criteria. It must be moisture-vapor proof to keep the fruits from drying out and from absorbing odors from other foods in the freezer. The loss of moisture from frozen foods creates a condition called *freezer burn*. Although this is not dangerous, it causes a toughness in texture and flavor and nutrient loss. To avoid freezer-burn, use suitable containers. Rigid plastic containers with snap-on tops are most convenient. They hold their form and, as long as they are tightly closed, they will offer protection against freezer-burn. Plastic freezer bags, aluminum foils, waxed paper, and collapsible freezer cartons made from cardboard are also used for freezing. These products are usually less expensive than the rigid plastic freezer containers, but they are not always as reliable.

Rigid containers are best for those fruits packed in liquids and they can be stacked up in the freezer. They will take up less space in the freezer than bags. Freezer containers are available in a wide variety of sizes. Do not use those with more than a half-gallon capacity for freezing fruits or the fruits will freeze too slowly—causing poor quality. Usually, the pint- and quart-size containers are the best. Use the smaller packages when members of your family are away and larger packages when you have company.

Preparing Fruit

All fruits do not freeze equally well. Many fruits of the same species will have cultivars (cultivated varieties) that freeze better than others. If you plan on growing a lot of fruit for freezing, it is best to choose those cultivars that are best suited to freezing. It will make a difference. For example, some strawberries such as Sparkle will freeze well. Other cultivars such as Fairfax are best suited for fresh use or in jams. Fairfax berries should not be frozen because they will turn soggy with an undesirable texture and off flavor when they thaw. The same is true of other fruits. To find those cultivars that are best suited for freezing, check the descriptions in your favorite nursery catalogue. Many growers raise several varieties; some are for freezing and others are for canning or fresh use.

Fruit that is selected for freezing should be of high quality. Freezing only preserves the quality of the fruit at the time it is frozen. It never improves quality. Unripe fruits will not ripen after they are frozen. They may have a bitter flavor. Pick ripe fruit that is free of bruises or blemishes. Freeze them soon after they are harvested. Some fruits, such as apples, apricots, or pears, might need to ripen further after harvesting to reach their peak eating stage. Take care that they don't get too ripe. Overripe fruit that is frozen will have a mushy texture and inferior flavor.

Wash fruit to rinse off dirt, dust, and other airborne particles. Wash small quantities at a time so that each piece is thoroughly cleaned. Do not soak fruit in water for any prolonged period of time or it will lose flavor and food value.

Peel fruits that require peeling and remove pits and seeds where practical. Nobody expects seedless raspberries. Slice fruits that are large. Some fruits, such as berries, can be left whole, but remove hulls and stems. Work with small amounts of fruit at a time. This is especially important if it is a fruit that tends to darken quickly.

Pack fruit by syrup packs, sugar packs, or unsweetened packs. Most fruit has a better texture and flavor when packed sweetened. Gooseberries, currants, cranberries, and rhubarb do best in unsweetened packs.

Anti-Darkening Agent

Many fruits darken during freezing. This is especially true if the liquid content does not cover over the solid pieces. Darkening occurs as the result of exposure to air. Because a small amount of air is even in the liquid, some darkening can occur even in fruits fully submerged. The darkening problem is sometimes exaggerated. (My peaches didn't darken in the freezer). If darkening is a problem, there are steps you can take to deal with it. To retard darkening, vitamin C (ascorbic acid) should be added to the fruit during preparation. Crystalline forms of vitamin C are easier to dissolve in liquid than powder or tablet forms. It can be readily obtained in drug stores or places that sell freezing supplies.

Ascorbic acid mixtures containing sugar, and sometimes citric acid, are also available. Follow the manufacturers' directions for use of these products.

Filling Containers

With freezing, as with canning, there will be some expansion of the finished product. Do not fill containers to the brim. Pack foods tight into the containers. Because most foods expand during freezing, leave headspace between the packed food and the lid. Figure on ¾ to 1 inch headspace.

Containers that are any good for freezing must be capable of a tight seal. Rigid containers should have an air-tight fitting lid. Lids that bounce off will not protect your fruits.

Storing Frozen Fruit

After packing and sealing fruits, label containers with the name of the fruit, the type of pack used (such as sugar pack or unsweetened) and the date when packed. Freeze food as soon as possible after packing. Place containers into the freezer, a few at a time, as they become ready for storage.

Freeze fruits at 0 degrees Fahrenheit or below. Leave a space between each package so that containers freeze properly. Do not load the freezer with more fruit than can be properly frozen at one time. Figure on the fruit being frozen within 24 hours. After that time, you can place the fruit containers closer together and rearrange items in the freezer to a permanent location. No more than 2 to 3 pounds of fruit per cubic foot should be frozen at one time. This will enable food to be frozen quickly. If you freeze foods too slowly, there will be a loss in quality.

Keep your freezer free of frost to ensure optimum efficiency. Stack containers all in one location so that they don't get lost. Frozen fruits stored at 0 degrees Fahrenheit or below will keep up to a year without quality loss. Unsweetened fruits will lose quality faster than sweetened fruits. Fruits kept frozen longer than a year will also start to lose quality.

Note: Freezing fruits is an easy operation. Unlike vegetables, fruit does not need to be blanched before freezing.

DRYING FRUITS

The latest trend in preserving fruits at home is by drying them into fruit leathers. Although an ancient technique to food preservation, drying has regained popularity with the introduction of home drying equipment. Drying requires less storage space than other methods of preservation.

Fruit can be dried in sunlight, in an oven, or in a commercial dehydrator. For beginners, a dehydrator is the easiest way. Drying fruits removes most of their moisture content. Dehydrator units are available in many sizes and for various budgets. Solar drying ovens are also available commercially or you can build one yourself using plans that are generally available (for a small fee) from your county extension office.

Fruits can be dried into individual pieces or slices or pureed and dried into a thin sheet as a leather.

Fruit Selection

The fruits selected for drying should be ripe and high in quality. Drying will not improve the quality of the fruit. Fruits that are not fully ripe or are overripe should be avoided because they will not make a very good dried product. Green fruits will lack flavor and color. Overripe fruits will be too tough and fibrous.

Prepare the fruits as soon as they are harvested. Thoroughly rinse off each piece of fruit to remove any trace of dirt. Sort and discard any defective fruits with molds, bruises, or signs of decay. A bad piece of fruit can ruin the entire batch. With larger fruits, such as apples, it is best to cut them into smaller pieces that can dry more quickly and uniformly. A shrunken apple, complete with core, is not an attractive product.

Fruits contain enzymes that are primarily responsible for the color and flavor changes that occur during ripening. These enzymes also cause many light-colored fruits—such as apricots, apples, and pears—to darken during drying and storage. There are ways to deal with this aesthetic problem. Dipping fruits in a solution of vitamin C is very effective in preventing color changes. There are also commercial salts available. To obtain a *candied fruit*, blanch the fruit in syrup to retain the color.

Drying

It is best to make small batches at a time. Follow the instructions that come with your dehydrator. Drying time will vary according to the fruit being dried, size of the pieces, and method of drying being used. A commercial dehydrator is recommended for beginners. If you use a conventional oven, a temperature of 135 to 140 degrees Fahrenheit is recommended.

Remember that the purpose is to *dry* the food not cook it. If temperatures are too high, the fruit will not dry properly. This is not a rush-type procedure. Your dehydrator will let you know the precise timing required. If you use an oven you will need to rely on some common sense. Do not try to dry fruits in a microwave oven. Dried fruits should be leathery and pliable. Home-dried fruits will need to be drier than commercially dried fruits if they are to be stored for any length of time.

Storage

Fruits that are cut into pieces and dried should be allowed to "sweat" after drying for about a week to equalize the moisture among the pieces. This should be done before the fruit is put into long-term storage containers. To achieve this process, place fruit in a glass container (do not use aluminum or plastic) and put the container in a dry well-ventilated and protected area. Stir the fruits gently every day for about a week. After that, put dried fruits into their permanent storage containers.

You won't have insect contamination while drying fruits in a dehydrator. Nevertheless, sun-dried fruits can become contaminated and they should be treated before storage. Insects, or their eggs, can be killed by heating the fruit at 150 degrees Fahrenheit in the oven for 30 minutes (after drying). Remove any visible traces of insects before placing fruits into storage.

Dry fruit should be allowed to cool off before it is packaged. Package all dry fruits only in insect-resistant containers. Glass canning jars are ideal. Label jars as to the contents and date dried. Store containers in a cool, dark, dry place. It is a good practice to check containers from time to time to see that they have not reabsorbed moisture. If there is any sign of spoilage (mold or discoloration) throw it away. All dried fruits will lose some vitamins, flavor, color, and aroma during storage. Low storage temperatures will prolong storage life.

JELLIES, JAMS, AND PRESERVES

Some popular ways to preserve fruits are to make jellies, jams, and preserves. These are excellent ways to make use of those fruits that are of lower quality. Naturally, you will not want to use rotten fruits, but you do not have to use your prime fruits when making jelly. Set aside your blemish-free fruits for eating fresh.

Definitions

Jelly is made from fruit juice. It is clear and firm enough to hold its shape when removed from the jar. *Jam* is made from crushed fruit. Less firm than jelly, it spreads easier. *Conserves* are jams made from a mixture of fruits (and sometimes nuts) including citrus. *Preserves* are whole fruits or large pieces of fruit in syrup. *Mar-*

malades are usually made from pulpy fruits with the skin and pulp suspended in a clear, jellied liquid. *Butters* such as apple butter are made by cooking fruit pulp with sugar and spices to a thick consistency that spreads evenly.

Making Jelly and Jams

It is relatively easy to make jelly as long as you follow recipe instructions. *Pectin* is the jellifying substance. Some fruits, such as apples, contain enough natural pectin and acid that they will form a good gel without additional pectin. Many fruits will need pectin added to help them gel. Pectin is available commercially in most grocery stores. It usually comes in liquid or powdered forms. Choose the form you find most convenient. Most commercial pectins carry instructions for their use. Follow the instructions.

Jams, conserves, preserves, marmalades, and fruit butters are not as easy to make as jelly. All of these products should be processed in a boiling-water bath. This will help destroy fermenting yeasts and molds and give the product a good seal.

You will find recipes to make these products inside the package along with the pectin. You generally can obtain recipes from your county home economist at the extension office.

Chapter 30

Why Fruit Plants Fail

There are two things that will cause great discomfort to any fruit grower. The first is if your fruit plants fail to bear fruit; that's embarrassing. The second is if your fruit plants fail to live; that can break your heart. It might be easier to cope with plant death than to try to explain to everybody why your fruit plants never produce. And everybody will ask so there is no hiding. Neither case will do much for your gardening prowess.

Things usually do not go wrong without some reason. There will be circumstances beyond your control, but many times you will be able to influence the situation. Sometimes only a little awareness on your part for the needs of your plants can mean the difference between fruit and no fruit or plant life and plant death.

Success in growing fruit is like success in any endeavor; it does not happen by accident. You will have to set your goals and then you must plan to meet those goals. When growing fruit, the care you put in—selecting stock, planting, watering, pruning, and fertilizing—all will be returned in the dividends of production. That means top-quality fruit. And quality fruit is what you will want so keep this in mind while choosing varieties. Sure it has to grow in your area, but it should be something you want to eat.

The need to control pests is a must. If you grow "wormy" apples, everyone will remember your apples. Who wants to be remembered for their wormy apples? Do not let anyone blame it on natural gardening methods. You can grow worm-free apples. Most of the time, if you stay ahead of the situation, you will be prepared for the challenges when they come.

FAILURE TO BEAR FRUIT

Let's deal with a situation that is as frustrating as it is embarrassing: the failure of your bearing-age fruit plants to produce. Usually, the reasons are quite simple and you might even be surprised at how easy it will be to identify the cause of your troubles.

Frost Injury

Fruit buds are more sensitive to frost injury than are leaf buds. Fruit plants that bloom early in areas with habitually late spring frosts are not likely to be as productive as those plants that bloom late enough to escape those frosts.

If frost injury keeps your buds from bearing fruit, there are steps that you will be able to take to control the situation. Sprinkler irrigation is the easiest and most satisfactory means of protecting fruit buds from frost damage. When frosts are predicted, simply turn on your garden sprinkler. Set it to a fine mist spray. Keep your fruit plant under a constant mist until outside temperatures have warmed so there is no longer any threat of frost injury. The water mist will usually protect fruit buds from frosts.

Another method that is more cumbersome and involves more risk is to cover plants with cloth or burlap to protect them from frost. One problem here is that if you uncover plants too early the frost can get the buds anyway. If you do not remove the cover, inside temperatures can cause heat damage. It is safer and simpler for the beginner to use sprinklers to protect fruit plants from frost.

Temperate Fruits Need Some Chill

Insufficient chill is not a problem for Northern growers, but in the South it can be a major problem. All temperate-zone fruits require some exposure to cold in order to break dormancy. Trees that are grown in climates that do not meet their chill requirement will bear poorly or perhaps not even bear any fruits at all. The cold requirement varies for each species and within species.

New fruits are being developed by plant breeders with low-chill requirements. An example is the apple Ein Shemer, that was developed for growing in the Middle East. It is a golden delicious type of apple. In the United States, the Beverly Hills apple will grow in such nonapple-growing areas as Southern California. There are other cultivars available. Check your nursery to see what they offer.

Pollination

Most fruits require cross-pollination to produce fruit. This is something people often forget. Some plants are capable of self-pollination, but most fruits are not. They will need another variety of the same fruit growing nearby. If your fruit plant always bloom but never bear any fruit, your problem could be lack of pollination.

If this turns out to be the case, the solution is simple enough. Just plant another variety of the same kind of fruit for it to cross-pollinate. While you are waiting for your newly set fruit to reach bearing age, you might want to check around your community to see who else has a fruit of bearing age. Perhaps they will give you a small twig of blossoms. You can hand pollinate your fruit so that it will bear while you are waiting for the second plant to grow. Always ask people if you can have some blossoms and tell them why you need them. Do not just walk into somebody's yard and snip blossom-laden twigs off their tree.

Thin for Annual Bearing

Most of the fruit buds that open in the spring will have been formed the previous summer. Sometimes a heavy crop of fruit will prevent the formation of fruit buds for next year's crop. If this happens, fruit production can become an every-other-year occurrence. To prevent this situation, thin out fruits during years of bumper crops. This will help to maintain annual production of high-quality fruits.

Fruit Needs Sunlight

Most fruit plants require full sunlight to perform their best. There are exceptions. Fruits such as sour cherries, currants, and mulberries all can be grown in partial shade—some even prefer it. Shade will lower the productivity of some fruits and some might not produce any fruit at all.

When setting out plants, set the shade-tolerant plants in areas where there is some shade and the rest of your fruit plants in areas that receive full sunlight. Sometimes you can create more sunlight in your yard by opening up the branches of some of your shade trees.

Winter Bud Injury

Severe cold during the winter dormancy can injure and kill fruit buds. This is especially true of fruits that are not quite hardy enough for the region where they have been transplanted. To save yourself grief, it is wise to plant only fruits that are adapted to your area. Winter cold hardly ever damages cold-hardy plants. If you lose too many fruit buds to winter bud injury, your fruit plant is probably not sufficiently hardy for your region.

PLANT DEATH

There are few things more heartbreaking than to watch your fruit plants die. After all the work and attention you devote to them, it will seem like such a waste if they fail, you will be left with a frustrated and empty feeling. Sometimes there are specific causes for plant death, but usually a combination of factors—rather than one easily recognizable cause—is involved.

Alone, one factor probably will not kill the plant—at least outright. Usually what happens is that an injury occurs that creates a stress situation for the plant, sapping its resources. The injury might not be obvious, but the plant will react to it by putting its resources into repelling the invader and healing its wounds. Less effort will go into fruit production. If any fruits are produced, they will be of a lower quality.

When too many factors combine, the stresses can overpower the plants' ability to resist and repair damage. Sometimes plants seriously weakened can manage to hang on for a few years. Afterward they will never be able to bear up to par and they are likely to enjoy a much-shortened life span. Any condition causing irreparable damage to roots, crowns (area of the plant at the soil line) or cambrium (regenerating tissue right under the bark) will always result in plant death.

Improper Transplanting and Care

Improper transplanting and poor maintenance are among the major reasons for fruit plant failure. Most nursery companies will include a pamphlet of instructions with your order. It is a good idea to read these instructions before planting. Often people are impatient and do not want to be bothered with details. These details can mean the difference between success or failure.

If you do not have the time to set your plants out immediately, read the directions for proper storage of dormant fruit plants. This way you will be able to keep your plants in good condition until you have the time to plant them.

All fruit is not planted the same. There are even differences in techniques used by various nurseries. One important consideration to make is that the guarantee you receive from the nursery company is based on the assumption that you followed their instructions.

It is not difficult to transplant fruit trees, bushes, or vines, but it is crucial to do it right. Your fruit plants are very much alive when dormant and they should be handled with tender loving care. Commercial growers routinely set out transplants with very few losses. Take the extra effort and care to transplant your fruits—as instructed.

The proper maintenance of your fruit plants is necessary. Neglected plants will not be as healthy or perform as well as plants that are properly taken care of. During the first two seasons of growth, special attention will be vital to the plant's survival. Newly set plants are always the most likely to be hurt and the quickest to respond to a stress situation. If you neglect young fruit plants, it can impair their development and delay fruiting.

Winter Injury

Winter injury is a leading cause of fruit plant death. Low temperatures are not the only factor. Cold, wind, and sunlight all combine to create damage. Most often the injury is the result of the drying out or dehydration of plant tissue. The dormant plant loses essential (life-supporting) moisture to the air and wind, and is unable to replace this loss because of frozen ground.

Winter injury occurs most often in the lower trunk, the crown region, or in the roots near the soil surface. If damage is severe enough to destroy the cambrium tissue, death will usually follow (shortly after growth begins in the spring). The trunks of young trees should be protected with tree wrap. The roots should be covered with mulch.

The extent of winter damage usually is not noticable until spring when some branches bloom and others do not. A simple scratch test can tell if your plant is healthy. Scratch the bark with your thumbnail. If it is greenish-yellow underneath, it is healthy. If it is brown, (that portion of your plant might be dying or already dead. Even if you suspect your plant is dead, wait until growth begins in spring. There might still be live tissue underground or on lower portions of the plant. If your plant starts to come up from the root, prune off the dead portions.

Even limited cold injury to bark makes fruit trees more susceptible to insect damage (especially borers) and crown or root diseases. The best way to minimize losses to winter injury is to plant only hardy varieties in your area.

Poorly Drained Soils

Poor soil drainage is a common cause of fruit plant failure. Excessive moisture can occur in soils with a high clay content, an impervious subsoil (called hard pan), or in areas with a high water table. Always select well-drained sites for planting. If necessary correct improper drainage before you plant. Use of organic matter such as composts or peat moss will help loosen tight clay soils. If you live in an area with a high water table or have hard pan, contact your county agent for advise or referral to professional services that can supply you with drainage tiles or other means to correct your soil drainage problems.

Prolonged periods of very wet soil conditions can damage most fruits. Brown inner bark tissue will identify root and crown damage caused by poor drainage. Various soil-borne disease might invade the injured tissue.

Drought

Drought, by itself, seldom kills healthy, well-established plants. Newly-set plants, with their smaller root systems, or plants damaged by insects, diseases, or winter injury can be seriously hurt by lack of adequate moisture. A long period of drought can create moisture stress on fruit plants, stunting newly set plants, and severely weakening them. Weak plants are always more susceptible to insect and disease attacks. On occasion, a prolonged drought can kill even large trees.

There are some insects that can aggravate drought conditions. High populations of spider mites will sap large amounts of moisture from your plants, making matters worse, and their chewing of plant tissues will create wounds from which valuable moisture will escape.

The only cure for drought is to be certain to supply ample amounts of water to your fruit plants during these dry spells. Control spider mites by introducing ladybugs to your fruit plants.

Excess Fertilizer

Nutritional deficiencies are not usually a problem, but they can occur. Most often people overfertilize their young fruit plants. The excessive application of fertilizer, especially the chemical kind that is immediately available to the plant for uptake, can overpower the plant's system—causing injury or even death.

Most fruit plants will not need fertilizer prior to reaching bearing age. If you fertilize young plants, do so sparingly. Composted manure will work nicely. If you use a commercial fertilizer, read the directions on the label. Do not add more than they say you need.

Herbicides

Herbicides are not recommended for use in the home garden. Excessive or improper use of herbicides frequently cause fruit-plant death. Contact herbicides can seriously injure tender foliage and bark, killing young trees. Systemic herbicides can be lethal to fruit plants and enter into the fruit itself. The long-term use of herbicides can cause a build-up in the soil that injures roots and results in plant death.

Insects

Insects are seldom the direct cause of a fruit plant's death, but some insects can be harmful (especially in large numbers). Insect damage, as with disease, weakens and injures plants, and can lead to their eventual decline and death.

Trunk and crown borers and root-feeding insects, like grubs, can kill plants in a very short time. Insects that defoliate part or all of a plant's leaves will greatly reduce the health of that plant and its ability to resist disease and other environmental stresses.

Disease

Diseases are not as common as insect pests. When they do occur, usually an insect is involved in transmitting it. Insect control is a good way to control disease. There are three basic types of plant diseases: viral, bacterial, and fungal. If your plant has a disease, contact your county agent for assistance.

Chapter 31

Natural Methods for Control of Insects and Diseases

Pest control, particularly of insects, is of natural concern to fruit growers. Yet there has been too much publicity about the menace of insects and all bugs have been given a bad name. This overemphasis on insect pests has produced many unfounded fears and even discourages some people from even trying to grow their own fruits. That is a real tragedy.

There are nearly 1 million insect species and most are relatively harmless. Some insects are actually beneficial and helpful in the garden. In most cases, only a few common insects will do all the damage. The symptoms of the damage they do can identify them to the experienced eye. There is a tremendous amount of information available on the common pests of fruits and much is known about their life cycles and habits. The home fruit grower can prevent many problems by following good sanitation and cultural habits and using resistant cultivars when possible.

Many insects will look alike to the inexperienced eye. If you incorrectly identify an insect, you might use the wrong treatment and make matters worse. If you are having serious insect pest problems, do not try to play doctor. Consult your county agricultural extension agent for expert assistance.

Once a pest is identified, the proper treatment can be made for its control or eradication. The use of natural insect predators or biological controls, such as insect-disease-spores, are alternatives that can be relied upon in the place of chemical sprays.

The best gardening methods are those that work in harmony with nature. A healthy fruit garden is a clean one that is free of noxious pests and dangerous chemicals. The use and misuse of pesticides is of concern to conscientious home growers. There is much misinformation available; most of it is in the form of ads put out by vested interests. They often will resort to scare tactics or name calling and insist that only by using the products they make can one successfully grow fruit. Of course that is not true, but many people are gullible enough to be taken in. That main objection that naturalists have to pesticides is the side effects they can produce.

The use of chemical pesticides has polluted the environment, created new races of "super-insects" resistant to the most deadly poisons, and subjected fruit plants to a lethal world where the cure is worse than the problem. Even more devastating is that many pesticides do not go away. Many of the most effective pesticides remain toxic for relatively long periods of time. Some have a tendency to accumulate in the soil after repeated exposures. For example, lead arsenate compounds were for many years sprayed on fruit trees to protect them from codling moth and other common fruit pests. Unfortunately, these compounds don't degrade very well. The result is a buildup of excessive levels of lead and arsenic in the soil. Many old orchard lands are now no longer fit for growing fruit trees. That might seem like an extreme example, but it is only one example of how short-sighted gains can have detrimental effects in the long term.

There can also be health risks involved in the use of some of these chemical products. Only recently have we begun to investigate the large number of carcinogens (cancer-causing agents) released into the environment. Another problem with the use of most pesticides is that they are nonselective. They will kill all insects and not just the troublemakers. This is detrimental for two main reasons. Many fruit plants are insect pollinated. Insects could be eliminated that normally might help to control the situation by preying upon the pests. These beneficial insects then have a harder time re-establishing themselves. This frequently results in an increase in the number of pests.

All fruit trees need to be pollinated. Although frisky breezes might gain you an apple or two, severe reductions in bee populations pose a serious problem for fruit and vegetable growers. The use of insects for pollination is so crucial that many commercial growers have their own honeybee hives.

If you must garden with chemicals, use them strictly according to the directions on the label. This includes disposing of the container in the proper way. Protect the health of your family, pets, neighbors and avoid possibly contaminating yourself or someone's water supply. Do not use chemical pesticides.

Insects are usually the leading pest problem you will encounter. Weeds and diseases can also become a problem if preventive steps are not taken. The best way to prevent problems is to plant resistant varieties, engage in cultural control, and—where warranted—practice biological control of target pests.

RESISTANT VARIETIES

It is a good idea to talk to your neighbors, before planting, to find out what kind of pest problems they are having. Your county extension office, listed in your local phone book, can tell you the major pest problems to watch out for in your county. They can recommend disease- and insect-resistant varieties for planting. This free advice can save you much grief.

No variety is 100 percent disease- or insect-resistant, but the selection of resistant varieties will better your chances for success. *Resistance* refers to the fact that some plants can tolerate pests better than others and are, therefore, less likely to suffer as much damage or be injured by certain pests. Resistant plants are not totally immune to pests, but they are tolerant of them. This *tolerance factor* gives your fruit plants a better chance for survival under unfavorable or adverse conditions. It gives them an edge on staying alive and healthy. Resistance can be by either the fruit plant itself or, in the case of fruit trees, the rootstock to which that the fruit is grafted.

CULTURAL CONTROL

Cultural control is the easiest way to keep fruit plants healthy and pests down to a minimum. All fruit plants are not alike. Do not treat them the same. The culture of each fruit must be addressed individually. See individual chapters for determining each fruit's cultural requirements.

There are some basic practices that make good sense. For example, do not plant fruit in a hostile location. If your fruit plant has to struggle just to survive, it will never bear up to its potential—if it bears at all. Isolate fruits from the wild. Cultivated fruits should never be planted near their wild cousins. These wild fruit plants could contain diseases that will attack your tame fruits or they might harbor insect pests. Many virus diseases will not be noticable except in the reduced yield from your fruit plants.

Control weeds. Weeds can and do harbor noxious pests—including diseases, insects, and rodents. Weeds also compete with your fruit plants for water and nutrients. Tall weeds can shade out fruits. This is especially true for newly set plants. Weeds can be controlled by mulching plants and by hand cultivation. Weed control will not be a chore if it is performed on a routine basis. If neglected, weeds can take over and be a major nuisance.

Prune broken and diseased branches to control the spread of disease and the insect pests that are attracted to dying and decaying wood.

Keeping your garden free of decaying fruit, debris, and weeds is probably the most important step you can take to have a pest-free garden. A healthy fruit garden is a clean one. Think of your garden as an extension of your home. In a way it is. You don't let garbage pile up in your kitchen do you? If you did it would attract bugs. The same principle is true of your fruit garden. Garbage always attracts bugs.

Windfallen fruits should not be allowed to decay under trees or bushes. They must be picked up and removed regularly. Rotting fruits attract insect pests and can also harbor diseases that can later attack healthy plants.

Removing insect cocoons in early spring is another sanitary measure. Many insect pests will form cocoons in which they overwinter. If you remove these cocoons, before the insects hatch, and burn them you will substantially reduce the pest population. It's very simple to do. Wear rubber gloves if you're the least bit squeamish.

Cultivation means simply tilling the soil underneath and around fruit plants to kill many insect pests that overwinter in the soil. The soil can be tilled in late fall and again in spring. This is very effective for controlling some hard-to-control pests. Be careful about tilling around shallow-rooted plants.

Simple soap and water will provide control of many pests. Mites like to live on the dusty underside of leaves. Aphids, mealy bugs, and scale insects can all be controlled by soap and water. Do not use detergent to wash plants. Detergents strip away the natural plant waxes that help protect them. Treat your plants the same way you would treat your own skin; use a mild soap. A bar of Ivory and a bucket of water will do the trick. Give your plants a bath, but do not scrub too hard or you might tear the leaves.

Another sanitary method is to remove dead plants. If a tree or fruit bush is hopelessly ill or has already died, remove it from your garden. Dead plants attract diseases and insect pests. Leaving diseased plants around is more than unsightly; it is also a good way to invite trouble. Once a plant is dead, dig it up—roots and all—and burn it. Do not, however, jump the gun. Be sure the plant is dead before you remove it. Sometimes fruit plants will only suffer from dieback. This is where only the top parts have died, but the rest of the plant is still alive. In cases when you have spotted signs of life, prune the plant to the living tissue and remove the prunings of the decaying materials and destroy them.

BIOLOGICAL CONTROL

There are natural insect predators, parasites, and diseases that can reduce pest populations to controllable levels. You won't usually have all the possible insect pests, but you might have more than one. Know your enemy. Before you can successfully control the problem pest, you should identify it. Make use of the services of your county agricultural extension service. Either invite your county agent out to examine the damage or trap a pest insect (place it in a small bottle filled with rubbing alcohol) and take it to your extension office. They will be able to identify the pest.

Most common fruit pests have been around a long time and they are quite well known. Your county agent will probably offer control recommendations. Often an agent will suggest a chemical control. Nevertheless, there are other approaches that will be open to you once you have identified the pest insect (or disease).

There are a number of insects that are predators upon insects pests. These are called *beneficial insects* because they help control pest populations. Some of these insects are commercially available. These include Trichogramma wasps, ladybugs, lacewings, and praying mantids.

Trichogramma wasps are tiny (almost mosquito-size) wasps. They do not sting and they will not hurt people. They kill pest insects by laying their eggs in them. A parasite of many pests, these creatures have a short life span and need to be released on a schedule basis to be most effective. Instructions for their use will come with your order. Your nursery catalog will usually list the insect pests that it is most effective against.

Ladybugs are really beetles. They have brightly colored coats, usually a bright orange or red, and are a handsome insect. The ladybug feeds on aphids, scale insects, and the eggs of other insect pests. Introduce them to your fruit plants and they will be very effective patrolling your garden for "enemies." If you are offended by the sight of insects, this is one of the least offensive-looking creatures.

Lacewings are among the most useful insect predators. In their larval stage, they are called aphid lions. They eat aphids, scales, mealy bugs, leafhoppers, moth eggs, and caterpillers. Unfortunately, they also eat some ladybugs. You might want to try one or the other. In their adult stage, lacewings have large eyes and light green lacelike wings. Not exactly cute, but they are better-looking than the pests they control.

Fig. 31-1. Black Knot Fungus. Prune these "knots" to control this disease of plums and cherries (courtesy USDA).

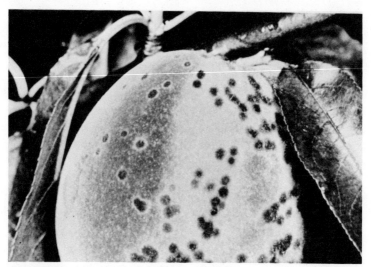

Fig. 31-2. Peach Scab on fruit (courtesy USDA).

Praying mantids are rather ugly creatures and grow to 5 inches or more long. They will eat larger insect pests such as grasshoppers.

No single insect-control method will ever give 100 percent kill. Nevertheless, by combining several methods you can greatly di-

Fig. 31-3. Root Rot on peach. This tree was planted in poorly drained soil (courtesy USDA).

Fig. 31-4. Leaf spot infection of strawberries (courtesy USDA).

minish the pest population and reduce the amount of your fruit loss to insects. The more strategies you employ the better your chances for success.

DISEASES

Diseases (Figs. 31-1 through 31-6) will not be your main

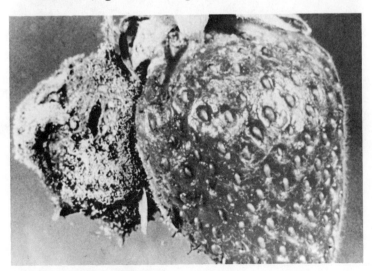

Fig. 31-5. Fruit rot of strawberries.

Fig. 31-6. Bacterial spot disease on peach leaf (courtesy USDA).

problem when you are growing fruit—insects will. Diseases are spread by insects so controlling insects will help to control disease problems. For combating specific diseases, see the appropriate chapters.

Chapter 32

Sources for the Beginner

Many places sell fruit plants. Where you buy your fruit plants will be an important decision. The higher the quality of the nursery stock, the better will be your chances for success. Always buy from a reputable nursery that is willing to stand behind their merchandise. You will want quality plants that will bear true to name. There are few things more frustrating than for a grower to think he is planting one kind of fruit and then end up with another. If you plant a McIntosh apple tree, you won't want a tree that bears Northern Spy apples. The government had to crack down on some nurseries a few years back. They were apparently hiring people who did not read English and so were not fulfilling orders with the right varieties. Although such occurrences are rare, they do happen.

A good nursery will offer a wide selection of fruits. Some will offer a choice with tree fruits (dwarfs or standards). A few nurseries will even recommend fruits for your area. Often there will be hardy varieties of your favorite fruits or new resistant types that many growers are excited about. Whether you are looking for a favorite variety, a new variety, or one of the old varieties that are rare—but oh so good. Someone is likely to have what you want.

Chances are that no matter where you live there is some kind of fruit that you can grow successfully. Remember when you are making selections to pick only fruits that will be hardy in your area.

MAIL-ORDER HOUSES

Mail-order nursery houses are usually excellent sources of quality fruit plants. They are often the best sources. All mail-order businesses are strictly regulated by the United States Postal Service. Any incidence of consumer fraud should immediately be reported to your postmaster. Chances are that if you've been ripped off you stand a good chance of getting your money back.

Mail orders are very convenient. You can shop in the comfort of your own home at your leisure. Shopping by mail allows you to keep an accurate account of how much money you are actually spending. With mail orders, there's no rush and no high-pressure sales clerk who will tell you anything to make a sale. Best of all there's no traffic to battle. And your fruit plants will arrive at the proper planting time—delivered to your doorstep.

Unless you specify an exact date, most companies will ship your plants during the planting time best suited to your region, weather permitting. Some companies might not offer you the option of choosing a date. Any date that you set should be realistic. For example, don't ask for your plants to be shipped in February if you live in Wisconsin. Winter will not be over and late freezes could kill newly set plants. For most of the country, June 1 is the last day you will want to do any spring planting. After that time, the weather will be too hot and chances of plant loss will rapidly increase.

Reputable mail-order nurseries will have temperature-controlled warehouses where dormant plants are stored prior to shipping. This special care in the handling of dormant plants makes for the best transplants. There is no danger of plants breaking dormancy from sitting out in the hot sunlight in parking lots. You might find this to be the case in many retail outlets that lack the expertise to handle dormant nursery stock. The grocery boy might have many good qualities and be well-instructed in many areas, but he is not likely to know beans about pomology (the science of growing fruit). Most mail-order nurseries have qualified personnel who will inspect all plants before shipping. They will take extra care to see that your plants arrive in the best possible condition.

Naturally, there are things to watch out for when ordering through the mails. Be suspicious of anything priced too inexpensively or that boasts extravagant claims. It's OK to shop for bargains, but do not let low price be the only factor in selecting plants. Quality is almost always worth the price. If an item is priced too low, it might be an inferior grade or not virus free. Most importantly, remember to buy only from an established firm offering a guarnateee. No guarantee will mean money down the drain should your plants die and need replacement.

RETAIL OUTLETS

Unless the retail outlet is a nursery, you are probably better off sticking to the mail-order houses. Many types of retail stores and grocers sell fruit plants in the spring. Some people do have success with these plants. Most of the retail outlets do not have a controlled-environment for the best storage of dormant plants.

Often you will see fruit trees sitting in the sunlight. They will be tall and some will be leafed out or have flowers. This often impresses many people because Americans always seem to be in a hurry and like to see instant results. These are not the best plants to buy. The fact that they leafed out indicates that they already have broken dormancy. They will be weaker when planted and you are apt to lose them. The roots of the fruit plants need about two weeks to grow and establish themselves in a new location before the plant breaks dormancy.

Many plants in these "parking-lot situations" have not been properly pruned. With dormant plants, the size of the root system is more important than the height of the scion (top) in determining a successful transplant.

GUARANTEES

Let's face it, sometimes your fruit plants will die through no recognizable fault of your own. It is important to buy from a nursery that will replace dead plants with viable ones, refund your money, or in some other way minimize your loss. One of the signs of a reputable nursery is that they will offer a guarantee. The guarantee should be located somewhere in their garden catalog. All guarantees are not alike. Read it very carefully so that there will be no misunderstandings later.

Your guarantee will usually be just a brief paragraph or two stating the company's policy. There are some points of reference that are fairly common to all guarantees. These are the period of time the guarantee covers, the refund or replacement policy, and directions for filing a complaint.

Period Of Time Covered. All guarantees cover only a limited period. With nursery stock, only the first season's growth is usually covered. This includes the period of time from planting in the spring up until August 1 or September 1 of the same year. Again, each guarantee is different so read it carefully.

If you live in an area where fall planting is common, you will discover that fall-planted stock carries a different guarantee. Fall-planted nursery stock is usually guaranteed only to the first spring's growth after planting. In both cases, this means only a few months.

Refund or Replacement Policy. Some companies will offer a partial or full refund for plant losses. Most will offer a replacement policy to replace your losses. Some will offer to replace the fruit plant free, charging only for shipping costs. Other companies will offer to replace plants for one-half of the original purchase price, plus shipping and handling charges. Most will not ask you to return the original nursery stock or present proof that your plant actually died.

Filing a Complaint. Most companies will specify in their guarantee the instructions for filing a complaint. If there are no written guidelines, just write to the company and refer to your order number. Always keep the papers that come with your order. You will need these to offer some proof of purchase when filing for refund or replacement. Your order number makes it easier for the nursery to check their files.

Do not wait until the last date on the guarantee to file a complaint. But don't jump the gun and complain just a week after you've planted the tree; it simply might not have broken dormancy yet. Give the plant ample time to leaf out. If by early summer the plant still has not leafed out, apply the scratch test. Take your thumbnail and scratch the bark of the tree. If the inner bark is green, your tree is healthy and you have nothing to worry about. If it is brown—worry. Call your county agent if you are in doubt. If your fruit plant is dead, take out your guarantee, locate all other papers, and file your complaint as soon as possible. It does not do any good to file a complaint after the time has expired on the guarantee.

What Guarantees do not Cover. What companies will not guarantee is to replace plants killed by neglect, pests, mechanical damage, weather, improper planting procedures, or natural disasters. Most companies will try to be fair with you. Do not abuse their goodwill by asking them to accept responsibility for things beyond their control. If you had a fire and got wiped out, don't blame it on the nursery. If vandals injure your fruit plants, it is not the nursery's fault.

Do not be afraid to file legitimate complaints, but don't hold a grudge against a company without giving them fair opportunity to do right. If you have any difficulty getting a company to make good on their guarantee, report them to your state attorney general's office.

If it is a mail-order nursery, a complaint to your postmaster will get quick results.

INSURANCE

To protect yourself from fire, vandalism, and natural disasters, you should consider insuring your fruit plants. Many homeowner's insurance plans offer the option of insuring your landscape plants. Some companies include tree and small fruits in this coverage. Check with your insurance representative to see what plans are available. It is always a good idea to protect your investment.

ADDRESSES

The following are reputable mail-order nursery firms. You should be able to obtain information on local firms or other nurseries from your county agent. The firms are listed in alphabetical order. With each address is information as to what types of fruit the company offers and cost of its catalog or price list.

Adams County Nursery, Inc.
P.O. Box 108
Aspers, PA 17304
Fruit trees; free catalog

Ahrens Strawberry Nursery
Route 1
Huntington, IN 47542
Small fruits; free catalog

Armstrong Nurseries, Inc.
P.O. Box 4060
Ontario, CA 91761
Fruit trees; free catalog

Bountiful Ridge Nurseries, Inc.
Box 250
Princess Anne, MD 21853
All fruits; free catalog

Brittingham Plant Farms
P.O. Box 2538
Salisbury, MD 21801

Bunting's Nurseries, Inc.
Box 306
Selbyville, DE 19975
All fruits; free catalog

Burgess Seed & Plant Co.
905 Four Seasons Road
Bloomington, IL 61701
Tree and small fruits; free catalog

California Nursery Co.
P.O. Box 2278
Fremont, CA 94536
Tree fruits; free catalog

Cumberland Valley Nurseries
Box 430
McMinnville, TN 37110
Tree fruits; free catalog

Emlong Nurseries
Stevenville, MI 49127
Tree and small fruits, free catalog

Farmer Seed & Nursery
Faribault, MN 55021
Trees, small, and native fruits; free catalog

Henry Field Seed & Nursery Co.
Shenandoah, IA 51602
Tree, small, and native fruits; free catalog

Finch's Blueberry Nursery
Route 1
Bailey, NC 27807
Blueberries for the south; free catalog

Dean Foster Nurseries
Route 2
Hartford, MI 49057
Tree and small fruits; free catalog

Fowler Nurseries, Inc.
525 Fowler Road
Newcastle, CA 95658
Tree and small fruits; price list

Gurney Seed & Nursery Co.
Yankton, SD 57079
Tree, small, and native fruits; free catalog

Hastings
P.O. Box 4274
Atlanta, GA 30302
Southern fruits; free catalog

Inter-State Nurseries, Inc.
Hamburg, IA 51640
Tree, small and native fruits; free catalog

Jackson & Perkins Co.
201 Rose Land
Medford, OR 97501
Tree and small fruits; free catalog

Johnson Orchard & Nursery
Route 5
Ellijay, GA 30540
Tree and small fruits; free catalog

J.W. Jung Seed Co.
Randolph, WI 53956
Tree and small fruits; free catalog

Krider Nurseries
Middlebury, IN 46540
Trees and small fruits; free catalog

Lakeland Nurseries
Hanover, PA 17331
Tree, small and native fruits; free catalog

Lawson's Nursery
Route 1
Ball Ground, GA 30104
Old-fashioned and unusual fruit trees; free catalog

Lawyer Nursery
Route 2
Plains, MT 59859
Tree fruits; free catalog

Henry Leuthardt Nurseries
P.O. Box 666
East Moriches, NY 11940
Tree fruits, espaliered fruit trees, and small fruits; price list

Makielski Berry Farm
7130 Platt Road
Ypsilanti, MI 48197
Small fruits; specializing in raspberries; free catalog

Earl May Seed & Nursery Co.
Shenandoah, IA 51601
Tree, small, fruits, and native fruits; free catalog

Mellinger's Inc.
North Lima, OH 44452
Tree, small, fruits, and native fruits; free catalog

J.E. Miller Nursery
Canandaigua, NY 14424
Tree and small fruits; free catalog

National Arbor Day Foundation
Arbor Lodge 100
Nebraska City, NE 68410
Tree and small fruits; free catalog

Neosho Nurseries
Neosho, MO 6r850
Tree and small fruits; free catalog

Nourse Farms, Inc.
Box 485
South Deerfield, MA 01373
Strawberry and raspberry plants; free catalog

L.L. Olds Seeds Co.
P.O. Box 7790
Madison, WI 53707
Tree and small fruits; free catalog

Pike's Peak Nurseries
Route 1
Penn Run, PA 15765
Tree fruits; price list

Raintree Nursery
265 Butts Road
Morton, WA 98356
Disease-resistant fruits; catalog $1

Savage Farms Nursery
P.O. Box 125
McMinnville, TN 37110
Tree and small fruits; free catalog

R.H. Shumway Seedsman, Inc.
P.O. Box 777
Rockford, IL 61101
Tree and small fruits; free catalog

Stark Bro's Nurseries & Orchards Co.
Louisiana, MO 63353
Tree and small fruits; free catalog

Stern's Nurseries, Inc.
Geneva, NY 14456
Small fruits; price list

Vanbourondien Bros.
Babylon, NY 11702
Tree and small fruits; free catalog

Van Well Nursery
P.O. Box 1339
Wenatchee, WA 98801
Apples and tree fruits; free catalog

Waynesboro Nurseries
Box 987
Waynesboro, VA 22980
Tree and small fruits; free catalog

Dave Wilson Nursery
Hugson, CA 95326
Fruit trees and small fruits; free catalog

Wolf River Nurseries
Buskirk, NY 12028
Tree fruits and small fruits

Index

A

Apple insect pests, 129
Apples, 118
Apples, crab, 242
Apples, pollination of, 125
Apples, pruning, 122
Apple tree diseases, 134
Apricots, 160

B

Bacterial spot disease, 284
Beach plums, 227
Blackberries, 75
Black Knot Fungus, 281
Blueberries, 214
Botanical names, 39
Bush cherries, 224

C

Canning, 257
Canning, cold pack, 259
Cantaloupe, 249
Cherries, 151
Cherries, bush, 224
Cherry tree diseases, 158
Cherry tree inspect pests, 156
Cherry trees, pruning, 156
Chokecherries, 228
Cold packing canner, 259
Cold packing pressure cooker, 261
Compost, 25

Crab apples, 242
Cranberries, 207
Cranberries, highbush, 213
Currants, 98

D

Deer, 16
Dewberries, 75
Disease control, natural methods for,
   276
Drought, 274
Drying fruit, 266
Dwarf apple trees, 127

E

Elderberries, 105
European Mountain Ash, 238
European plums, 168

F

Fertilizer, excess, 274
Fireblight, 140
Food spoilage, causes of, 254
Freezer burn, 263
Frost injury, 270
Fruit canning basics, 258
Fruit, freezing, 262
Fruit, preparing, 263
Fruit, storing frozen, 265
Fruit garden, plan your, 2
Fruit plants, winter injury to, 273

Fruit rot, 283
Fruits, drying, 265
Fruits, unusual, 228
Fruit trees, planting, 32
Fruit trees, training, 35
Fruit varieties, 12

G

Gooseberries, 98
Grape classifications, 95
Grape insect pests, 94
Grapes, 86
Grapes, training systems for, 90
Guarantees, 287

H

Herbicides, 275
Honeydew, 249
Huckleberries, 220
Huckleberries, true, 223

I

Insect control, natural methods for, 276
Insurance, 289

J

Jams, 267
Japanese flowering quince, 145
Japanese plums 171
Jellies, 267
Jelly and jams, making, 268
Jelly fruits, 238
Juneberries, 202

K

Kettle, open, 262

L

Ladybugs, 280
Leaf spot, 283

M

Mail-order houses, 286
Melons, 244
Melons, dessert, 245
Mulberries, 194
Mulch, 27
Muskmelon, 249

N

Nectarines, 186

P

Pawpaw, 235

Peaches, 177
Peach scab, 282
Peach tree diseases, 183
Peach tree insect pests, 183
Peach tree pruning, 182
Pears, 136
Persimmons, 232
pH, 6
Photoperiodism, 38
Plant death, 272
Plants, cultural control of, 278
Plants, resistant varieties of, 278
Plums, 168
Plums, beach, 227
Pollination, 30, 271
Predators, biological control of, 280
Preserves, 267
Pressure cooker, 261
Produce, fresh storage of, 255
Produce, preserving, 254

Q

Q 10 factor, the, 39
Quinces, 145

R

Raspberries, 62
Raspberries, black and purple, 64
Raspberries, red, 64
Raspberries, yellow, 65
Raspberry diseases, 72
Raspberry insect pests, 70
Rhubarb, 109
Rhubarb, forcing for indoor growth, 115
Rodents, 13
Root rot, 282
Rosehips, 240
Russian olives, 241

S

Safety, 20
Soil fertility, 22
Sources, addresses of, 289
Strawberries, 42
Strawberries, diseases of, 53
Strawberries, everbearers, 44
Strawberries, Junebearers, 44
Strawberries, pick-your-own operations for, 58
Strawberries, training systems for, 47
Sunlight, fruit needs, 271

T

Time schedule, your, 10

Tools, 29
Topography, 7
Transplanting and care of plant, 272
Trees and shrubs, existing, 9

W

Watermelons, 249
Water sprouts, 124
Weather, 20